"Caner and Caner offer an interesting and enlightening treatment of the Christian Crusades and Christian justifications for war and violence. This important book marks one of the first forays by evangelicals into these thorny issues. The Caners have documented a phenomenon within the church— succeeding generations moving away from the pacifism that characterized the earliest generations of the church and progressing incrementally into a willingness to engage in war and murder in Jesus' name. Highly recommended."

—PHILIP L. BARCLIFT, PH.D.
Director of Liberal Studies, Seattle University

"*Christian Jihad* is a chilling reminder that we are closer to the truth when we 'love the sinner, and hate our own sins.' Every Christian should read this book—especially right now!"

—MARK LOWRY
Nationally known speaker, author, comedian, and Gaither Vocal Band member

Other Books by the Caners:

Unveiling Islam

"In a fascinating book written by two Arab Muslims who converted to Christianity, Ergun Mehmet Caner and Emir Fethi Caner give an eye-opening account of Islam's prophet in *Unveiling Islam: An Insider's Look at Muslim Life and Beliefs*."

—ANN COULTER
Political commentator
Author, *Slander: Liberal Lies About the American Right*

"Must reading for all C

—ZIG ZIGLAR

"[The Caners are] articu̲.̲.̲.̲ ̲ ̲ ̲ ̲ in excellent grasp of the politics, theology, beliefs, and thinking of a majority of Muslims."

—VICTOR OLADOKUN
CBN International

More Than a Prophet

"Christians need [this book] to be prepared witnesses and the Muslim needs it if he really wants to know the truth about the One who is 'more than a prophet.'"

—Dr. James Merritt
Former President, Southern Baptist Convention
Senior Pastor, First Baptist Church, Snellville, Ga.
CEO, *Touching Lives,* national television broadcast

Voices Behind the Veil

"*Voices Behind the Veil* is a powerful reminder that the most liberating message the world can hear is that 'God loves you unconditionally.' This book will help Christian women lovingly share with those women who are *trapped* behind the veil, that those whom the Son has set free are free indeed."

—Janet Parshall
Nationally syndicated radio host and columnist

"Dr. Ergun Caner is quickly becoming known as the authority in pulling back the veil of Islam. This compilation from the hearts of Christian women reveals the love of Christ for the women of Islam. All of these women are speakers and authors in their own right, and they have come together for a project of infinite importance. Get this book! There is not a more timely or critical book."

—Dr. Mac Brunson
Senior Pastor, First Baptist Church, Dallas, Tex.
President, Southern Baptist Convention Pastor's Conference

CHRISTIAN
JIHAD

Two Former Muslims Look at the Crusades
and Killing in the Name of Christ

CHRISTIAN JIHAD

ERGUN MEHMET CANER

EMIR FETHI CANER

Kregel
Publications

Christian Jihad: Two Former Muslims Look at the Crusades and Killing in the Name of Christ

© 2004 by Ergun Mehmet Caner and Emir Fethi Caner

Published by Kregel Publications, a division of Kregel, Inc., P.O. Box 2607, Grand Rapids, MI 49501. For more information about Kregel Publications, visit our Web site: www.kregel.com.

Library of Congress Cataloging-in-Publication Data
Caner, Ergun Mehmet.
     Christian jihad: two former Muslims look at the Crusades and killing in the name of Christ / by Ergun Mehmet Caner and Emir Fethi Caner.
        p. cm.
Includes bibliographical references.
     1. War—Religious aspects—Christianity—History. 2. Crusades. I. Caner, Emir Fethi. II. Title.
BT736.2.C27   2004
270.4—dc22   2004007563

ISBN 0-8254-2403-8

Printed in the United States of America

1 2 3 4 5 / 08 07 06 05 04

To Eren and Eda

CONTENTS

INTRODUCTION

T*he taste of blood always made him pray.*

A single trail of sweat dripped from Tom's furrowed brow into his left eye, which was clenched tightly. In the oppressive heat of the midday sun, Tom felt like he could almost taste the air, and on his palate he thought he could taste blood.

Perhaps it was a cut in his mouth.

Perhaps it was from his frequent nosebleeds.

Regardless, the faint taste of iron excited him. Long ago, Tom had trained himself to view blood as a spiritual sign, a type of imprimatur. God was blessing his work.

The burning of the sweat in his eye cavity did not make him flinch. Focusing all of his attention on the task at hand, it did not even seem that he breathed or twitched a muscle. With the precision of one who had practiced his maneuver hundreds of times, Tom lay in the bushes across the street from the "house of the devil's work."

Whenever Tom spoke of the place, which was now directly in his crosshairs, he regarded it with dripping disdain. It was a cauldron center of his deep burning anger and did not deserve to be spoken of with the respect due true centers of prayer.

Tom was a swarthy man, obviously of mixed descent. His hairy knuckles were turning white as he gripped the stock of his high-powered rifle. His right eye, covered by a thick mat of hair, a "unibrow," was directly in line with the scope.

It seemed all of his life hinged on this moment—on the precise execution of this act. His legacy—his reputation before the other martyrs, his divine mandate—coalesced into this moment. In just a minute, the pagans would leave their services. He was to greet them with eternity.

He took short, shallow breaths, so as to avoid having to sight the rifle again. He avoided any sudden movement. His mind raced over the hundreds of times he had anticipated this hour: *Find a low bush and nestle in the undergrowth. Make sure you are in the sight line of the front doors. Exhale slowly when you spot the target. Release the safety with your right thumb. Wait for a clear shot at the heart or head, and then squeeze gently.* In one clarion moment, it would be over.

He had not planned an exit strategy. In fact, in the years of traveling, meeting with the network of leaders, flying across the globe, organizing in basements in hushed tones, hiding in caves—he had never thought he needed one. He longed achingly to mix his blood with that of the other martyrs. He often said this, passionately. He had said it so often that it had become a type of mantra for the other followers. He was to be a martyr, pure and simple. His action would spill the blood of the infidel, and for that he too would be killed. His blood, in turn, would call others to join him. Together they would be holy warriors.

His mind raced. The distraction of a small mosquito did not even move him from his locked position beneath the gardenia cover. He felt something crawling up the right leg of his pants . . . a worm? A snake? He dared not move, however, for there were pedestrians nearby.

His mind raced. A cacophony of meetings and strategies and prayers had prepared him for this moment. He was emotionally exhausted by the relief that his personal struggle would soon be over. He knew his destiny for this act of courage: Eternal bliss. Promised and specific blessings. The approval of God. Soon, he would join the other martyrs in paradise.

His mind raced. In recent days, the police had raised a terror alert, a notice that there were unsavory characters about. Tom was certain he was under the radar, however, and his natural caution gave him a confidence that his prospective victim did not share. Tom's target had apparently assumed he was at risk, though, because he was now traveling with compatriots. Accessories, Tom called them. He rarely traveled in public alone, often walking with groups to eat.

Of course, his name was not really "Tom." In fact, as he lay motionless in the dirt, he struggled to remember his true name. He had used so many in the interim: Tom. Anthony. Raul.

The names were always generic and nondescript. He had to mix into the indigenous group.

He momentarily closed his right eye to concentrate on the various names he had taken over the past number of years. In a world of falsified passports, he traveled easily across borders and through immigration centers in various countries. His network of fellow believers had carried him well, even establishing bank accounts in his assumed names. He never stayed in one location for long; a month here, a month there. But in these days of "terrorist security," he had to be careful.

In one particular instance (three or four years ago . . . he couldn't remember) he had even dared to get a driver's license in his assumed name. The purpose was simple. To take lessons to become an airplane pilot, he needed a driver's license. Maintaining his low profile, he needed to take jobs that were menial, like driving a taxi. The license was a necessary risk. Yet the process of flight lessons and the scrutiny was too elaborate and too intrusive. They asked too many questions. He could not risk it, so he settled on monotonous jobs that were far beneath his high intellect: Dishwasher at a diner. Hotel night clerk. Lawn care man. These were jobs for which few people ever asked questions, and anonymity was at a premium.

It had been three years since he attempted to take flying lessons. Approaching a pilot in that Florida airfield, Tom felt confident enough to ask about the cost of lessons. He began small—taking guided flights in the Cessna. Gradually, he worked his way up to the Piper Seneca V, which was a six-seat plane, if all the occupants were thin. As many of his colleagues were doing the same, it seemed important at the time. He truly enjoyed the weightlessness and exhilarating freedom he felt when airborne. Still, the suspicion of the trainer set off alarms with

Tom, and he quit the lessons abruptly. Almost as quickly, he moved out of the region, settling some 150 miles away.

Moving into a new community always unsettled Tom. The process of integrating himself as unobtrusively as possible was painstaking. Every government worker, it seemed, looked at him with piercing suspicion. Surely their suspicion was only in his mind, he thought. People sign up for water, electricity, and utilities every day. Yet every time he entered his falsified Social Security number, he secretly wondered if this would be the moment he would be exposed.

Of course, he had long since learned to hide any anxiety. He had developed an easygoing manner, a fatherly laugh, and a gentle demeanor. His once thick, coarse beard was kept shaven. Whatever facial hair he kept was also nondescript and easily modified.

It did not matter if he settled in dense urban centers or outlying farming communities. In the urban centers, the government employees often wore the glazed, scornful look of a carnival worker—the look of someone who had carried out the same tedious task countless times. Often they would not even glance up to look at him. Still, the urban centers were linked by massive computer banks, and the inherent risk of raising a flag was large.

Ironically, the smaller cities were often more distrusting. New people rarely moved in, and their natural friendliness grated against Tom's desire for obscurity. He remembered one bank teller in particular.

"So, how does your family like our town so far, Mr. . . . . Ahmed?" the woman had asked. She was short in stature, but carried the weight of someone much larger. She smiled with her mouth but, Tom noticed, not with her eyes. She struggled with his assumed last name like one who had been raised in the American suburbs and had never learned any other languages.

"So far—fine," he replied tersely. He cursed himself for having a last name so distinctive. They should have given him "Brown" or "Wilson." Yet he was committed now.

His usual manner of grace and ease was not accessible at the moment. It usually took some hours for him to work up the ability to mix and mingle. Her question had interrupted his thoughts, and he replied more coarsely than he would have liked. Struggling to regain his composure, he added, "This is a beautiful area. We love the countryside."

"Oh, well you must get out on the parkway," she rejoined, "it is gorgeous in the fall." She gushed on for about another minute as she completed his transaction, speaking of fishing ponds and bike trails and mountain hikes. Tom attempted to add his own version of small talk, but he paused as she examined the check again, this time more closely.

She looked up a moment, told him she would be right back, and walked to the main teller, seated at a desk. They spoke in hushed tones for a moment, and Tom felt a trickle of sweat descending his back along the spine. Beads of sweat broke out on his forehead, and Tom felt his heart race. *Have they discovered some telling mistake?* Tom wondered, but he dared not flinch. She returned to her station window, and said with a smile, "Now, these funds will not be accessible for five days. We have a policy like this for all out-of-state deposits."

Tom exhaled slowly and smiled. "Of course," he said matter-of-factly, "I understand." In his momentary paranoia, Tom had felt some small detail had caused her to question either his validity or the validity of the check. Or . . . it could have been his looks.

His looks. It was a constant source of concern for Tom. His swarthy complexion, almost like soft leather, made him look like a seasoned migrant worker. The sun had burnt him into a soft olive tone, and his eyes betrayed an old soul. The bags under his eyes . . . the black, coarse hairs on his cheeks which would creep toward his eye sockets . . . his natural hairiness . . .

Ouch!

The pain shooting up his right leg shocked Tom from his daydreams. Whatever had crawled up his leg was now stinging him fiercely, like a needle into tender flesh.

The severity of the sting actually caused Tom to jolt in the underbrush, as if he were experiencing a leg cramp. He attempted to shake whatever it was loose, but he finally used his left arm to reach around and smack the spot hard. In the motion of the swinging of his arm,

Tom noticed that his left shoulder had cramped under his weight. How long had he been resting in this locked position, putting almost all of his torso weight on his left elbow?

Tom glanced around. No one seemed to have noticed his sudden movement. In fact, there were very few people in sight, except for an old man sitting on the curb in the distance. Very gingerly, Tom turned his wrist to look at his watch. The moment of truth was at hand. He readjusted his position, attempting to awaken the numbed nerves in his left arm. He peered through the scope and saw that his movement had not affected it too much. He eased back into his prone position beneath the leaves of the bush . . . and waited.

He spotted the white, Cossack-like coat of his target first. It gleamed in the sun's brightness. Though the target was surrounded by associates, he was clearly in the line of sight. It was now "go time."

Tom inhaled silently. He muttered a prayer under his breath, the prayer he had practiced for years. This climactic moment was now upon him. The purpose for his entire existence now faced him . . . and Tom froze.

What is wrong with me? he thought. *Why am I so nervous? We have planned for this occasion for years, and now I freeze? This is unlike me.*

Yet the reason for his reticence was clear as well: *Tom had never actually killed before.* This man, this target, this perpetrator of the decadence he so lamented . . . was to be his first.

His stomach felt queasy, like he was at the top of a roller coaster ride. It was the feeling when anticipation meets abject fear. His legs felt weak, almost jelly-like. The numbness he felt in his feet was creeping up his shins. He sensed a slight tremor in his right forearm. He needed to calm down quickly.

Summoning his courage, he thought of the defenseless victims for whom he was fighting. In one crystalline moment, they would have a voice. "God be praised," he exhaled. And then he gently squeezed the trigger.

The bullet ripped through flesh in an instant. It was like an exploding light bulb—a flash, a crack, and a quick echo. There was no cry from the victim, only a shriek from his compatriots. Those standing closest to his target ducked, then crouched beside the lifeless form, wailing loudly. They looked feverishly around, attempting to locate Tom among the shrubs and bushes. One of the bystanders, freckled crimson with the victim's blood, spotted the gleam of the metal of the gun stock, and raised his right hand, index finger extended, to Tom's location at ground level.

His arm never reached shoulder height. Tom squeezed the trigger again, exploding the chest of the would-be informant. His body cartwheeled in midair and crumpled beside the first man. A woman cringing and screaming attempted to shield her face, but it was to no avail. Tom finished God's work by taking off the top of her skull with his final discharge.

Each subsequent shot was easier than the previous one had been. His resolve grew as each victim fell. They deserved death, didn't they? Tom secretly wished their deaths were not so swift. If he could have spoken to them before their souls left their bodies, perhaps he could have prepared them for eternity by giving them a chance. Instead, Tom reasoned, they were now entering hell's darkest fury.

His mission now completed, Tom knew exactly what he needed to do. Show aggression or run. The police would certainly shoot him on sight. Surrender quickly and in the American judicial system he would be allowed to speak. American lust for tragedy being what it was, the world would listen. He would be allowed to vent and address the court. He would speak to the world, and others would join him in the war.

Using his forearms, Tom pushed himself backward from under the bush. His muscles, stiff from inertia, twitched involuntarily as he rose to full height. The silence of the moment was shattered by the sirens of distant emergency vehicles. Standing rigidly in the full sun, Tom raised both arms in the air, leaving his weapon under the bush. They would find it in due time.

A slight smile crossed Tom's face.

The work was done.

The mission was complete.

Tom had killed the infidels, and he knew that Jesus Christ was glorified by his work.

Does the story of Tom offend your senses as a Christian?

We pray it does.

Is it an implausible scenario?

Tragically, no. It is all too real.

The details are drawn from incidents of the early 1990s in which Christians murdered doctors in abortion clinics. One such man, Paul Hill, whom many hold in high esteem as a Christian warrior, declared that he was called of God to fight for the unborn. When he was executed, he ascended in the eyes of his admirers to the level of a Christian martyr. He said he had acted upon the expressed wishes of Jesus Christ to defend those who could not defend themselves.

Was he, in fact, a martyr?

As abhorrent as the evangelical community finds abortion, can we ever justify killing someone in the name of Christ? If we can, are such acts somehow ordained and approved by God as righteous acts of indignation? And if such acts of violence are acceptable to God, can such an indulgence be extended to other venues or other perpetrators of the evils that so beset our sin-saturated world?

If God *does* ordain such acts, one can come to only one conclusion: Jesus Christ commands his followers to jihad. But is that the case?

That is the express question of this book.

This book is designed to be conspicuously controversial.

By way of disclosure, we need to admit some pertinent details at the start. The authors are two evangelical Christians, teaching at two decidedly evangelical Christian institutions of higher learning. We are also both former Muslims who have spent much time in the past years decrying the acts of jihad performed by Muslims, intent on pleasing Allah.

And now we intend to turn the spotlight of criticism of jihad onto Christian history.

Why?

Because as uncomfortable as this may make the reader, it must be said: Christianity has been guilty of its own form of jihad as well. In our corporate history, we have killed in the name of our God, drawn blood from those we have considered infidels, and even promised salvation for those who fought under the banner of the cross.

Since the bombing of the World Trade Center towers and the subsequent publication of our books describing the Islamic world from which we came, we have heard the constant refrain from fellow Christians: How can they believe killing us gets them into heaven?

Before we jump too quickly to criticize Islamic doctrine, we must first face our own history. *We too have killed in the name of our God.* The Crusades. The Inquisitions. These are just two of the more notorious examples of dark moments in our collective history when people identifying themselves with the Christian faith abandoned the teachings of Jesus to love our enemies and attempted to convert by the sword.

In fact, this book is a call for authenticity. True authenticity demands that we denounce acts in history in which innocent nonbelievers were slaughtered for the sole crime of being a nonbeliever. True authenticity demands that we confront and learn from dark chapters in the past.

Faith is never coerced, and salvation does not come at the end of a bayonet. We must remember our history because it calls us to humility. We must remember our history because it forces us to evaluate our future. We must remember our history . . . because the Muslims do.

Difficult as it may be to fathom, there was a time when Christians butchered Muslims and Jews in the name of Jesus Christ and declared our own version of jihad. *Christian* jihad.

Chapter 1

We Shed No Blood
but Our Own

The Early Church and Warfare
(A.D. 30–300)

As Christians, we are forbidden to wage war, and that
our loyalty to our country, to humanity, to the Church
Universal, and to Jesus Christ our Lord and Master, calls
us instead to a life-service for the enthronement of Love
in personal, commercial and national life.[1]
—Fellowship of Reconciliation
(summer 1914 in Switzerland)

P opular culture—and the world of modern academia—purports
that the early Church, beginning with the institution of the church
at Pentecost, was defiantly pacifist—that is, that Christians refused to
participate in any conflict, including any defensive act of protection.

Are they right?

The history of the Amish, Quaker, and Mennonite communities
are built upon this premise.

The pacifist movement, consisting of millions of mainstream Chris-
tians, unites Christian tradition with the movements of Hinduism,
Buddhism, and secular activists. They cite such church fathers as
Tertullian and Origen, such medieval and Reformation authors as
Francis of Assisi and Menno Simons, and such modern Christian
authors as Thomas Merton.

In the United States, pacifist movements have been anchored in such groups as the American Friends Service Committee, the Fellowship of Reconciliation, and the Mennonite Central Committee. Those groups and others have joined with secular pacifists to protest acts perceived as violence to humanity—war, capital punishment, or defensive armament.

As the Fellowship of Reconciliation (FoR) notes in their history, their justification is the centrality of Christianity itself:

> The FoR was founded in Cambridge in 1914 by a group of pacifist Christians. During the summer of 1914 an ecumenical conference of Christians who wanted to avert the approaching war was held in Switzerland. However, war broke out before the end of the conference and, at Cologne station, Henry Hodgkin, an English Quaker, and Friedrich Siegmund-Schulze, a German Lutheran, pledged themselves to a continued search for peace with the words, *"We are at one in Christ and can never be at war."*[2]

The basis for their formation was explicitly Christian in nature, with references to the kingdom of Christ rather than nationalistic fervor. They continued the reasoning:

> Inspired by that pledge, about 130 Christians of all denominations gathered in Cambridge at the end of 1914 and set up the FoR, recording their general agreement in a statement which became "The Basis" of the FoR, namely:
>
> 1. That love as revealed and interpreted in the life and death of Jesus Christ involves more than we have yet seen, that is the only power by which evil can be overcome and the only sufficient basis of human society.
>
> 2. That, in order to establish a world order based on Love, it is incumbent upon those who believe in this principle to accept it fully, both for themselves and in relation to others and to take the risks involved in doing so in a world which does not yet accept it.

3. That therefore, *as Christians, we are forbidden to wage war,* and that our loyalty to our country, to humanity, to the Church Universal, and to Jesus Christ our Lord and Master, calls us instead to a life-service for the enthronement of Love in personal, commercial and national life.

4. That the Power, Wisdom and Love of God stretch far beyond the limits of our present experience, and that he is ever waiting to break forth into human life in new and larger ways.

5. That since God manifests himself in the world through men and women, we offer ourselves to his redemptive purpose to be used by him in whatever way he may reveal to us.

The FoR supported conscientious objectors during World War I and was a supporter of passive resistance during World War II. In 1919, representatives from a dozen countries met in Holland and established the International Fellowship of Reconciliation, which now has many branches on all five continents.[3]

Is their logic sound?

Is the history of Christianity clearly on the side of peaceful resistance against all warfare?

Certainly in the context of today's conflicts on the world stage, such questions nag Christians even within the military.

It is our premise that, while early Christians certainly did not seek out conversion through conquest and bloodshed, they did not espouse a pacifistic stance as purported by modern pacifist theologies.

Instead, the Christian community slowly refined a position that allowed Christian participation in the military within certain parameters of combat—that defined as a "just war." The Christian community moved from social and citizen passivity to a system that allowed Christians to be in the military. Explicit rules were designed to keep Christian soldiers from becoming drunk with blood and power. These rules would come to be known as the *Just War criteria.*

Tragically, any adherence to such a position was cast aside, once the leaders determined that *holy war* was more feasible and profitable than *just war*. It is this horrific junction in Church history that led to Christian declarations of jihad.

Was the Early Church Pacifistic?

In the generations following Jesus Christ's ascension, pacifism was not held as an absolute demand of the Lord. Christians tended toward a strong pacifism, which was ironic, given the various Roman emperors' proclivity to persecute them. The more vigorously the various Roman leaders immolated Christians as human torches, the less appealing any form of violence was to the believers. *Foxe's Book of Martyrs* compiled early church writings about the brutal treatment of Christians by various emperors, such as Nero (reigned 54–68) and Diocletian (284–304). At times of local or world persecution, Romans condemned the Christians of treason, since they were unwilling to offer worship to the emperor as a god or promise absolute allegiance to his authority.

Under that overall criminality, Christians were assumed to be guilty of various crimes, many of which reflected their fellowship and doctrines. As early as A.D. 35, the Roman Senate issued a decree calling the Christians "*strana et illicita*," meaning "strange and unlawful." They were called cannibals, because the Lord's Supper celebration included the words of Jesus Christ: "this is my body" and "this is my blood" (Matthew 26:26, 28). They were called incestuous, because they referred to their spouses and children as "brothers" and "sisters." Their genuine love for all humanity made them seem seditious to emperors bent upon world domination.

From this general time period comes a striking description of Christians that was received by a man identified only as Diognetus:

> Christians are not different because of their country or the language they speak or the way they dress. They do not isolate themselves in their cities nor use a private language; even the

life they lead has nothing strange. . . . They live in their own countries and are strangers. They loyally fulfill their duties as citizens, but are treated as foreigners. Every foreign land is for them a fatherland and every fatherland, foreign.

They marry like everyone, they have children, but they do not abandon their newborn. They have the table in common, but not the bed. They are in the flesh, but do not live according to the flesh. . . . They dwell on earth, but are citizens of heaven. They obey the laws of the state, but in their lives they go beyond the law. They love everyone, yet are persecuted by everyone. No one really knows them, but all condemn them. *They are killed, but go on living.* They are poor, but enrich many. They have nothing, but abound in everything. But in that contempt they find glory before God. Their honor is insulted, while their justice is acknowledged. When they are cursed, they bless. When they are insulted, they answer with kind words. They do good to others and are punished like evil-doers. When they are punished, they rejoice, as if they were given life. The Jews make war against them as if they were a foreign race. The Greek persecute them, but those who hate them cannot tell the reason for their hatred.[4]

Among the primary sources, there is no record until the time of Marcus Aurelius (160–180) of Christians in the military, except those soldiers who were converted under the apostles. Among the church leaders, it was clear that enlistment in military was problematic for the Christian, and participation in actual bloodshed and combat was against the very nature of the Christian life. Regional leaders such as Justin Martyr in Rome, writing in about 155, and Irenaeus in Gaul writing in about 180, saw the prophetic dimension of the Christian's eternal citizenship as most important, over against participation in any military conflicts. Since eternity would last longer than any political regime, why should they invest themselves in warfare, which would demand they shed blood? Certainly the horrific persecution of the believers by the various emperors caused the Church as a whole to look somewhat skeptically at believers being forced into military service by the emperors.

Yet as the Church developed a history, the Christian in the military became an issue of detailed discussions among such leaders as Arnobius in North Africa and Lactantius. Clearly by the beginning of the fourth century, Christians were numbered in the military, as tales of their martyrdom and tomb inscriptions will attest. The nature and breadth of their service, however, was questioned, in light of the teachings of Christ concerning enemies on the one hand and loyal citizenry on the other hand.

While it can be said that this period culminated in the participation of believers in various armies, the protocols for such involvement did not develop until the fifth century. What did finally develop differed greatly from the rules of engagement for an actual "Christian army" that Pope Urban II commanded hundreds of years later.

Church Voices of Pacifism: Christ Is Returning Soon!

At the dawning of the second century after Christ, the attention of the Church was focused on the imminent return of Jesus Christ. As Christ had come to literally transform society and man's relation to man, this kingdom work left no room for participation in warfare for his followers. Nowhere can this be more clearly illustrated than in the writings of Justin Martyr and Irenaeus. Reading the preserved works of these leaders, one gets the impression that Jesus Christ's coming had inaugurated an era of peace. The concept of warfare was, by its nature, antithetical to Christian life.

Justin Martyr, an apologist and minister writing from Rome around 150, implored a man named Trypho to understand this radical change in those who were followers of Jesus Christ. While the children of God may have, at one time, gloried in the horrors of warfare, they were now completely transformed and could no longer live by such violence. He notes:

> [We] have fled for safety to the God of Jacob and God of Israel; and we who were filled with war, and mutual slaughter, and

every wickedness, have each through the whole earth changed our warlike weapons,—our swords into ploughshares, and our spears into implements of tillage,—and we cultivate piety, righteousness, philanthropy, faith, and hope.[5]

This shift in lifestyle did not *justify* the former actions of God's people, but it did explain them. Indeed, with painful honesty, Justin cites the previous tendencies toward violence and the new repulsion to warfare as a sign of the Christians' transformed hearts. The implication was clear—to become a believer, one must lay aside the former ways and become a warrior for peace. In *Apologia*, Justin further states:

We who formerly used to murder one another do not only now refrain from making war upon our enemies, but also, that we may not lie nor deceive our examiners, willingly die confessing Christ. For that saying, "The tongue has sworn but the mind is unsworn," might be imitated by us in this matter. But if the soldiers enrolled by you, and who have taken the military oath, prefer their allegiance to their own life, and parents, and country, and all kindred, though you can offer them nothing incorruptible, it were verily ridiculous if we, who earnestly long for incorruption, should not endure all things, in order to obtain what we desire from him who is able to grant it.[6]

To Justin, the swearing of an oath to a military commander or country was more than just a violation of Scriptural injunction; it was also short-sighted. What can the country or emperor offer the soldier in return for his vow and allegiance? Nothing of any eternal significance. Since the believer has sworn himself only to Jesus Christ, his allegiance speaks to the inheritance of an incorruptible and perpetual reward. If death at the hands of those desiring to force the Christian to kill is the price for this inheritance, Justin argued, then the victor is actually the vanquished, and the martyr endures only brief pain.

Irenaeus, a pastor in Lyons, writing shortly after Justin, built upon the biblical imagery Justin had begun. Also citing Isaiah, Irenaeus continues the analogy of swords and plowshares. In *Against Heresies,* he argues that one of the major purposes for Christ coming to the earth was the complete end of warfare. Those who continue to fight, even after the conquest of death by Jesus Christ, are doing so in direct violation of the millennial reign of Jesus Christ. He noted:

> From the Lord's advent, the new covenant which brings back peace, and the law which gives life, has gone forth over the whole earth, as the prophets said: "For out of Zion shall go forth the law, and the word of the Lord from Jerusalem; and he shall rebuke many people; and they shall break down their swords into ploughshares, and their spears into pruning-hooks, and they shall no longer learn to fight."[7]

In the case of both Justin and Irenaeus, the citation from Isaiah had both prophetic and messianic connotations. Isaiah himself had said:

In the last days
>the mountain of the LORD's temple will be established
>>as chief among the mountains;
>it will be raised above the hills,
>>and all nations will stream to it.

Many peoples will come and say,

>>"Come, let us go up to the mountain of the LORD,
>>>to the house of the God of Jacob.
>>He will teach us his ways,
>>>so that we may walk in his paths."
>>The law will go out from Zion,
>>>the word of the LORD from Jerusalem.
>>He will judge between the nations
>>>and will settle disputes for many peoples.

> They will beat their swords into plowshares
> and their spears into pruning hooks.
> Nation will not take up sword against nation,
> nor will they train for war anymore.[8]

In the mind of Justin and Irenaeus, the coming of Christ not only brought redemption, but also a new geopolitical approach—loving your enemies and seeking peace, over the old ways of war and conquest. Even the preparation for warfare was paradoxical to the very purpose of the Incarnation.

If the early church fathers felt the pursuit of warfare did not befit the Christian life, then it would follow that such participation would be a betrayal of the Lord's commission. A compatriot of Justin in Rome, Tatian (160), pointedly declined an invitation to become a military commander. He was clearly disgusted with the idea that he would have to participate in any type of warfare or conflict:

> I do not wish to be a king; I am not anxious to be rich; I declined military command; I detest fornication; I am not impelled by an insatiable love of gain to go to sea; I do not contend for chaplets; I am free from a mad thirst for fame; I despise death; I am superior to every kind of disease; grief does not consume my soul.[9]

By associating warfare with such sins as fornication and greed, Tatian suggested that all such acts are evil. Based on faulty motives and pursuits, the pursuit of adventure in military conflict is an arrogance ("mad thirst for fame") of position, as opposed to a noble act of the defense of freedom.

Church Voices of Pacifism: Our Weapon Is Prayer!

As the Church entered the third century, the position of Christian pacifism remained intact, but the reasoning for the position slowly shifted. As the years passed without the return of Jesus Christ, the bishops and theologians began to teach an ethical pacifism. This position held that warfare and killing was inconsistent with the Christian's call to unconditional love of all peoples, regardless of politics or positions. This view was especially evident in North Africa, where the bishops were explicit in their admonitions to their churches.

Clement of Alexandria, writing at the dawn of the third century, illustrated the transformed nature and ethic of the believer. He wrote in a letter entitled *Paedagogus* ("The Instructor"),

> But let us . . . fulfill the Father's will, listen to the Word, and take on the impress of the truly saving life of our Savior. . . . For it is not in war, but in peace, that we are trained. War needs great preparation, and luxury craves profusion; but peace and love, simple and quiet sisters, require no arms nor excessive preparation. The Word is their sustenance.[10]

His argument was that Christ as our Commander also prepares his troops, except that our battle is the battle for peace and love. Such training and preparation is imminently important and vital, and is the clarion call for all believers. To invert the argument, Christians fighting in a war disobey their own Commander and are guilty of insubordination for not explicitly following the commands of God. Our training is for peace, not war.

Clement's pupil, and the subsequent leader in Alexandria, Origen (230) contributed to the argument toward Christian pacifism during his famous argument with the philosopher Celsus. Apparently, Celsus had claimed that, because of Christian pacifism, the king was "left in utter solitude and desertion" and that "the affairs of the world fall into the hands of the most impious and wild barbarians."[11] In *Contra Celsus* 8.69, Origen answers that by praying, Christians are in fact participating in a higher aim of victory. He advocates,

> We say that "if two" of us "shall agree on earth as touching anything that they shall ask, it shall be done for them of the Father" of the just, "which is in heaven;" for God rejoices in the agreement of rational beings, and turns away from discord.[12]

This weapon of *prayer*, as designed by the Father, will cause men to put down arms, which is a far more esteemed victory than slaughter. In returning to the topic of warfare later in the work, Origen dedicates an entire chapter to the explanation of their perceived insubordination. In fact, Origen would argue, Christians are doing their part by praying, which is the higher call and the more precise weapon. He enjoins:

> In the next place, Celsus urges us "to help the king with all our might, and to labor with him in the maintenance of justice, to fight for him; and if he requires it, to fight under him, or lead an army along with him." To this our answer is, that we do, when occasion requires, give help to kings, and that, so to say, a divine help, "putting on the whole armor of God." And this we do in obedience to the injunction of the apostle, "I exhort, therefore, that first of all, supplications, prayers, intercessions, and giving of thanks, be made for all men; for kings, and for all that are in authority"; and the more any one excels in piety, the more effective help does he render to kings, even more than is given by soldiers, who go forth to fight and slay as many of the enemy as they can.[13]

Origen regards those who demand military allegiance from the Christians to be "enemies of our faith." To that end, he offers two explanations for their nonparticipation. First he notes that even the priests of pagan temples are excused from military service. "Do not those who are priests at certain shrines, and those who attend on certain gods . . . keep their hands free from blood, that they may with hands unstained . . . offer the appointed sacrifices to your gods; and even when war is upon you, you never enlist the priests in the army?"[14]

Secondly, Origen reasons that the warfare that Christians are fighting is far more dangerous and harmful, because they are battling the demonic realm itself. In fact, he explicitly states that the common soldier could not fight such a foe:

> If that [military conflict], then, is a laudable custom, how much more so, that while others are engaged in battle, these too should engage as the priests and ministers of God, keeping their hands pure, and wrestling in prayers to God on behalf of those who are fighting in a righteous cause, and for the king who reigns righteously, that whatever is opposed to those who act righteously may be destroyed! And as we by our prayers vanquish all demons who stir up war, and lead to the violation of oaths, and disturb the peace, we in this way are much more helpful to the kings than those who go into the field to fight for them.[15]

As Origen challenges at the end of his letter,

> If Celsus would have us to lead armies in defense of our country, let him know that we do this too, and that not for the purpose of being seen by men, or of vain glory. For "in secret," and in our own hearts, there are prayers which ascend as from priests in behalf of our fellow-citizens.[16]

In the first two centuries of the Christian church, perhaps no voice was as forcefully raised against Christian participation in warfare than that of Tertullian, Cyprian's predecessor in Carthage. Writing at the beginning of the second century, Tertullian acknowledged that the question of whether to accept military personnel into Christian fellowship was an issue. In his opinion, military service in combat was a real ethical dilemma for a Christian, because all violence contradicts the Christian life. In his book *On Idolatry*, he wrote:

> Now inquiry is made about this point, whether a believer may turn himself unto military service, and whether the military may be admitted unto the faith, even the rank and file, or each inferior grade, to whom there is no necessity for taking part in sacrifices or capital punishments. There is no agreement between the divine and the human sacrament,

the standard of Christ and the standard of the devil, the camp
of light and the camp of darkness. One soul cannot be due
to two masters—God and Caesar. And yet Moses carried a
rod, and Aaron wore a buckle, and John (Baptist) is girt with
leather and Joshua the son of Nun leads a line of march; and
the People warred: if it pleases you to sport with the subject.
But how will a Christian man war, nay, how will he serve
even in peace, without a sword, which the Lord has taken
away?[17]

As can be seen, the entire issue hinged on the question—could a
person who was already a believer enlist in the military, even if their
specific task in the military would not expressly involve the death of
another? Tertullian sees this as an issue of idolatry. To serve in the
military, the believer must swear allegiance to Caesar (the commander),
which is impossible since Christians have sworn allegiance to Jesus
Christ. This "dual citizenship" is not allowed in Tertullian's position,
and would bespeak a negation of any personal faith.

The problem with this dual citizenship is intrinsic to the nature of
true Christianity, for Christ has disarmed all men. Tertullian concludes,
"for albeit soldiers had come unto John, and had received the formula
of their rule; albeit, likewise, a centurion had believed; still the Lord
afterward, in disarming Peter, [unarmed] every soldier. No dress is
lawful among us, if assigned to any unlawful action."[18]

Elaborating on this theme further in *De Corona Militis,* Tertullian
expands the discussion to involve many other forms of military service. In fact, he lists thirteen reasons why soldiers could not be allowed in the churches.

To begin with the real ground of the military crown, I think
we must first inquire whether warfare is proper at all for
Christians. What sense is there in discussing the merely ac-
cidental, when that on which it rests is to be condemned?
Do we believe it lawful for a human *oath* to be superintended
to one divine, for a man to come under promise to another

master after Christ, and to abjure father, mother, and all nearest kinsfolk, whom even the law has commanded us to honor and love next to God himself, to whom the gospel, too, holding them only of less account than Christ, has in like manner rendered honor? Shall it be held lawful to make an *occupation* of the sword, when the Lord proclaims that he who uses the sword shall perish by the sword? And shall the son of peace *take part* in the battle when it does not become him even to sue at law? And shall he *apply the chain*, and the prison, and the torture, and the punishment, who is not the avenger even of his own wrongs? Shall he, (therefore), either *keep watch* for others more than for Christ, or shall he do it on the *Lord's day*, when he does not even do it for Christ himself? And shall he *keep guard* before the temples that he has renounced? And shall he take a *meal* where the apostle has forbidden him? And shall he diligently *protect* by night those whom in the daytime he has put to flight by his exorcisms, leaning and resting on the spear the while with which Christ's side was pierced? Shall he carry a *flag*, too, hostile to Christ? And shall he ask a *watchword* from the emperor who has already received one from God? Shall he be *disturbed* in death by the trumpet of the trumpeter, who expects to be aroused by the angel's trump? And shall the Christian be *burned* according to camp rule, when he was not permitted to burn incense to an idol, when to him Christ remitted the punishment of fire?[19]

These thirteen questions all seem to beg a negative answer from Tertullian's view. Could a Christian, in good conscience,

1. swear an oath to another master?
2. be employed in a vocation that promises reciprocal death ("sword")?
3. take part in battle when it is unlawful for him to even go to court?

4. fasten anyone in chains, when Christ is the only avenger of justice?
5. give more allegiance to anyone other than Christ ("keep watch")?

Furthermore, could he,

6. fight on the Sabbath?
7. guard pagan temples?
8. eat forbidden food?
9. protect the demonic against whom he is to pray?
10. carry the flag of a regime that persecutes believers?
11. receive orders from a lesser commander ("watchword")?
12. wake to the wrong trumpet?
13. be buried in an unchristian manner?

Tertullian sees all such acts as an expressed denial of Jesus Christ's sovereignty over humanity, and the call for the Christian to act in a manner unfitting to his changed character. He continues:

Nowhere does the Christian change his character. There is one gospel, and the same Jesus, who will one day deny every one who denies, and acknowledge every one who acknowledges God,—who will save, too, the life which has been lost for his sake; but, on the other hand, destroy that which for gain has been saved to his dishonor. With him the faithful citizen is a soldier, just as the faithful soldier is a citizen. A state of faith admits no plea of necessity; they are under no necessity to sin, whose one necessity is, that they do not sin. For if one is pressed to . . . the sheer denial of Christ by the necessity of torture or of punishment, yet discipline does not connive even at that necessity; because there is a higher necessity to dread denying and to undergo martyrdom, than to escape from suffering, and to render the homage required.[20]

Still, an important point must be made here. It seems that Tertullian is unwilling to completely disallow the Christian service in the military. Instead, he leaves it to the conscience of the individual fellowships and Christians. He concludes the chapter:

> Touching this primary aspect of the question, as to the unlawfulness even of a military life itself, I shall not add more. . . . Indeed, if, putting my strength to the question, I banish from us the military life, I should now to no purpose issue a challenge on the matter of the military crown. Suppose, then, that the military service is lawful, as far as the plea for the crown is concerned.[21]

Church Voices of Pacifism: Take No Blood!

Though it shall be illustrated that Christians were serving in the military by the third century of the church, the early pastors and ministers in the leading churches still held to an anti-warfare stance well into the fourth century. Arnobius, writing around 300, derided all forms of public violence as homicide, and called Christians to task for even participating in capital punishment trials. In *Against the Heathen,* he wrote:

> It is not therefore befitting that those who strive to keep to the path of justice should be companions and sharers in this public homicide. For when God forbids us to kill, he not only prohibits us from open violence, which is not even allowed by the public laws, but he warns us against the commission of those things which are esteemed lawful among men. Thus it will be neither lawful for a just man to engage in warfare, since his warfare is justice itself, nor to accuse any one of a capital charge, because it makes no difference whether you put a man to death by word, or rather by the sword, since it is the act of putting to death itself which is prohibited. Therefore, with regard to this precept of God, there ought to be no exception

at all but that it is always unlawful to put to death a man, whom God willed to be a sacred animal.[22]

To Lactantius, even the testimony of a Christian in a trial which ends in the death of the accused is sinful, for it is participation in the process of death, which is to be left to God. Though his view may not have been in the majority, certainly he indicated a decided distaste for Christian cooperation in death.

In Book Six of *The Divine Institutes,* Lactantius takes perhaps the strongest pacifistic stance among the early church leaders:

> For he who reckons it a pleasure, that a man, though justly condemned, should be slain in his sight, pollutes his conscience as much as if he should become a spectator and a sharer of a homicide which is secretly committed. . . . So far has the feeling of humanity departed from the men that when they destroy the lives of men, they think they are amusing themselves with sport, being more guilty than all those whose blood-shedding they esteem a pleasure.[23]

If violence and death is endemic to humankind, how then does the Christian avoid all contact with acts of violence? As complete isolation is not an option, the Christian is called upon to provide a visual example of Jesus Christ's sacrifice when violence rises. Arnobius (300), writing from northern Africa, calls Christians to offer themselves in death, rather than cause the death of another human being. He writes:

> For since we, a numerous band of men as we are, have learned from his teaching and his laws that evil ought not to be re-quited with evil, that it is better to suffer wrong than to inflict it, that we should rather shed our own blood than stain our hands and our conscience with that of another, an ungrateful world is now for a long period enjoying a benefit from Christ, inasmuch as by his means the rage of savage ferocity has been

softened, and has begun to withhold hostile hands from the blood of a fellow-creature.[24]

Though a complete consensus of the opinion of the leadership of the early church cannot be stated emphatically, the common desire to avoid any participation in armed conflict is evident. Virtually every bishop who wrote treatises and addressed the subject spoke passionately against any Christian partaking in the shedding of blood, innocent or otherwise. Even in the midst of armed conflict, the Christian's chief weapon was considered to be that of active prayer and labor for peace. As citizens of heaven (*polituema*), this was the Christian's most effective service.

Conclusion: The Empathy of the Hunted

If the above ministers actually represented the majority of Christian opinion, what would the motivating factor for their universal love be? How could they be so irenic in the face of such a tumultuous time? Perhaps the answer can be found in the tumult itself. The Christians, in a profoundly visceral way, empathized with the vanquished.

All the Christians wanted to do was to worship their Savior and to share his love. Yet, at seemingly every turn, they were confronted with persecution, hatred, and scorn. While they—this minority band of followers of the Man who had been crucified—simply sought freedom, they were hounded by conscription and coercion. Perhaps their sympathy for the defeated foes, even to Rome's throne, was actually empathy. They understood only too well what it meant to be on the receiving end of warfare.

John Foxe's *Book of Martyrs* devotes the entire second chapter to stories he could collect of the horrors of the persecution of the early Christians. Though it is profoundly disturbing, perhaps it is good for Christians to once again visit the lives of our forefathers. In this final section of the chapter, he illuminates the torture of our fellow believers in the ten most intense periods of early Church persecution. From these selected and edited examples, the reasons early believers despised bloodshed become evident.

1. The First Persecution, Under Nero (67)

The first persecution of the Church took place in the year 67, under Nero, the sixth emperor of Rome. This monarch . . . gave way to the greatest extravagancy of temper, and to the most atrocious barbarities. . . . Nero even refined upon cruelty, and contrived all manner of punishments for the Christians that the most infernal imagination could design. In particular, he had some sewed up in skins of wild beasts, and then worried by dogs until they expired; and others dressed in shirts made stiff with wax, [were] fixed to axle trees, and set on fire in his gardens, in order to illuminate them.

2. The Second Persecution, Under Domitian (81)

The emperor Domitian, who was naturally inclined to cruelty, first slew his brother, and then raised the second persecution against the Christians. . . . Timothy was the celebrated disciple of St. Paul and bishop of Ephesus, where he zealously governed the Church until A.D. 97. At this period, as the pagans were about to celebrate a feast called Catagogion, Timothy, meeting the procession, severely reproved them for their ridiculous idolatry, which so exasperated the people that they fell upon him with their clubs, and beat him in so dreadful a manner that he expired of the bruises two days later.

3. The Third Persecution, Under Trajan (108)

In this persecution suffered . . . [Ignatius,] being sent from Syria to Rome, because he professed Christ, was given to the wild beasts to be devoured. . . . Having come to Smyrna, he wrote to the Church at Rome, exhorting them *not* to use means for his deliverance from martyrdom, lest they should deprive him of that which he most longed and hoped for. *"Now I begin to be a disciple. I care for nothing, of visible or invisible things, so that I may but win Christ. Let fire and the cross, let the companies of wild beasts, let breaking of bones and tearing of limbs, let the grinding of the whole body, and all the malice of the devil, come upon me; be it so, only may I win Christ Jesus!"* And even when he was sentenced to be thrown to the beasts, such was the burning desire that he had to suffer, that he spake, what time he heard the lions roaring, saying: *"I am the wheat of Christ: I am going to be ground with the teeth of wild beasts, that I may be found pure bread."*

In Mount Ararat many were crucified, crowned with thorns, and spears run into their sides, in imitation of Jesus Christ's passion. Eustachius, a brave and successful Roman commander, was by the emperor ordered to join in an idolatrous sacrifice to celebrate some of his own victories; but his faith (being a Christian in his heart) was so much greater than his vanity, that he nobly refused it. Enraged at the denial, the ungrateful emperor forgot the service of this skillful commander, and ordered him and his whole family to be martyred.

4. The Fourth Persecution, Under Marcus Aurelius Antoninus (162)

The cruelties used in this persecution were such that many of the spectators shuddered with horror at the sight, and were astonished at the intrepidity of the sufferers. Some of the martyrs were obliged to pass, with their already wounded feet, over thorns, nails, sharp shells, etc. upon their points, others were scourged until their sinews and veins lay bare, and after suffering the most excruciating tortures that could be devised, they were destroyed by the most terrible deaths.

Germanicus, a young man, but a true Christian, being delivered to the wild beasts on account of his faith, behaved with such astonishing courage that several pagans became converts to a faith which inspired such fortitude.

Polycarp, the venerable bishop of Smyrna, hearing that persons were seeking for him, escaped, but was discovered by a child. . . . The proconsul then urged him, saying, *"Swear, and I will release thee; —reproach Christ."*

Polycarp answered, *"Eighty and six years have I served him, and he never once wronged me; how then shall I blaspheme my King, Who hath saved me?"* At the stake to which he was only tied, but not nailed as usual, as he assured them he should stand immovable, the flames, on their kindling the fagots, encircled his body, like an arch, without touching him; and the executioner, on seeing this, was ordered to pierce him with a sword, when so great a quantity of blood flowed out as extinguished the fire. But his body, at the instigation of the enemies of the gospel, especially Jews, was ordered to be consumed in the pile, and the request of his friends, who wished to give it Christian burial, rejected.

5. The Fifth Persecution, Commencing with Severus (192)

Perpetua, a married lady, of about twenty-two years was martyred at this time. Those who suffered with her were Felicitas, a married lady, big with child at the time of her being apprehended, and Revocatus, catechumen of Carthage, and a slave. The names of the other prisoners destined to suffer upon this occasion were Saturninus, Secundulus, and Satur. On the day appointed for their execution, they were led to the amphitheater. Satur, Saturninus, and Revocatus were ordered to run the gauntlet between the hunters, or such as had the care of the wild beasts. The hunters being drawn up in two ranks, they ran between, and were severely lashed as they passed. Felicitas and Perpetua were stripped, in order to be thrown to a mad bull, which made his first attack upon Perpetua, and stunned her; he then darted at Felicitas, and gored her dreadfully; but not killing them, the executioner did that office with a sword. Revocatus and Satur were destroyed by wild beasts; Saturninus was beheaded; and Secundulus died in prison. These executions were in the year 205, on the eighth day of March.

Speratus and twelve others were likewise beheaded; as was Andocles in France. Asclepiades, bishop of Antioch, suffered many tortures, but his life was spared.

Cecilia, a young lady of good family in Rome, was married to a gentleman named Valerian. She converted her husband and brother, who were beheaded; and the maximus, or officer, who led them to execution, becoming their convert, suffered the same fate. The lady was placed naked in a scalding bath, and having continued there a considerable time, her head was struck off with a sword (222).

6. The Sixth Persecution, Under Maximinus (235)

Calepodius, a Christian minister, thrown into the Tyber; Martina, a noble and beautiful virgin; and Hippolitus, a Christian prelate, tied to a wild horse, and dragged until he expired. During this persecution, raised by Maximinus, numberless Christians were slain without trial, and buried indiscriminately in heaps, sometimes fifty or sixty being cast into a pit together, without the least decency.

7. The Seventh Persecution, Under Decius (249)

Julian, a native of Cilicia, as we are informed by Chrysostom, was seized upon for being a Christian. He was put into a leather bag, together with a number of serpents and scorpions, and in that condition thrown into the sea.

Agatha, a Sicilian lady, was not more remarkable for her personal and acquired endowments, than her piety; her beauty was such, that Quintian, governor of Sicily, became enamored of her, and made many attempts upon her chastity without success. In order to gratify his passions with the greater conveniency, he put the virtuous lady into the hands of Aphrodica, a very infamous and licentious woman. This wretch tried every artifice to win her to the desired prostitution; but found all her efforts were vain; for her chastity was impregnable, and she well knew that virtue alone could procure true happiness. Aphrodica acquainted Quintian with the inefficacy of her endeavors, who, enraged to be foiled in his designs, changed his lust into resentment. On her confessing that she was a Christian, he determined to gratify his revenge, as he could not his passion. Pursuant to his orders, she was scourged, burnt with red-hot irons, and torn with sharp hooks. Having borne these torments with admirable fortitude, she was next laid naked upon live coals, intermingled with glass, and then being carried back to prison, she there expired on February 5, 251.

8. The Eighth Persecution, Under Valerian (257)

Began under Valerian, in the month of April 257, and continued for three years and six months. The martyrs that fell in this persecution were innumerable, and their tortures and deaths various and painful. The most eminent martyrs were the following, though neither rank, sex, nor age were regarded.

Stephen, bishop of Rome, was beheaded in the same year, and about that time Saturninus, the pious orthodox bishop of Toulouse, refusing to sacrifice to idols, was treated with all the barbarous indignities imaginable, and fastened by the feet to the tail of a bull. Upon a signal given, the enraged animal was driven down the steps of the temple, by which the worthy martyr's brains were dashed out.

9. The Ninth Persecution, Under Aurelian (274)

Faith, a Christian female, of Acquitain, in France, was ordered to be broiled upon a gridiron, and then beheaded (287).

Quintin was a Christian, and a native of Rome, but determined to attempt the propagation of the gospel in Gaul, with one Lucian, they preached together in Amiens. Quintin remained in Picardy, and was very zealous in his ministry. Being seized upon as a Christian, he was stretched with pullies until his joints were dislocated; his body was then torn with wire scourges, and boiling oil and pitch poured on his naked flesh; lighted torches were applied to his sides and armpits; and after he had been thus tortured, he was remanded back to prison, and died of the barbarities he had suffered, October 31, 287. His body was sunk in the Somme.

10. The Tenth Persecution, Under Diocletian (303)

Victor was a Christian of a good family at Marseilles, in France; he spent a great part of the night in visiting the afflicted, and confirming the weak; which pious work he could not, consistently with his own safety, perform in the daytime; and his fortune he spent in relieving the distresses of poor Christians. He was at length, however, seized by the emperor Maximian's decree, who ordered him to be bound, and dragged through the streets. During the execution of this order, he was treated with all manner of cruelties and indignities by the enraged populace. Remaining still inflexible, his courage was deemed obstinacy. Being by order stretched upon the rack, he turned his eyes toward heaven, and prayed to God to endue him with patience, after which he underwent the tortures with most admirable fortitude. After the executioners were tired with inflicting torments on him, he was conveyed to a dungeon. In his confinement, he converted his jailers, named Alexander, Felician, and Longinus. This affair coming to the ears of the emperor, he ordered them immediately to be put to death, and the jailers were accordingly beheaded. Victor was then again put to the rack, unmercifully beaten . . . and again sent to prison. Being a third time examined concerning his religion, he persevered in his principles; a small altar was then brought, and he was commanded to offer incense upon it immediately. Fired with indignation at the request, he boldly stepped forward, and with his foot overthrew both altar and idol. This so enraged the emperor Maximian, who was present, that he ordered the foot with which he had kicked the altar to be immediately cut off; and Victor was thrown into a mill, and crushed to pieces with the stones.

Timothy, a deacon of Mauritania, and Maura his wife, had not been united together by the bands of wedlock above three weeks, when they were separated from each other by the persecution. Timothy, being apprehended as a Christian, was carried before Arrianus, the governor of Thebais, who, knowing that he had the keeping of the Holy Scriptures, commanded him to deliver them up to be burnt; to which he answered, "Had I children, I would sooner deliver them up to be sacrificed, than part with the Word of God." The governor being much incensed at this reply ordered his eyes to be put out, with red-hot irons, saying, "The books shall at least be useless to you, for you shall not see to read them." His patience under the operation was so great that the governor grew more exasperated; he, therefore, in order, if possible, to overcome his fortitude, ordered him to be hung up by the feet, with a weight tied about his neck, and a gag in his mouth. In this state, Maura his wife, tenderly urged him for her sake to recant; but, when the gag was taken out of his mouth, instead of consenting to his wife's entreaties, he greatly blamed her mistaken love, and declared his resolution of dying for the faith. The consequence was, that Maura resolved to imitate his courage and fidelity and either to accompany or follow him to glory. The governor, after trying in vain to alter her resolution, ordered her to be tortured, which was executed with great severity. After this, Timothy and Maura were crucified near each other (304).

Notes

1. "Fellowship of Reconciliation, England (1916–1992)," in the British Library of Political and Economic Science, COLL MISC 0456. Found in many collections, and on the web at library-2.lse.ac.uk/archives/handlists/Fellowship/m.html. Accessed October 16, 2003.
2. Ibid.
3. Ibid.
4. Chrétiennes 33 bis, 62–67. Emphasis added.
5. Justin Martyr, *Dialogue with Trypho* 110, in *Ante-Nicene Fathers*, 38 vols., ed. A. Cleveland Cox (Grand Rapids: Eerdmans, 1987), 1:254 (hereafter cited as *ANF*).
6. Justin Martyr, *1 Apologia* 39, in *ANF,* 1:175–6.
7. Irenaeus, *Contra Haereses* 4.34.4, in *ANF,* 1:349.
8. Isaiah 2:2–4.
9. Tatian, *Oratio ad Graecos* 2, in *ANF,* 2:381.
10. Clement of Alexandria, *Paedagogus* 1.12, in *ANF,* 2:511.
11. Ibid.
12. Origen, *Contra Celsus* 8.69, in *ANF,* 5:666. Origen also illustrates that the Lord to whom they are praying is the one who said to the Hebrews, "The Lord shall fight for you and ye shall hold your peace." This citation from Exodus 14:14 (KJV) seemed to indicate a complete pacifism, which then calls God to the task of vengeance.
13. Ibid., 8.73.

14. Ibid.
15. Ibid.
16. Ibid.
17. Tertullian, *On Idolatry* 19, in *ANF*, 3:73.
18. Ibid.
19. Tertullian, *De Corona Militis* 11, in *ANF*, 3:99–100.
20. Ibid. Tertullian sees the Roman homage as a violation. He continues, "In fact, an excuse of this sort overturns the entire essence of our sacrament, removing even the obstacle to voluntary sins; for it would be possible also to maintain that inclination is a necessity, as involving in it, forsooth, a sort of compulsion."
21. Ibid.
22. Arnobius, *Against the Heathen* 1.6, in *ANF*, 6:415.
23. Lactantius, *The Divine Institutes* 6.20, in *ANF*, 7:186.
24. Arnobius, *Against the Heathen* 1.6, in *ANF*, 6:415.

Chapter 2

THE THUNDERING LEGION

How the Slaughtered Saints Became Sporadic Soldiers
(A.D. 150–325)

We used to murder one another. Now, we not only refrain from warring with our enemies, but we don't even
lie or deceive our examiners. We willingly die, all the while
confessing Christ. Your soldiers—who have taken the
military oath—prefer their allegiance to you over their
own lives, and you can offer them nothing of eternal consequence. How much more do we who long for the incorruptible prize endure all things, in order to obtain what
we desire from Christ, who is able to grant it.[1]

—Justin Martyr

We attacked the city [of Jerusalem] from all sides, day
and night, on Wednesday and Thursday. But before we
attacked the city, the bishops and priests, by preaching
and exhortation, ordered everyone to hold a procession
in honor of God all around the city and arranged for
prayers, almsgiving and fasting. . . . Soon our men were
running all around the city, seizing gold and silver. . . .
Rejoicing and weeping for joy, our people came to the
sepulcher of Jesus our Savior to worship and pay their
debt.

At dawn our men cautiously went up to the roof of the
Temple and attacked the Saracen [Muslim] men and
women, beheading them with naked swords. . . .

Our men ordered that all the dead Saracens should be cast out of the city because of the great stench, since the city was filled with their corpses. The living Saracens dragged the dead outside the gates and made great heaps of them, as large as houses.

No one ever saw or heard of such a slaughter of pagan peoples, for funeral pyres were formed of them like pyramids and no one knows their number except God alone.[2]

—Report of the Conquest of Jerusalem

July 17, 1099

Quite a difference, isn't it? Eight hundred fifty years after Justin penned his description of the irenic Christian community at Rome, the Crusade Chronicler writes this horrific summary of the explicitly "Christian" army beheading the Muslim inhabitants of Jerusalem. With graphic details usually reserved for the most blatant horror movies, the Chronicler revels in the bloodshed by the Christian soldiers, and even describes the prayers that preceded the slaughter. The inclusion of women among the victims comes without a hint of remorse in the narrative, and the demonstration of an outdoor crematorium comes without a tear.

Was this shift caused by some cataclysmic event that shocked the leadership of the Church? No, it was not.

Although the first three centuries of the Christian movement were marked by an almost universal stance of pacifism, one can trace a perceptible—albeit grudging—easing of the prohibition against Christian involvement in warfare.[3] While the bishops and leaders certainly did not advocate active killing in war, they did begin to allow believers to serve under strict conditions.

As historian Roland Bainton notes, the ascension of Constantine in 324 marks the point of transition in the teaching of the church regarding warfare. It is the position of the authors that this transition marked the first step of descent into a sanctioned theology of holy war. Each subsequent level was marked not only by a greater participation of Christians in the military, but in truth a greater influence by Church leaders on the purposes, motives, and strategies of war. *This point cannot be overstated.*

The descent can be viewed in four levels, as seen in the chart on the following page.

This chapter will trace the subtle shift in Christian thought toward participation in armed warfare from Augustine's careful prohibitions in the fifth century to Urban's *Christi militia* in the eleventh century.

Let Some of Them In: Conditional Provisions for Military Service

In the third century, a minister named Hippolytus was trained by Irenaeus and became the bishop of Portus. Though he was a Greek, his "history was Roman," and he lived during the reign of Severus.[4] As the Christian community began to become more acceptable and established in regions around Europe and North Africa, many congregations struggled with the problem of whether to accept into membership those who served in positions that seemed contradictory to the faith. Hippolytus listed twenty-four forbidden or restricted vocations for believers in his book, *Apostolic Traditions*.[5]

Among the twenty-four restricted professions, the church found consensus on those that explicitly violated the common biblical ethics. Prostitutes, sodomites, sculptors and painters of idols, and astrologers must abandon their employment if they professed Jesus Christ. Interestingly, the list also denied membership to those whose occupations were based on deception or entertainment, such as magicians and actors.[6]

The most pervasive restriction was against occupations that involved *violence*. Eight of the twenty-four involved brutality, including chariot drivers, gladiators, civil servants in gladiatorial shows, and executioners.[7] With regard to the soldier, Hippolytus allows some conditional involvement. If the man was a soldier at conversion, he was allowed to continue in this work, but he was not allowed to take active part in killing an enemy, executing a prisoner, or taking a vow of allegiance.[8]

Level of Involvement	Approximate Dates	Title	Graphic	Description
First	A.D. 30–175	The Hunted	**State** → **Church**	Christians are not regarded as joining the military until about 173. The period is marked by an adversarial relationship between Church and state, with the Church being persecuted. *Christians are mostly prohibited from serving in the army until the fourth-century reign of Constantine.*
Second	A.D. 175–324	The Courtship	**State** / **Church** (State over the Church)	In small increments, the Christians become involved in the military, and by the time of Constantine, are the protected and preferred soldiers in the state's army. *Christians now serve in the army for God's work.*
Third	A.D. 324–1000	Unholy Matrimony	**State = Church** (State and the Church being equal partners)	From Charles Martel to Hildebrand, Christian soldiers come to believe that they accomplish God's work in warfare. The climax of this period is the anointing of Charlemagne as emperor of the Holy Roman Empire by the pope, and the vestment of the pope's staff by Charlemagne. *Christians command the army under temporal Kings.*
Fourth	A.D. 1000–1300	The Church as a Mistress	**Church** / **State**	The Church becomes drunk on temporal authority, and its leaders assume that it controls the state. In fact, the secular rulers use the Church and tossed it aside when no longer needed. The Crusades are the demarcation of this period. *Christian armies go to war under the direction of the pope as commander-in-chief.*

In this vein, Hippolytus seems to agree with Tertullian. This Latin Father of the second and the third centuries was loath to allow combatants to join the church, but also made provision for nonviolent soldiers who served in the military prior to their conversion.[9]

Even Clement of Alexandra, who had given such a vigorous condemnation of Christian involvement in the military ("For it is not in war, but in peace, that we are trained"[10]) gives a qualified acceptance of the Christian in the army. In *Stromata,* he writes of the transformed nature of the Christian soldier, as well as the change in ethics for workers in all other occupations. When a man or woman becomes a Christian, *allegiance* and *alliance* radically change, but not necessarily occupation. The former idols are destroyed, and the new believer is transformed into a servant of Jesus Christ.

> And as, if one devote himself to Ischomachus, [Christ] will make him a farmer; and to Lampis, a mariner; and to Charidemus, a military commander; and to Simon, an equestrian; and to Perdices, a trader; and to Crobylus, a cook; and to Archelaus, a dancer; and to Homer, a poet; and to Pyrrho, a wrangler; and to Demosthenes, an orator; and to Chrysippus, a dialectician; and to Aristotle, a naturalist; and to Plato, a philosopher: so he who listens to the Lord, and follows the prophecy given by him, will be formed perfectly in the likeness of the teacher—made a god going about in flesh. Accordingly, those fall from this eminence who follow not God whither he leads. And he leads us in the inspired Scriptures.[11]

This provisional acceptance of the peaceful military officer may have been for the purposes of service to the state, as in civil service or desk work. If the soldier were to transfer his commission into a field of peaceful order, then military service would not be prohibited. As Bainton notes:

> That the objection to war lay in the scruple against killing rather than in social indifference is borne out by the willingness of a

number of early Christian writers to sanction even military service provided it were restricted to police functions and did not entail bloodshed. A soldier might serve for a lifetime without killing in an empire at peace where the army is vested with the functions of a police force. For example, in the city of Rome fire protection and the keeping of the peace were assigned to a military unit known as the *Vigiles*. We have evidence of Christian participation in two branches of the service devoted primarily to police work.[12]

Therefore, a Christian could serve in some state protection function without violating the commands of Scripture or offending the bishops and churches. The Christian soldier would in fact act in a servant role to humanity in so doing. Such work would actually be seen in a positive light. Bainton continues,

> Their functions included the guarding of the emperor's person, the custody of prisoners, care of public transport and the mails, supervision of ordinance, and even secretarial duty— the two latter both in military and civilian administration.[13]

Yet in any regard, this was a far cry from actual participation in warfare, as would become the case in just a number of years.

The Thundering Legion: First Christians in the Military (ca. 173)

Cecil John Cadoux states there is no evidence of Christians serving in the military until the time of Marcus Aurelius (160–180).[14] If there were Christian soldiers, little or nothing was said about their faith. Certainly the clearest example of early Christian involvement in the military was found in the famous *Legio XII Fulminata*, the "Thundering Legion," which served under Aurelius. Around 173, Aurelius's forces included some Christian recruits from Armenia. While fighting in the region of Germany, the intense heat and lack of water almost killed the soldiers. Drought, coupled with the heat, was leading to massive dehydration. As Eusebius recounts, the Christian soldiers prayed, and miraculously rain began to fall. Eusebius writes:

> It is reported that Marcus Aurelius Caesar, brother of Antoninus, being about to engage in battle with the Germans and Sarmatians, was in great trouble on account of his army suffering from thirst. But the soldiers of the so-called Melitene legion, through the faith which has given strength from that time to the present, when they were drawn up before the enemy, kneeled on the ground, as is our custom in prayer, and engaged in supplications to God. This was indeed a strange sight to the enemy, but it is reported that a stranger thing immediately followed. The lightning drove the enemy to flight and destruction, but a shower refreshed the army of those who had called on God, all of whom had been on the point of perishing with thirst.[15]

Perhaps the story is a legend. However, Bainton notes that even Tertullian uses the story to illustrate Christian involvement in civil affairs.[16]

Did the purported Christian soldier somehow refute the admonitions of bishops such as Tertullian and Iranaeus? Was he being disobedient? In certain instances, the presence of Christians in the military actually helped the bishops and writers illustrate the usefulness of the Christian community to the state. Tertullian, in his detailed letter to the leaders of the Roman Empire, details the almost schizophrenic nature of the Christian living in a warring land. On the one hand, he cites,

> If we are enjoined then to love our enemies . . . whom have we to hate? If injured, we are forbidden to retaliate, lest we become as bad ourselves: who can suffer injury at our hands?[17]

Yet before the politicians and leaders begin to believe that the Christian community is completely useless, he writes passionately,

But we are called to account as harm-doers on another ground, and are accused of being useless in the affairs of life. How in all the world can that be the case with people who are living among you, eating the same food, wearing the same attire, having the same habits, under the same necessities of existence? We are not Indian Brahmins or Gymnosophists, who dwell in woods and exile themselves from ordinary human life. We do not forget the debt of gratitude we owe to God, our Lord and Creator; we reject no creature of his hands, though certainly we exercise restraint upon ourselves, lest of any gift of his we make an immoderate or sinful use. So we sojourn with you in the world, abjuring neither forum, nor shambles, nor bath, nor booth, nor workshop, nor inn, nor weekly market, nor any other places of commerce. We sail with you, and *fight with you,* and till the ground with you.[18]

By the dawn of the fourth century, there was clearly a Christian presence in military combat. Eusebius of Caesaria begins Book Eight of his encyclopedic *History of the Church* with painfully candid description of the moral decline in Christian society around 303. The mark of the beginning of a fresh persecution was directed toward, in his estimation, the "brethren in the army." Galerius was Diocletian's lieutenant, and he sought to rid the army of all Christians. The mere mention of a concerted effort to purge Christians from the legions suggests that there must have been a number of them. He writes:

But when on account of the abundant freedom, we fell into laxity and sloth, and envied and reviled each other, and were almost, as it were, taking up arms against one another, rulers assailing rulers with words like spears, and people forming parties against people, and monstrous hypocrisy and dissimulation rising to the greatest height of wickedness, the divine judgment with forbearance, as is its pleasure, while the multitudes yet continued to assemble, gently and moderately harassed the episcopacy. *This persecution began with the brethren in the army*. But as if without sensibility, we were not eager to make the Deity favorable and propitious; and some, like atheists, thought that our affairs were unheeded and ungoverned; and thus we added one wickedness to another.[19]

Christian Martyrs in the Military

Further evidence of a developing presence of Christians in the military was the citation of Christian soldiers who died in battle. Beginning in the third century, certain authors and bishops offered evidence that they recognized a presence of believers in the armies of the land. Modern liberal scholarship, from Adolf von Harnack (1851–1930), acknowledges the presence of Christian soldiers in battle.[20]

In the third century, Cyprian, the leading minister in Carthage, wrote Celerinus to encourage other believers, reminding them of his godly heritage. Included in this account was the story of Celerinus's soldier uncles, viewed as godly men, though they were also soldiers:

> Nor is that kind of title to glories in the case of Celerinus, our beloved, an unfamiliar and novel thing. He is advancing in the footsteps of his kindred; he rivals his parents and relations in equal honors of divine condescension. His grandmother, Celerina, was some time since crowned with martyrdom. Moreover, his paternal and maternal uncles, Laurentius and Egnatius, who themselves also were once warring in the camps of the world, but were [also] true and spiritual soldiers of God, casting down the devil by the confession of Christ, merited palms and crowns from the Lord by their illustrious passion.[21]

With the pressure from the bishops to avoid military service, certainly some prospective enlisted men must have refused to swear allegiance to the Empire. In writing a refutation to Celsus, Origen states plainly, "We do not indeed fight under [the king], although he requires it."[22]

The Slow Shift toward
Christian Participation in Warfare

Prior to the ascension of Constantine as emperor of both the Eastern and Western Roman Empire in 324, there is evidence of a weakening of the prohibition against warfare in the Church, even among the leadership and clergy. The Thundering Legion under Aurelius became an example for at least Eusebius and Tertullian. Christians were taking part in all civic affairs, even accepting election and appointment to public office. Such occupations were now acceptable within the Christian community. In 278, Paul of Samosata became the first Christian bishop to hold the post of civil magistrate in Palmyra, and he even employed a bodyguard during his time of service.[23] The presence of a bodyguard and the garnering of a political position had been foreign to the Christian community just a few generations before. Now, as they were becoming accepted, Christians were taking a prominent place in society.

Eusebius tells an extraordinary tale of Christian bloodshed that shows how loose the pacifistic stance had become. In the same region of Armenia from which the Thundering Legion came, the Christians in the fourth century united against an emperor who was severely persecuting them. Whereas in previous centuries Christians would have passively faced martyrdom, this time they rose up against the emperor, took up weapons, and defeated him. Eusebius seems to regard this as the judgment of God against the pagan king:

> In addition to this, the tyrant was compelled to go to war with the Armenians, who had been from ancient times friends and allies of the Romans. As they were also Christians and zealous in their piety toward the Deity, the enemy of God had attempted to compel them to sacrifice to idols and demons, and had thus made friends foes, and allies enemies. All these things suddenly took place at one and the same time, and refuted the tyrant's empty vaunt against the Deity. For he had boasted that, because of his zeal for idols and his hostility against us,

neither famine nor pestilence nor war had happened in his time. These things, therefore, coming upon him at once and together, furnished a prelude also of his own destruction. He himself with his forces was defeated in the war with the Armenians, and the rest of the inhabitants of the cities under him were terribly afflicted with famine and pestilence, so that one measure of wheat was sold for twenty-five hundred Attic drachmas. Those who died in the cities were innumerable, and those who died in the country and villages were still more.[24]

Theodoret, writing his own version of Church history, also includes the account of Bishop James of Nisibis, who inspired the army against the Persians in the fourth century by calling down the judgment of God on the approaching heathen. The pestilence that followed was directly attributed to the hand of God, and included mosquitoes and gnats to upset the horses and elephants on which the enemy was traveling. He writes of the bishop with a stirring sense of reverence:

For that holy man, through prayer, filled with valor both the troops and the rest of the townsfolk, and both built the walls, withstood the engines, and beat off the advancing foe. And all this he did without approaching the walls, but by beseeching the Lord of all within the church. . . . Jacobus [mounted] the wall to see the barbarians and to let fly at them the darts of his curse. So the divine man consented and climbed up into a tower but when he saw the innumerable host he discharged no other curse than to that mosquitoes and gnats might be sent forth upon them, so that by means of these tiny animals they might learn the might of the Protector of the Romans. On his prayer followed clouds of mosquitoes and gnats; they filled the hollow trunks of the elephants, and the ears and nostrils of horses and other animals. Finding the attack of these little creatures past endurance they broke their bridles, unseated their riders and threw the ranks into confusion. The

Persians abandoned their camp and fled head-long. So the wretched prince learned by a slight and kindly chastisement the power of the God who protects the pious, and marched his army home again, reaping for all the harvest of the siege not triumph but disgrace.[25]

Such a narrative marks a clear distinction for the relationship between the civil authorities and the Christian citizens. By the time of Constantine, more Christians were serving in the military. The formerly adversarial relationship between faith and government was less strident. In fact, the Christians themselves believed that their service could be used by God.

Constantine and the Official Christian Church Military (A.D. 324)

The dramatic change from Diocletian's persecution to Constantine's acceptance of Christianity was a problem for theologians. Beyond the pressure for rulers to move from orthodoxy to more inclusive beliefs, the issue was whether a "Christian" leader who demanded that his entire force be baptized was any better than a pagan. Killing the enemies of the state was still the conclusion. Was Constantine's appropriation of Christian purpose reason enough to join the military forces wholeheartedly and to kill with sanctified glee?

The Church had been able to distance itself from the military, to the point of martyrdom. The taking up of arms was seen as a contradiction to the teachings of Jesus Christ, even if the pagan forces against which they were fighting were intent upon their death. The emperors, regardless of name or degree of persecution, asked for a sworn oath of loyalty that the Christian could not take in light of Jesus Christ's firm admonitions.

Thus, the very issue of the oath was irreducible for the teachers and bishops. Yet what was the Church to do when the emperor is willing to forego the oath, or to adapt the oath to become a vow unto the Lord God? The *Constantinian synthesis* became a vexing issue for

Church leaders. Now they were faced with one who was supposedly fighting for the truth of Christ and his kingdom. Was the end result of murder in the temporal realm somehow justified if the purpose for such an endeavor was one of spiritual dimension?

Some leaders of the era attempted to justify the warfare as one of *kerygma*—a temporal deed of warfare for the purposes of proclamation of the essence of the gospel. But could the end result of spreading the message of Jesus Christ really excuse the methods used?

Eusebius of Caesarea in later writings regarded the Roman Empire's victories against the pagans as a divine blessing and developed a theological apologetic for the Empire's successes. In his *Oration of Eusebius Pamphilus: In Praise of the Emperor Constantine*, pronounced on the thirtieth anniversary of the beginning of Constantine's reign, Eusebius presumes that there is an intersection of the purposes of God in the rule of Constantine.[26]

He begins by noting the "supremacy" of God, even with the approval of the emperor:

> Today is the festival of our great emperor: and we his children rejoice therein, feeling the inspiration of our sacred theme. He who presides over our solemnity is the Great Sovereign himself; he, I mean, who is truly great; of whom I affirm (nor will the sovereign who hears me be offended, but will rather approve of this ascription of praise to God), that he is above and beyond all created things the Highest, the Greatest, the most Mighty One.[27]

Thus, we see a perplexing conundrum for the Church: What if the emperor is willing to acknowledge God as sovereign? Does that substantively change the nature of warfare? Apparently, it elicited Christian allegiance in the eyes of Eusibius.

Secondly, Eusebius saw the hand of God upon the protections the Roman Empire enjoyed:

> This only begotten Word of God reigns, from ages which had

no beginning, to infinite and endless ages, the partner of his Father's kingdom. And [our emperor] ever beloved by him, who derives the source of imperial authority from above, and is strong in the power of his sacred title, has controlled the empire of the world for a long period of years. Again, that Preserver of the universe orders these heavens and earth, and the celestial kingdom, consistently with his Father's will.[28]

Finally, Eusebius notes that Constantine became the force of restraint against the demonic onslaught of the heathens, and in so doing, the emperor was acting within the very will of God, even in warfare.

For whereas we are composed of two distinct natures, I mean of body and spirit, of which the one is visible to all, the other invisible, against both these natures two kinds of barbarous and savage enemies, the one invisibly, the other openly, are constantly arrayed. The one oppose our bodies with bodily force the other with incorporeal assaults besiege the naked soul itself. Again, the visible barbarians, like the wild nomad tribes, no better than savage beasts, assail the nations of civilized men, ravage their country, and enslave their cities, rushing on those who inhabit them like ruthless wolves of the desert, and destroying all who fall under their power. But those unseen foes, more cruel far than barbarians, I mean the soul-destroying demons whose course is through the regions of the air, had succeeded, through the snares of vile polytheism, in enslaving the entire human race, insomuch that they no longer recognized the true God, but wandered in the mazes of atheistic error.[29]

Constantine, in his own *Oration* on the occasion of Easter, makes a connection that is later picked up by Urban at the Council of Clermont. In the center of his speech (chapters 16–22 in Eusebius's account), Emperor Constantine hearkens back to the Old Testament armies, which operated as a killing force for God's purposes. This must be noted as significant in developing an argument that would be taken up to justify the First Crusade. Moses, Joshua, and Gideon had all shed blood as warriors for God. Note Constantine's justification for the Old Testament warfare, and by proxy, his war to unite the Roman Empire under him:

> By these not the slaughter of animals alone, but the sacrifice of human victims, and the pollutions of an accursed worship, had been devised: as, for example, by the laws of Assyria and Egypt, the lives of innocent men were offered up in images of brass or earth.[30]

The purpose, in Emperor Constantine's rationale, was clear: *War for the purpose of defending the innocent, even if it means the slaughter of the enemy, is not only honorable and virtuous, but also God-ordained.* Constantine, as Pope Urban II later, ignores the moral implications of the teachings of Jesus Christ and simply uses Old Testament anecdotal evidence to justify the "warring church."

Get a Piece of the Roman Peace: Christians, Come Join Us!

As Emperor Constantine restored order to the Empire—and gave complicit authority to the Christian church—the bishops, theologians, and authors became emboldened to an almost eschatological and millennial hope for a temporal peace under the direction of God. This coalition of church and state, in both legislative and militaristic peace, carried serious implications for the formerly pacifistic Christian community. Would the Church now be complicit in warfare and defense? Would bishops preside at executions? The Christian leaders certainly seemed prepared to unite with the state, following centuries of antagonism. As Bainton notes, "to the confession of one faith, one lord, and one baptism could now be added that of one empire and one emperor."[31]

Diodor of Tarsus, echoing the beliefs of many theologians of that age, "declared that through Christianity and Rome, God had caused wars to cease to the ends of the earth and had mingled cities and people through the preaching of the city of God."[32]

Thus, not only did the Christian community give its benign approval to warfare, but by the time of Constantine the Church was giving explicit approval of warfare as a restraint of evil. So effusive was the Church in its praise that during the reign of Theodosius II (408–450), all pagans were purportedly discharged from military service, and only Christians were permitted to serve.[33]

What did this shift in Christian life and ethic do to their belief that Jesus Christ was returning soon, so they did not need to invest themselves in the affairs of men? There developed an almost postmillennial relief among the Christians. Rather than awaiting the return of Jesus to rescue the persecuted, the Christians, now respected by many in the Roman society, felt it was their job to usher in the kingdom of God by enforcing Christian rules in the laws of men. As Robert Lightner writes:

> Postmillennialism and theonomy (from the Greek for *God* and *law*) usually go together. Postmillennial theonomy advocates argue that the church, like Israel of old, has the solemn responsibility to pressure civil governments to confirm God's laws, including those given through Moses—the precepts and the penalties. In this way the secular state will be brought into submission to God and his laws. When this has been realized, God's kingdom on earth will have arrived. [34]

The Christian community had suffered through the horrors of persecution, famine, and sword. Now, as the official religion of the Roman Empire, they were allowed to participate in the civic affairs of men, including military service. Would they be willing to be an influence in political affairs to a godly end, or would they become infested with the lust for power like all who had gone before them? As the Church entered the next centuries, we would find both godly (Augustine) and ungodly (Henry IV) leaders attempting to reconcile this uneasy union.

Notes

1. Adapted from Justin Martyr, *1 Apologia*. In the *Apostolic Fathers*, trans. by A. Cleveland Cox (Grand Rapids: Eerdmans, 1987), 39.

2. Guibert, Abbot of Nogent, *Historia quae dicitur Gesta Dei per Francos*. In *Recueil des historiens des croisades, Historiens occidentaux*, 5 vols., author's translation (Paris: Bibliotheque, 1844–1895), 38–39.

3. Roland Bainton, *Christian Attitudes Toward War and Peace* (Nashville: Abingdon, 1960), 66. Bainton's seminal work serves as the basis for this chapter, along with the primary sources cited in the *Ante-Nicene Fathers*.

4. *ANF*, 5:3. The life of Hippolytus was roughly 170–236.

5. Hippolytus, *Apostolic Traditions*, ed. Gregory Dix (London: SPCK, 1937). The *Traditions* are extant mostly in the Coptic versions of Sahidic and Boharic.

6. Hippolytus, *Apostolic Traditions*, 27.

7. Ibid.

8. Ibid. He also notes, however, that the leader or commander must resign his commission to enter the church.

9. Tertullian, *On Idolatry* 11; and *1 Apologia* 43, in *ANF*, 49, 67.

10. Clement of Alexandria, *Paedagogus* 1.12, in *ANF*, 2:511.

11. Ibid., *Stromata* 7.16, in *ANF*, 2:464.

12. Bainton, *Christian Attitudes Toward War and Peace*, 79.

13. Ibid.

14. Cecil John Cadoux, *The Early Church and the World* (Edinburgh: T. & T. Clark, 1925), 276. Bainton agrees with Cadoux, as does Hornus. See Bainton, *Christian Attitudes Toward War and Peace*, 67ff.; and Jean-Michel Hornus, *It Is Not Lawful for Me to Fight* (Kitchener, Ont.: Herald, 1980), 122; as cited in Bainton, *Christian Attitudes Toward War and Peace*.

15. Eusebius, *History of the Church* 5.5, in *A Select Library of the Nicene and Post-Nicene Fathers of the Christian Church*, ed. Philip Schaff (Buffalo: Christian Literature, 1886), 1:127 (hereafter cited as *NPNF*).

16. Tertullian, *1 Apologia* 5, in *ANF,* 3:22.

17. Ibid., 37, in *ANF,* 3:45.

18. Ibid., 42, in *ANF,* 3:49. Emphasis added by author.

19. Eusebius, *History of the Church* 8.1, in *NPNF,* 143. Emphasis added by author.

20. Adolf von Harnack, *Militia Christi* (Tübingen, Germany: Tübingen University Press, 1905), 117–21.

21. Cyprian, *Epistolae* 33.3, in *ANF,* 5:313.

22. Origen, *Contra Celsus* 8.73, in *ANF,* 4:668.

23. Ibid., 7.30, in *NPNF,* 132. As cited in Bainton, *Christian Attitudes Toward War and Peace.*

24. Eusebius, *History of the Church,* 9.8, in *NPNF,* 2–4. This could be evidence of a growing schism between the Eastern provinces and the western Church as well. Certainly, the eastern regions and bishops seemed more amenable to warfare than their western counterparts.

25. Theodoret, *Historia Ecclesiastica* 2.26, in *NPNF,* 13:111.

26. Eusebius, *Oration,* 857, in *NPNF,* 2.243.

27. Ibid, 859.

28. Ibid., 861.

29. Ibid., 873. Italics added.

30. Ibid, 54.

31. Bainton, *Christian Attitudes Toward War and Peace,* 87.

32. Ibid.

33. Theodosius II, *Theodosiani Libri* XVI, 10. December 7, 416, in *Patrologia Latina,* ed. Jacques Migne (Rome: Gregg International, 1982), 16:21.

34. As cited in Wayne Grudem, *Systematic Theology* (Leicester, England: Inter-Varsity, 1994), 249.

Chapter 3

The Unholy Marriage

When the Church Became a Mistress
(A.D. 476–1087)

Among true worshipers of God, those wars are looked
on as peacemaking which are waged neither from ag-
grandizement nor cruelty but with the object of securing
peace, of repressing the evil and supporting the good.[1]
—Thomas Aquinas

One could imagine that their newfound acceptance in Roman society was shocking to the system of the Christian community. Slowly, Christians infiltrated virtually every venue of society—political, judicial, legislative, and military. After spending three
centuries in either seclusion or oppression, the Christians acclimated
slowly into the mainstream of culture. When Rome fell in 476, and
the various regions of Europe and Africa fought for sovereignty, the
Christians fought alongside them. By the dawning of the sixth century, the local Christian communities were firmly entrenched in local
politics, intrigue, and drama.

Yet the period also saw Rome developing into the central and leading voice for Christianity throughout the civilized world. Immediately following the apostolic era, five cities rose in both influence and
power among Christians: Jerusalem, Constantinople, Alexandria,
Antioch, and Rome. Out of this group, Rome rose to preeminence in

both ecclesiastical and political power. Increasingly, the bishops in Rome began to speak not only to the various Christian churches, but for them. By the time of Pope Leo I (440–461), Rome was actively unifying its power among the churches of the West. After Constantine made Christianity the "official" Roman religion, Rome began establishing its ties to the political machinations in various regions such as Germania and Gaul.

Why is this important?

Because the six hundred years between 476, when the last emperor of the Western Roman Empire was deposed, and the calling of the First Crusade in 1095 served as a bridge in between the Church persecuted (30–324) and the Church powerful and political (1095–1300). This period, one we will call the *Church protected*, saw the Christian community work itself incrementally into the fabric of geopolitical intrigue. As the examples and events during this period could fill an encyclopedia itself, we will limit ourselves to five major events, each of which clearly defines a fresh move into the secular arena.

The importance of these events cannot be understated. Quite simply, before Pope Urban II could have the ability and capacity to unite a Christian army under his leadership, the Church had to enter into an unequally yoked marriage with the state. This frightening union saw the development of a central premise that guides the study of Church history: *Whenever the church and the state enter into a relationship, inevitably the church ends up becoming the state's whore. She is used for the political expedience of the state, and then when she is no longer useful, she is tossed aside as an unwanted mistress. It is an unholy relationship, and the state is inevitably an abusive spouse.*

Through the early medieval centuries, the Roman Church became intoxicated with temporal power, until finally Rome unleashed the worst horror in the history of Christianity—the Crusades. Christianity declared its own jihad against Muslims, Jews, and anyone else who got in the way.

Setting Parameters: Augustine Attempts to Formulate Just War Criteria

Christians only slowly became invested in all avenues of societal and political life. This investment was particularly disturbing in the field of battle. The shedding of blood, which had been abhorrent to Christians before Constantine, became common after his rule. Somehow, the Christian community had to find some way to set limits on the actions of those who confessed Jesus Christ. This new ethic of warfare had to have constraints to distinguish Christians from pagans in deeds, goals, and motivations.

Appendix A will examine the Just War criteria and apply them to current global conflicts, but here it is necessary to clarify the development and criteria for a "just war." In fact, if Pope Urban had not abandoned the Just War thesis, perhaps the Crusades would not be as dark a spot on the map of Christian history.

Augustine (354–430), bishop of Hippo Regius in northern Africa, was a philosopher who converted to Christianity as an adult and had an amazing grasp of Greek philosophy and Christian theology. Over thirty years of writing, he studied the works of his mentor, Ambrose of Milan (339–397) and others in an attempt to formulate a blueprint for ethically Christian engagement in war. As one author has noted,

> Augustine led the way in revising Christian attitudes toward war by formulating a series of rules to regulate violence and permit believers to fight for the empire. He combined the Old Testament with the ideas of Aristotle, Plato and Cicero into a Christian doctrine of the just war.[2]

Exactly how could a Christian engage in a battle without violating his conscience and disobeying the admonitions of Jesus Christ to love one's enemies? The answer, according to Augustine, was in both intent and action. Specifically, Augustine believed a Christian must be constrained to fight as a last resort. For a Christian, even effective military campaigns were only to be undertaken from a defensive posture.

Augustine further taught that the motivation for a war was also important. A believer could not engage in a random war for political reasons. "War should have as its goal the establishment of justice and the restoration of peace. It must be fought under the authority of the legitimate ruler."[3] These standards block any attempt at a coup or the instigation of warfare.

Additionally, the conduct of believers in the military must be honorable. Looting of homes or businesses in the war zone and the killing of unarmed civilians were both prohibited in a just war. Finally, Augustine argued, monks, priests, and ministers should be exempt from military service, although they might be present among the soldiers to offer comfort.[4]

Other medieval theologians, such as Isidore of Seville (560–636) and Thomas Aquinas (1225–1274), contributed further to the delineation of the Just War criteria, so that a general outline could guide all believers as to whether a conflict in fact meets the standards. These can be outlined in six categorical criteria:

1. *Just Cause*: Force may be used only to correct a threatening and public evil, such as the massive and deadly violation of the basic rights of whole people groups. Physical force may be used in self-defense or to preempt an anticipated attack.

2. *Legitimate Authority*: Only legitimately constituted public authorities may use deadly force or wage war. Even just causes cannot be undertaken by the violent actions of individuals or groups of rebels who do not constitute an authority sanctioned by the government that society deems legitimate.

3. *Right Intention*: The ultimate goal or intention of the use of force is to reestablish peace, specifically a peace that is preferable to the peace that would have prevailed had the war not been fought.

4. *Probability of Success*: Arms may not be used in a futile cause; there must be a reasonable chance of success.

5. *Proportionality of Violence*: The overall destruction expected from the use of force must be outweighed by the good to be

achieved. A nation or army cannot go to war without considering the effect of its action on others and on the collateral damage such a war will inflict.

6. *The Principle of Last Resort:* Force may be used only after all peaceful alternatives have been genuinely attempted and exhausted.

(As we will state emphatically in the appendix and in later chapters, in our opinion, the application of these criteria qualified the wars declared by the United States in both Afghanistan and in Iraq as just, moral, and necessary military actions.)

The Muslims Are Coming: The Battle of Tours (732)

The second shift during this period which affected the stance of the Church with regard to warfare was the onslaught of the Islamic armies following the death of Muhammed. It was the first significant test of the Just War criteria, as well as the first major war between Islam and Christian forces. As we cited in our first book, *Unveiling Islam,*[5] after the death of Muhammed, Islam experienced a civil war between the two major factions, the Sunni and the Shi'ia. Once that struggle was resolved, the Islamic forces united to conquer Africa and southern Europe. By 732, Islam's rate of expansion was astounding:

647	Island of Cyprus
670	Tunisia and Kabul (Afghanistan)
672	Island of Rhodes
677	Siege of Constantinople
700	complete control of North Africa
711	Spain
715	complete control of China-Turkestan border
772	Morocco

By the end of its first century, Islam stretched to the western borders of China and the southern borders of France, with complete domination of North Africa.

Within this period, Damascus, Syria, became the capital of the Islamic world. Wealth and conquest went almost unhindered. One of the greatest leaders, Caliph Mu'awiya, described his military expertise, "I apply not my sword where my lash suffices, nor my lash where my tongue is enough. . . . When men pull, I loosen, when they loosen, I pull."[6]

Two great edifices were constructed that are still monumentally important. First, the Dome of the Rock in Jerusalem was erected on the Jewish Temple Mount in 691. Intended to demonstrate the superiority of Islam over Judaism and its corruption, this site is considered to be the third holiest place in Islam. The building of such an edifice on such a holy site to Christianity caused alarm throughout Christendom, specifically in Rome.

The Great Mosque of Damascus was finished in 715 as a replacement for the Cathedral Church of St. John. Considered the fourth holiest place in Islam, this site is intended to demonstrate the superiority of Islam over corrupt Christianity.[7]

As the Muslim army continued to make its way north, the European regents, provinces, and city-states were directly threatened. For almost one hundred years, Islam seemed unstoppable.

Enter Charles Martel (688–741). Rising to be king of the Merovingian Franks in 717, he consolidated a Frankish-Austrasian confederation in 719. A powerful and wise military leader, Charles confronted the Islamic forces as a necessity. The Islamic governor of Spain, Abd-er-Rahman, crossed the Pyrenees mountains with an immense army, intent on conquering Italy. The Muslims advanced as far as the Loire River. In October 732, Charles met and defeated Abd-er-Rahman outside of Tours.

The most accurate account of the battle was described in vivid detail:

> [Abd-er-Rahman] destroyed palaces, burned churches, and imagined he could pillage the basilica of St. Martin of Tours. It is then that he found himself face to face with the lord of Austrasia, Charles, a mighty warrior from his youth, and trained in all the occasions of arms.
>
> For almost seven days the two armies watched one another, waiting anxiously the moment for joining the struggle. Fi-

nally they made ready for combat. And in the shock of the battle the men of the North seemed like a sea that cannot be moved. Firmly they stood, one close to another, forming as it were a bulwark of ice; and with great blows of their swords they hewed down the Arabs. Drawn up in a band around their chief, the people of the Austrasians carried all before them. Their tireless hands drove their swords down to the breasts [of the foe].

At last night [Muslim] combatants [surrendered]. The Franks with misgivings lowered their blades, and beholding the numberless tents of the Arabs, prepared themselves for another battle the next day. Very early, when they issued from their retreat, the men of Europe saw the Arab tents ranged still in order, in the same place where they had set up their camp. Unaware that they were utterly empty, and fearful lest within the phalanxes of the Saracens were drawn up for combat, they sent out spies to ascertain the facts. These spies discovered that all the squadrons of the "Ishmaelites" had vanished. In fact, during the night they had fled with the greatest silence, seeking with all speed their homeland. The Europeans, uncertain and fearful, lest they were merely hidden in order to come back [to fall upon them] by ambushments, sent scouting parties everywhere, but to their great amazement found nothing. Then without troubling to pursue the fugitives, they contented themselves with sharing the spoils and returned right gladly to their own country.[8]

The Muslim chronicler also recorded their version of the battle, with quite a different take. Almost in denial, he disclosed the conversation of the Caliph and a soldier named Musa:

Musa being returned to Damascus, the Caliph Abd-el Melek asked of him about his conquests, saying "Now tell me about these Franks—what is their nature?"

"They," replied Musa, "are a folk right numerous, and full of might: brave and impetuous in the attack, but cowardly and craven in event of defeat."

"And how has passed the war betwixt them and thyself? Favorably or the reverse?"

"The reverse? No, by Allah and the prophet!" spoke Musa. "Never has a company from my army been beaten. And never have the Moslems hesitated to follow me when I have led them; though they were two score to fourscore."[9]

Yet the results of the battle were not in dispute. For the first time in one hundred years, the Islamic forces had been defeated. Had Martel not stopped the Muslim battalions at Tours, Islam would have probably invaded Italy, and conquered Rome.

The importance of this event was that the small European kingdoms had united for a common cause—ultimately a religious one. They took what was, in their minds, a defensive posture. The Battle of Tours thus fulfilled the Just War principles. Over the following centuries, subsequent battles failed to meet those criteria, and the Christian witness was damaged because of it.

"You Scratch My Back . . ." : The Coronation of Charlemagne (December 25, 800)

The grandson of Charles Martel and the son of Pepin III (714–768), Charlemagne (742–814) stood in what would be a long dynasty of Frank rulers. Like his father and grandfather, Charlemagne, whose name literally means "Charles the Great," was a skilled soldier and leader. Yet his administration is most remembered for its part in the marriage between church and state.

Charlemagne actually began his reign as the king of the Franks in 768. The Frankish empire consisted of what is now France, the Netherlands, Belgium, and western Germany. Through his expertise as a military commander, he soon conquered Saxony, also a part of what is now Germany, and the northern portions of Italy. By Charlemagne's death in 814, the Carolingian dynasty was at its zenith. Many regard Charlemagne as the founder of Europe.

Charlemagne was also a devoted man of the Roman church. He regularly sought the advice of ministers, including his friend Benedict of Aniane. He had a congenial relationship with the various pontiffs and did much to further Rome's work. However, in 800 he took part in the culmination of a seven-hundred-year courtship between church and state.

In 795, a new pontiff, Leo III faced much opposition from his predecessor's (Pius IX) leaders. They plotted for years to remove him from the papacy and install a pope who would restore their power. In 799, a cadre of Pius IX's henchmen attempted to kill Leo. He fled to Charlemagne's court.

Together Charlemagne and Leo formed a union of convenience. Charlemagne needed the Church's approval, because his ever-increasing lands needed a common thread, and Christianity united them. Leo needed the protection of Charlemagne, and the power he could wield to back Leo's authority.

On Christmas Day, December 25, 800, in an elaborate public ceremony, Charlemagne was crowned emperor, a term that had fallen into disuse. His rule was described as a "Holy Roman Empire." The crown was placed upon his head by Leo III. Then, in equally elaborate fashion, Charlemagne handed his staff to the pontiff.

The marriage was reflected in the very name of the new empire. It was "holy" because the pope vowed that God in heaven had chosen Charlemagne. It was "Roman" because it hearkened back to the days of Constantine, when Christians and the state ruled together in harmony. It was an "empire," and thus Charlemagne was, in effect, giving his blessing to Leo personally. His blessing also meant his protection.

The story of the coronation itself betrays an entirely different relationship between the Roman Church and the state, an unequal yoking. The *Annales Laureshamenses* recalls the reasoning of the council that met:

> Since the title of emperor had become extinct among the Greeks . . . it seemed to Pope Leo and to all the holy fathers

who were present at the council and to the rest of the Christian people that Charles, king of the Franks, ought to be named emperor, for he held Rome itself where the Caesars were always accustomed to reside and also other cities in Italy, Gaul and Germany. Since almighty God had put all these places in his power it seemed fitting to them that, with the help of God, and in accordance with the request of all the Christian people, he should hold this title. King Charles did not wish to refuse their petition, and, humbly submitting himself to God and to the petition of all the Christian priests and people, he accepted the title of emperor on the day of the Nativity of our Lord Jesus Christ and was consecrated by Pope Leo.[10]

As the day of crowning approached, the format for such an auspicious occasion had been discussed by the council, so Pope Leo would show proper deference without losing face himself. Vita Leonis III (795–816) wrote of the actual ceremony:

On the day of the Nativity of our Lord Jesus Christ all [who had been present at the council] came together again in the same basilica of blessed Peter the apostle. And then the venerable and holy pontiff, with his own hands, crowned [Charles] with a most precious crown. Then all the faithful Romans, seeing how he loved the holy Roman church and its vicar and how he defended them, cried out with one voice by the will of God and of St. Peter, the key-bearer of the kingdom of heaven, "To Charles, most pious Augustus, crowned by God, great and peace-loving emperor, life and victory" (*Salus et victoria*). This was said three times before the sacred tomb of blessed Peter the apostle, with the invocation of many saints, and he was instituted by all as emperor of the Romans. Thereupon, on that same day of the nativity of our Lord Jesus Christ, the most holy bishop and pontiff anointed his most excellent son Charles as king with holy oil.

The dangers of this marriage are readily seen. The most glaring hazard in such an agreement is that it was entirely dependent on the actual pontiff and regent. As long as they were not at cross-purposes, the agreement between the two would work. When the pope would speak in matters of theology, he would get explicit permission from the king, so as not to disturb the balance of power. In return, the king would offer all due reverence and protection to Rome and the pontiff.

But what would happen if the king and pope clashed? Would the Church be cast aside as an antiquated mistress? Would the power of the king overrule the power of the one who supposedly held the keys to heaven?

Tragically, history did not have to wait long for an answer. The Church, fresh from the installation ceremony, began to become wholly intoxicated by its secular authority. One of the finest examples of such inebriation with the temporal realm is in the battle between Pope Gregory VII and King Henry IV.

The War to Settle the Score: Hildebrand and Henry (1077)

Henry IV (1050–1106) became king of the Germans when he was just six years old. Henry III's death in 1056 forced his son to depend on Empress Agnes as regent until he was trained and educated to assume the responsibilities. By all accounts, Henry was a quick study, and became a consolidating force in Europe—until he clashed with a popular and powerful papal administrator, Cardinal Hildebrand, who was elevated to the Roman See as Gregory VII (1073–1085).

Hildebrand had effectively controlled the finances of the Roman Church and was an indomitable counselor before he rose to the throne of Peter. Circumstances of his election were suspect, and the new pope had many enemies. A shrewd politician, Pope Gregory quickly developed a network that increased his political clout in Europe and beyond. Church and state were bound to collide over the question of submission in this uneasy marriage.

In 1075, Henry challenged Gregory's political power. Henry insisted on the right of the king as secular ruler to "invest" the clergy. Investiture meant that the king selected ecclesiastical rulers deemed to be loyal and helpful to the secular government. Henry was removing that right from the purview of the pope. This was especially troublesome in the investiture of bishops. The position of bishop was highly valued. Many favors could be gained by installing bishops with strong political connections. This "Investiture Controversy" quickly developed into a full-scale war of words between the state (Henry) and the Roman Church (Gregory).

On January 24, 1076, King Henry sent a letter to the pontiff containing a scathing critique and withering sarcasm. Though Henry was only twenty-six at the time, he boldly challenged the papal right to overrule him in matters he deemed to be political as well as theological. Even in his address, he called the pope by his birth name of Hildebrand and referred to him as a "false monk." In all of Christian literature, there has rarely been such a scathing condemnation and naked grab for power.

> [From] Henry, king not through usurpation but through the holy ordination of God, to Hildebrand, at present not pope but false monk:
>
> Such greeting as this hast thou merited through thy disturbances, inasmuch as there is no grade in the church which thou hast omitted to make a partaker not of honor but of *confusion,* not of benediction but of malediction. . . . Thou hast won favour from the common herd by crushing them; thou hast looked upon all of them as knowing nothing, upon thy sole self, moreover, as knowing all things. This knowledge, however, thou hast used not for edification but for destruction. . . . And we, indeed, have endured all this, being eager to guard the honor of the apostolic see. Thou, however, has understood our humility to be fear, and hast not, accordingly, shunned to rise up against the royal power conferred upon us by God, daring to threaten to divest us of it. *As if we had received our kingdom from thee! As if the kingdom and the em-*

pire were in thine and not in God's hand! And this although our Lord Jesus Christ did call us to the kingdom, did not, however, call thee to the priesthood. For thou hast ascended by the following steps. By wiles . . . thou hast achieved money; by money, favor; by the sword, the throne of peace.

And from the throne of peace thou hast disturbed peace, inasmuch as thou hast armed subjects against those in authority over them; inasmuch as thou, who wert not called, hast taught that our bishops called of God are to be despised. . . . For the wisdom of the holy fathers committed even Julian the apostate not to themselves, but to God alone, to be judged and to be deposed. For himself the true pope, Peter, also exclaims: "Fear God, honor the king." But thou who does not fear God, dost dishonor in me, his appointed one. Wherefore St. Paul, when he has not spared an angel of Heaven if he shall have preached otherwise, has not excepted thee also who dost teach other-wise upon earth. For he says: "If any one, either I or an angel from Heaven, should preach a gospel other than that which has been preached to you, he shall be damned." Thou, therefore, *damned by this curse* and by the judgment of all our bishops and by our own, descend and relinquish the apostolic chair that thou has usurped. Let another ascend the throne of St. Peter, who shall not practice violence under the cloak of religion, but shall teach the sound doctrine of St. Peter. I, Henry, king by the grace of God, do say unto thee, together with all our bishops: *Descend, descend, to be damned throughout the ages.*[11]

Henry had already gathered his forces and demanded that Gregory be removed from office. In turn, Gregory excommunicated Henry, in effect damning him to hell. In his excommunication, he also released all subjects to Henry from their responsibilities, and he convened a council in October of 1076 at Tribur to elect a new German king. King Henry was facing a revolt of those in his realm who confessed loyalty to the pope.

In January 1077, King Henry had no other option but to travel to the papal winter home in Canossa. Henry approached in the dead of winter, and sought the forgiveness of the Pope by publicly repenting. Legend has it that Pope Gregory refused to allow Henry to enter the castle, and to show his penitence, Henry stood exposed in the snow for days, until Pope Gregory allowed him in and accepted his repentance, with a number of conditions.

The struggle between the king and the pope did not end at Canossa. For three years, threats continued to be issued on both sides of the conflict, and on March 7, 1080, Pope Gregory again excommunicated King Henry in a formal statement. This time, however, Henry had been manipulating public opinion, and the people were not with Gregory. The usefulness of "mistress Rome" was wearing thin. On June 16 of that year, Henry called a council at Brixen, which removed Gregory from office and named the archbishop Guibert of Ravenna as his successor.

In 1081, Henry brought his charges to Rome, and at the formal indictment, Gregory was surprised when thirteen of his cardinals voted for his removal. On March 24, 1084, Guibert was named Clement III, as a competing pope (history calls them the "antipopes"). Clement quickly assumed a subservient role under the king's power. Gregory had to flee for his life. While he remained the actual pope according to Rome, which did not accept Clement III, he was a pope in exile.

The Reluctant Pope:
Victor III and the Feeble Reconstruction

Back in Rome, the papal leaders faced a quandary. The "antipopes" were often just vassals to the king. Church rulers had learned, however, that outright antagonism against the kings was fruitless. They needed a pope that would be able to embrace the king's political plans, while maintaining the dignity, and more importantly, power, of the papacy.

On his deathbed, Gregory told the cardinals that Desiderius of Benevento (1027–1087) could do it. Desiderius was loyal to Gregory and had served as a cardinal since 1059. On May 24, 1086, the cardinals selected him to become Pope Victor III. He was a decidedly reluctant pope. Because of his reticence, Victor was not even installed until May 9, 1087. Immediately following his appointment, he left for Monte Cassino, and the cardinals had to enlist Countess Matilda of Tuscany to convince him to return and begin to carry out the business of the papacy.

Finally, in August of 1087, Pope Victor III held a council in Benevento. It was his inaugural, albeit feeble, attempt at reconstructing the power Rome had enjoyed. He was not a strong leader, however, and he became ill during the sessions. He left the council and returned to Monte Cassino, where he died a month later, on September 16, 1087. His entire reign was sixteen months.

The Lessons Learned

The previous decades had proved quite trying for the Church at Rome. They deeply desired the political influence engendered by the marriage to the state, but the cost of such a union was high. The state inevitably overruled the ecclesiastical authorities in matters of importance, and the power of the papacy was fleeting at best. The folly of Gregory's fall taught that direct conflict with the state usually ended in horror. It would take a stronger leader than Pope Victor to ensure Rome's continuing influence.

The question of *whether* the Church should be invested in temporal authority was never raised. Sadly, the Church had become addicted to its power, politics, and intrigue. Militarily, the Church had approved of every conflict, given its blessing to every soldier, and cheered every victory. Following the coronation of Charlemagne, the line between Christians in the army and a Christian army had been blurred. It was the king, representing the state, who would lead the troops into battle and demand obedience of his men.

If only the Church at Rome could somehow supercede the power of the kings to command the troops, then the power of the Church would rise above the state. If the Church could find some way to unite all the European kings under the aegis of Christianity and under the banner of heaven, then the pope would become, in effect, the commander of all commanders-in-chief.

It would take a keen and astute pope to accomplish such a feat. Rome found him, and he became the successor to Victor III.

His name was Odo of Lagny, and he became Pope Urban II.

Notes

1. Thomas Aquinas, *Summa Theologia* (London: Blackfriars, 1951), II, II, ae, 40, 1.
2. R. G. Clouse, "War and Peace," in *New Dictionary of Theology*, ed. Sinclair B. Ferguson, David F. Wright, and J. I. Packer (Downers Grove, Ill.: InterVarsity, 1988), 715.
3. Ibid.
4. Ibid.
5. The following three paragraphs are modified from Ergun Caner and Emir Caner, *Unveiling Islam* (Grand Rapids: Kregel, 2002), 71–72.
6. George Braswell, *Islam* (Nashville: Broadman and Holman, 1996), 26.
7. Ibid.
8. *Isidore of Beja's Chronicle*, in *Readings in Ancient History: Illustrative Extracts from the Sources*, ed. William Stearns Davis (Boston: Allyn and Bacon, 1912–13), 2:362–64.
9. Arabian chronicler, ibid.
10. Brian Tierney, *The Crisis of Church and State 1050–1300* (Englewood Cliffs, N.J.: Prentice Hall, 1964), 113.
11. Ernest F. Henderson, *Select Historical Documents of the Middle Ages* (London: George Bell and Sons, 1910), 372. Emphasis added.

Chapter 4

"God Wills It!"

When Christ Commanded a Jihad
(November 27, 1095–July 17, 1099)

You, brothers and fellow bishops; you, fellow priests and sharers with us in Christ, make this same announcement through the churches committed to you, and with your whole soul vigorously preach the journey to Jerusalem. When they have confessed the disgrace of their sins, do you, secure in Christ, grant them speedy pardon. Moreover, you who are to go shall have us praying for you; we shall have you fighting for God's people. It is our duty to pray, yours to fight against the Amalakites. With Moses, we shall extend unwearied hands in prayer to Heaven, while you go forth and brandish the sword, like dauntless warriors, against Amalek.[1]

—Pope Urban II, "Admonition to the Bishops,"
Council of Clermont, 1095

The pressures on the papacy in Rome are intense in any year. Hundreds of millions of faithful adherents look to the Vatican for spiritual direction, guidance, and instruction. The economic considerations alone would keep the calmest saint awake at night. Hundreds of thousands of cardinals, bishops, monks, nuns, priests, and missionaries serve in every corner of the globe, in hundreds of languages among thousands of people groups. It is quite an enterprise.

Yet the era in which Pope Urban II (1088–1099) rose to power was fraught with dangers and peril rarely matched in Church history. As detailed in the previous chapter, the Church entered into an ill-advised relationship with the state, culminating in the coronation of Charlemagne by the pope to create a "Holy Roman Empire" in 800. This marriage led to the Roman Church's obsession with power, prestige, and position. In subsequent conflicts with the regents to whom Rome had been united, the Church always lost. The exile of Pope Gregory VII and installation of Clement III as the antipope, along with the failure of Pope Victor III, left the Church without direction and with a decreasing influence. Clearly, something had to be done, and quickly.

This chapter will detail the rise of Pope Urban II, and his call to Crusade on November 27, 1095 at the Council of Clermont. We shall attempt to provide a narrative for what is arguably the darkest day in Christian history—*the day Christianity declared a* jihad. The terrifying consequences of that dismal day were so harrowing that the effects still resonate throughout the Middle East, Europe, and Africa. Christianity has never recovered from the darkness of that decision to offer forgiveness and salvation to warriors bent upon the slaughter of any and all adversaries who stood between them and the liberation of Jerusalem.

The Papacy of Pope Urban II

The inception of the rule of Urban II found the Church in a state of almost total disintegration. On the twelfth of March of 1088, he assumed the leadership of a corporation on the brink of complete disarray. If he were unable to unite the people of the faith quickly, the Church would divide into warring factions bent on self-rule and domination. Civil war among the "Christian" nations in Europe was imminent, as the Gauls and Celts continued to strive with one another for land and regional control.

Urban's method of rescuing the church at Rome was simple. He proclaimed a larger cause that would stir the hearts of all—the recapture of the Holy Land of Jerusalem. Though Muslims had controlled the Holy Land for years, a ferocious band called the Seljuk Turks had come to power over all Asia Minor after a Seljuk army defeated the Byzantines at Manzikert in 1071. Access to the Holy Land was now constricted at best, and forbidden at worst. Pilgrims seeking the Holy Land had been denied access to the various holy sites, and Christian inhabitants of the land had fallen under intense persecution. Pope Urban II, after receiving repeated requests for aid from the Patriarch in Constantinople, decided that the urgency of the hour, coupled with his own political circumstances, demanded drastic measures.

Born to a wealthy family around 1035 at Chatillon-sur-Marne, Odo studied under a Catholic priest and educator named Bruno, who was the founder of the Carthusians. After taking the priestly vows and receiving ordination, he was quickly made canon and subsequently archdeacon in 1068.[2] Upon becoming a monk at Cluny, he soon rose to become a prior. He established himself as a shrewd diplomat and often served as a go-between for hostile factions within the Church. This poise of character and astute political maneuverings would serve Urban well in the papal seat.

After the death of Victor III in Monte Cassino in 1087, Odo was elected pope and took the name Urban II. His actual election took some time, because a group of cardinals opposed his election. These cardinals were intent on reforming the Church quickly, and Urban had been firmly allied with the camp of Hildebrand during his conflict with Henry IV. In addition, Urban had presided over the Synod of Quedlinburg of 1085 in Saxony, in which Clement III, the antipope, was condemned.[3] To cardinals intent on starting fresh with someone unencumbered with ecclesiastical baggage, Odo seemed an insider who was tainted by the failures of two previous administrations.

Upon ascending to the papal throne, Urban felt his purpose was clear. Facing stiff opposition from emperors, he set about to establish his position as the legitimate pontiff and return the papacy to its former luster. Urban also had to contend with the popularity and influence of the antipope.

Several strong motivations for the Crusades will be noted in coming chapters. Certainly one of the incentives for Urban's call of the First Crusade was his desire to unify the Roman Catholic Church under a single mantle. A common antagonist was a sure cure for civil disunity and war. A second motivation was reacquisition of the Holy Land. The land was held in reverence by the Christian community. The land of Christ seemed rightfully to be the property of the Church.

Though his efforts to unite the Church in crusade came to fruition in 1096, the groundwork was laid soon after his election in 1088. He was foremost a diplomat who sought to diplomatically walk on both sides of the controversy besetting the Church. His mantra was Gregorian reform, but he also modified the advances to appease the traditionalists. Like a good politician, Urban was gaining allies.

These diplomatic advances, however, did not ease his relations with Henry IV of Germany, who was still a powerful antagonist. When Henry captured Rome for Clement III in a campaign in 1090–1092, Urban fled with the Normans to southern Italy. Safely hidden, Urban patiently waited until Henry found himself trapped in conflict in Verona. Urban returned to Rome in the winter of 1093, and he quickly took back possession of the Vatican by means of bribery in 1094.[4]

His concessions were successful in other countries as well. In England, William II (1087–1100) finally recognized him in 1095 when Urban agreed to send only officials who had William's approval. In France, his cautious line with Philip I (1060–1108) and the scandal of Philip's adulterous affairs enabled Urban to garner a needed ally. In Spain, he successfully encouraged the recapture of the land from the Moors, and reorganized the country ecclesiastically. In Italy, Urban's closest allies were the Normans in southern Italy and Sicily.

Give Them a Common Enemy and a Common Leader

Leaders in Rome had been aware of Seljuk brutality toward Christians since 1071. Gregory VII had written to Count William of Burgandy on March 1, 1074, asking for help to defend the believers in Jerusalem. He appealed in vain to William's sense of outrage over the slaughter of Christian pilgrims:

Remember your promise . . . that you make ready the strength of your military forces to aid the liberty of the Roman church and that, if necessary, you come hither with your army in the service of St. Peter. We do not intend to assemble this multitude of soldiers in order to shed Christian blood. . . . For we hope . . . that when the Normans have been pacified we may cross over to Constantinople to help the Christians who have suffered exceedingly from the oft-inflicted stings of the Saracens and who have vainly besought us to lend our hand to help them.[5]

He followed up that same day with a letter released to all believers for the same purpose. In this letter, he vividly details the graphic violence inflicted on the Christians:

A pagan people has prevailed strongly against the Christian Empire, (and) they have already cruelly laid waste and occupied with tyrannical violence everything . . . they have slain many thousands of Christians, as if they were herds of beasts. . . . Brotherly love demands that we lay down our lives for the liberation of our brethren.[6]

Nine months later, Gregory was even compelled to write his arch nemesis, King Henry IV, and ask him for help as well:

Christians . . . [who] are being daily butchered like herds of cattle, have humbly sent to me . . . begging that I [help] in whatever way I can, lest—God forbid!—the Christian religion perish completely in our times. . . . I have taken steps to rouse and stir up certain Christians who long to lay down their lives for their brethren by defending the law of Christ. . . . Already more than fifty thousand men have prepared themselves so that, if they can have me as their Pontiff and leader, they may raise up their mailed fist against God's enemies and, under God's leadership, go all the way to the Lord's sepulcher.[7]

Yet with the ongoing civil wars in Europe, and Gregory's own shaky political position, he was incapable of mounting any meaningful offensive.

No Bloody Sundays:
Urban Reinstates the Truce of God of 1063

Pope Urban's situation, however, was more secure by 1095, when he embarked on a series of victorious synods to consolidate his power. As the Synod of Clermont began, Urban reinstated the Truce of God, which demanded the ceasing of all warfare on holy and Sabbath days. This *Truce of God* was actually a document written by Drogo, bishop of Terouanne, in 1063, which set boundaries on the days for carrying out warfare, and instituted heavy penalties for violators. Urban reinstated the "truce" so that he could inaugurate a war and still maintain the appearance of restraining violence. The ten points of *Truce of God* are a strange amalgam of courtesy and carnage:

> *Dearest brothers in the Lord,* these are the conditions which you must observe during the time of the peace which is commonly called the truce of God, and which begins with sunset on Wednesday and lasts until sunrise on Monday.
>
> 1. During those four days and five nights no man or woman shall assault, wound, or slay another, or attack, seize, or destroy a castle, burg, or villa, by craft or by violence.
>
> 2. If anyone violates this peace and disobeys these commands of ours, he shall be exiled for thirty years as a penance, and before he leaves the bishopric he shall make compensation for the injury which he committed. Otherwise he shall be excommunicated by the Lord God and excluded from all Christian fellowship.
>
> 3. All who associate with him in any way, who give him advice or aid, or hold converse with him, unless it be to advise him to do penance and to leave the bishopric, shall be under excommunication until they have made satisfaction.

4. If any violator of the peace shall fall sick and die before he completes his penance, no Christian shall visit him or move his body from the place where it lay, or receive any of his possessions.

5. In addition, brethren, you should observe the peace in regard to lands and animals and all things that can be possessed. If anyone takes from another an animal, a coin, or a garment, during the days of the truce, he shall be excommunicated unless he makes satisfaction. If he desires to make satisfaction for his crime he shall first restore the thing which he stole or its value in money, and shall do penance for seven years within the bishopric. If he should die before he makes satisfaction and completes his penance, his body shall not be buried or removed from the place where it lay, unless his family shall make satisfaction for him to the person whom he injured.

6. During the days of the peace, no one shall make a hostile expedition on horseback, except when summoned by the count; and all who go with the count shall take for their support only as much as is necessary for themselves and their horses.

7. All merchants and other men who pass through your territory from other lands shall have peace from you.

8. You shall also keep this peace every day of the week from the beginning of Advent to the octave of Epiphany and from the beginning of Lent to the octave of Easter, and from the feast of Rogations [the Monday before Ascension Day] to the octave of Pentecost.

9. We command all priests on feast days and Sundays to pray for all who keep the peace, and to curse all who violate it or support its violators.

10. If anyone has been accused of violating the peace and denies the charge, he shall take the communion and undergo the ordeal of hot iron. If he is found guilty, he shall do penance within the bishopric for seven years.[8]

"Retake the Land!" Urban's Unifying Call

On Tuesday, November 27, 1095, Urban sounded the summons for what would be a centuries-long movement. In Constantinople, Alexis had requested aid from the pope, and Urban saw this as his great opportunity. He urged the people to retake the Holy Land from the Turks, who had taken the land from their Muslim allies. With a booming and resonant voice, he built the crowd into a fever pitch. The essence of Urban's sermon concerned their sense of chivalry, patriotism, and allegiance to the Church for the purpose of promised salvation.

The land was their goal, he urged, and the crusaders were to be emissaries of God in conquest. One of the chroniclers of the historic synod, Robert the Monk, reported that Urban exclaimed:

> Jerusalem is the navel of the world; the land is fruitful above others, like another paradise of delights. This the Redeemer of the human race has made illustrious by his advent, has beautified by residence, has consecrated by suffering, has redeemed by death, has glorified by burial. This royal city, therefore, situated at the centre of the world, is now held captive by his enemies, and is in subjection to those who do not know God, to the worship of the heathens. She seeks therefore and desires to be liberated, and does not cease to implore you to come to her aid. From you especially she asks succor, because, as we have already said, God has conferred upon you above all nations great glory in arms. Accordingly undertake this journey *for the remission of your sins,* with the assurance of the imperishable glory of the kingdom of heaven.[9]

In one short paragraph as recorded by Robert the Monk, Pope Urban II overturned one thousand years of Church teaching. Urban summarized his fourfold justification for launching a Christian army, under the direction and leadership of the pope:

1.   We must go to recapture Jerusalem from the pagan Muslims.

2. We must go to come to the aid of fellow believers who are suffering.
3. We must go for the remission of our sins.
4. We must go because we are assured the imperishable glory of heaven.

If Robert's account is complete, Urban could have given his Latin speech in under two minutes, yet the darkest chapter in our entire history hinges on these words. Urban effectively declared a holy war on Muslims who held Jerusalem. Christians had taken on as much guilt as Muslims who declared a jihad. The Just War criteria had been replaced by a theology of retribution. Christians no longer had mere permission to serve in the army. The army was now explicitly Christian. It was not the state as the temporal authority that sanctioned military conflict. The pope himself gave the orders. Cessation of violence was not the ultimate aim of the war, but rather eternal forgiveness and the promise of heaven. The new war theory was both brutal and unbiblical. Urban promised that whoever lifted arms against the Muslims entered into a holy war and would be saved. Either by shedding the blood of the infidels, or by dying on the battlefield, the warrior was promised eternal salvation.

The Cry of "God Wills It!"

The congregation of bishops gathered for Urban's sermon reached an emotional climax, as recorded by Fulcher of Chartres:

> When Pope Urban had said these and very many similar things in his urbane discourse, he so influenced to one purpose the desires of all who were present, that they cried out,
> "It is the will of God! It is the will of God!"
> When the venerable Roman pontiff heard that, with eyes uplifted to heaven he gave thanks to God and, with his hand commanded silence, said:
> "Most beloved brethren, today is manifest in you what the

Lord says in the Gospel, 'Where two or three are gathered together in my name there I am in the midst of them.' Unless
the Lord God has been present in your spirits, all of you would
not have uttered the same cry. For, although the cry issued
from numerous mouths, yet the origin of the cry was one.

"Therefore I say to you that God, who implanted this in
your breasts, has drawn it forth from you.

"Let this then be your war-cry in combats, because this word
is given to you by God. When an armed attack is made upon
the enemy, let this one cry be raised by all soldiers of God: It is
the will of God! It is the will of God!"[10]

While persuasion of the masses had to be achieved, Urban first
needed the support of the bishops to gather and organize the essential
troops and inspire the fervor necessary for conquest. Urban did not
have to wait long for the response of the bishops. In his record of the
oration, Baldric of Dol notes:

As those present were thus clearly informed by these and other
words of this kind from the apostolic lord, the eyes of some
were bathed in tears; some trembled, and yet others discussed
the matter.

However, in the presence of all at that same council, as we
looked on, the Bishop of Puy, a man of great renown and of
highest ability, went to the Pope with joyous countenance and
on bended knee sought and entreated blessing and permission
to go.

Over and above this, he won from the Pope the command
that all should obey him, and that he should hold sway over
the army in behalf of the Pope, since all knew him to be a
prelate of unusual energy and industry.[11]

With his sales presentation, Urban not only had gained a consensus among the several hundred archbishops, bishops, abbots,
and others, but he also had a recruiting officer in Adhemar, bishop

of Puy. The bishop would lead those who spread the message through the countryside, marshalling forces and preparing for the long journey.

Urban had succeeded in rallying the warriors to battle. In so doing, he forever blurred the distinction Augustine of Hippo had drawn between an aggressive war and a defensive battle.[12] Instead of justice, the Roman Church sought a conquest. Under the new rules of engagement, warriors were ill prepared to fight for righteousness and were not instructed in handling the defeated foes ethically. This absence of civility cursed every subsequent Crusade and served as a devastating model for capricious violence. By the time of his death on July 15, 1099, two weeks after the reacquisition of Jerusalem by the crusaders, Urban had begun to receive reports of the carnage of the conquest.

The Sign and Tattoo of the Cross: Preparation for Crusade (Winter 1095)

During the winter of 1095, there seemed to be but one occupation throughout northern France and the Lower Rhine Valley—that of preparing for the Crusade exodus. Urban had suggested that the soldiers depart as soon as the roads were passable in the spring of 1096. All ranks of men thronged to receive the vestments of war. Along with the coat of armor and mail,

> [Urban] instituted a sign well suited to so honorable a profession by making the figure of the Cross, the stigma of the Lord's Passion, the emblem of the soldiery, or rather, of what was to be the soldiery of God. This, made of any cloth, he ordered to be sewed upon the shirts, cloaks, and byrra of those who were about to go. He commanded that if anyone, after receiving this emblem, or after taking openly this vow, should shrink from his good intent through base change of heart, or any affection for his parents, he should be regarded an outlaw forever, unless he repented and again undertook whatever his pledge he had omitted.[13]

To further cement the central premise of salvation for bloodshed, Urban designed an emblem of the Cross for the soldiers' uniforms, and demanded that if any man deserted from the force, or if his parents interfered and did not allow him to go to battle, then he would be considered an "outlaw." The implication was clear: *without the emblem of the cross, there would be no salvation.*

All priests were empowered to give the sacred symbol with full benediction. Many soldiers burned the sign of the cross into their flesh, like a tattoo. The rich sold their estates to raise the funds needed for the expeditions. Knights and esquires practiced incessantly to prepare for combat against the Muslims, who were perceived to be able, albeit vicious, warriors. Hermits left their retreats with the anticipation of seeing great miracles in the righteous cause. Robbers came out of hiding or were released from jails to join the army. Monks were substituting helmets for the cowls they wore. The fury of activity was a harbinger for the bloodshed and battles to come.

Foreigners from across Europe arrived to join forces with the mostly French battalions, even though they did not share a common tongue. Guibert wrote:

> I take God to witness that there landed in our ports barbarians from nations I did not even know. No one understands their tongues, but placing their fingers in the form of the Cross, they made the sign that they desired to proceed to the defense of the Christian faith.[14]

And a Hermit Shall Lead Them: The Crusade of the Crowds (March 1096)

By the springtime of 1096, the troops were ready for battle. During the First Crusade, the forces marched on *two* fronts: the *Crusade of the Crowds* (the unruly mercenaries headed by Peter the Hermit) and the *Crusade of the Chieftains* (soldiers trained and subject to nobles). The two armies joined forces at Nicea and defeated the Muslim soldiers in Jerusalem.

The Crusade of the Crowds was borne from Pope Urban's desire to include these warring peoples in the troop movements. The summons of the masses was presented as a remedy for lives lived in debauchery. In Urban's sermon at Clermont, Fulcher of Chartres recorded, the pontiff declared,

> Let those . . . who are accustomed to wage private wars wastefully even against Believers, go forth against the Infidels in a battle worthy to be undertaken now and to be finished in victory. Now, let those, who until recently existed as plunderers, be soldiers of Christ; now, let those, who formerly contended against brothers and relations, rightly fight barbarians; now, let those, who recently were hired for a few pieces of silver, win their eternal reward. Let those, who wearied themselves to the detriment of body and soul, labor for a twofold honor. Nay, more the sorrowful here will be glad there, the poor here will be rich there, and the enemies of the Lord here will be his friends there.[15]

The leader of this band of rescued savages was Peter the Hermit.[16] A man of small stature with prematurely white hair and piercing eyes, Peter was an unusual figure who often cried out against the apathy of the people so passionately that he would drive himself to exhaustion. He responded excitedly to Urban's call at the Synod of Clermont. His huge following among the peasants in the Rhine Valley enabled him to amass a large army with which to attack Jerusalem.[17]

Guibert offers a fascinating description of this leader of the common warriors. He was a barefoot warrior in a one-piece woolen potato sack, who was adored by the impoverished commoners:

> Therefore, while the princes who felt the need of many expenses and great services from their attendants, made their preparations slowly and carefully; the common people who had little property, but were very numerous, joined a certain Peter the Hermit, and obeyed him as a master while these

affairs were going on among us. He was, if I am not mistaken, from the city of Amiens, and we have learned that he lived as a hermit, dressed as a monk, somewhere in Upper Gaul. After he had departed from there—I do not know with what intention—we saw him going through the cities and towns under the pretense of preaching. He was surrounded by so great throngs of people, he received such enormous gifts, his holiness was lauded so highly, that no one within my memory has been held in such honor. He was very liberal in the distribution to the poor of what he had received. He restored prostitutes to their husbands with gifts. By his wonderful authority he restored everywhere peace and concord, in place of discord. For in whatever he did or said it seemed as if there was something divine, especially when the hairs were snatched from his mules for relics. . . . He wore a woolen shirt, and over it a mantle reaching his ankles; his arms and feet were bare. He lived on wine and fish; he hardly ever, or never, ate bread.[18]

Peter's reputation as a holy man of near-miraculous power facilitated his ability to marshal the masses to the Crusade movement. Albert of Aix, a canon at Aix-la-Chapelle (Aachen) in the mid-twelfth century, noted that Peter was the conduit through which many joined the Crusade:

In every admonition and sermon, with all the persuasion of which he was capable, he urged setting out on the journey as soon as possible. In response to his constant admonition and call, bishops, abbots, clerics, and monks set out; next, most noble laymen, and princes of the different kingdoms; then, all the common people, the chaste as well as the sinful, adulterers, homicides, thieves, perjurers, and robbers; indeed, every class of the Christian profession, nay, also, women and those influenced by the spirit of penance—all joyfully entered upon this expedition.[19]

Peter's appeal to the common people was simple: He promised the blessing of God upon the poor and starving masses to whom he ministered, and he stated that God would be favorable to the responsive businessman. In March of 1096, Peter led twenty thousand men and women[20] toward Jerusalem with the intention of first capturing Nicea.

Unprepared for battle, the hordes of enthusiastic crusaders of the streets met with disaster when they reached Nicea. The army consisted of Lombards, Longobards, and the Alemanni from the north, all under the direction of Peter the Hermit. On the south edge of the city, the crusaders captured an empty fortress called *Xerogord* and made quick use of the grain, wine, and meat.

While establishing the fortress as their first vanguard, Peter somehow lost control of a great many of the warriors. One contemporary chronicler notes, "Peter had gone to Constantinople . . . because he was unable to restrain that varied host, which was not willing to listen either to him or to his words."[21] Those remaining in the Nicean fort crowned a soldier named Reinald, the leader of the Lombards, master of the entire battalion. While drinking from the major water source, a river just outside of the fortress, the band of warriors did not foresee the onslaught of the Turks. While some died in the ensuing battle, many fled to the confines of the fortress, only to be cut off from their only water supply. For eight days, the soldiers fought both Turks and dehydration. One chronicler details the horrors of the hour, including their desperate drinking of blood and sweat:

> The Turks, who came on the day of the Dedication of St. Michael, found Reginald and those who were with them and killed many of them. Those who remained alive fled to the fortress, which the Turks straightway besieged, thus depriving them of water. Our people were in such distress from thirst that they bled their horses and asses and drank the blood; others let their girdles and handkerchiefs down into the cistern and squeezed out the water from them into their mouths; some urinated into one another's hollowed hands and drank; and others dug up the moist ground and lay down on their

backs and spread the earth over their breasts to relieve the excessive dryness of thirst.[22]

Finally, the devastation became unbearable for the tormented troops. After eight days, Reinald surrendered to the Turks, though he did it secretly, not wanting to look like a coward to his troops. After pretending to attack, he surrendered to the Muslims without a fight. The aftermath was a bloodbath. The captured warriors were told to deny Jesus Christ or die. Those who did recant to save their lives were also killed or sold into slavery. The chronicle continues:

> Those, however, who were unwilling to deny the Lord received the sentence of death; some, whom they took alive, [the Muslim leaders] divided among themselves, like sheep; some they placed as a target and shot with arrows; others they sold and gave away, like animals. Some they took captive to their own homes, some to Chorosan, some to Antioch, others to Aleppo, or wherever they themselves lived. These were the first to receive a happy martyrdom in the name of the Lord Jesus.[23]

Those who traveled with Peter met no less abominable a fate. While traveling to Constantinople, the group passed through a city directly north of Nicea called Civitote. There Peter's band of survivors was mugged.

> The Turks, indeed, rushed upon these people and killed many of them. Some they found sleeping, some lying down, others naked—all of whom they killed. With these people they found a certain priest celebrating mass, whom they straightway martyred upon the altar. Those who could escape fled. . . . Others hurled themselves headlong into the sea, while some hid in the forests and mountains. But the Turks, pursuing them, collected wood to burn them.[24]

By the summer of 1096, the first battalion of the Crusade was almost totally laid to waste.

Soldiers of Fortune: The Crusade of the Kings (June–December 1096)

It was at this time that the Crusade of the Chieftains was making final preparations. News of the defeat of the crusading mob reached their leaders, and they hurried to the defense of their brethren.

The "chieftains" were nobles of some standing, who were both able and well-financed. Four divisions prepared to travel different routes to arrive at the city of Nicea for the first assault. Each was headed by a nobleman or king so as to inspire confidence in the men. If they had learned anything from the loss of Peter's troops, it was the necessity of planning and preparation.

The first battalion to set out after Peter's defeat was led by Hugh of Vermandois. As the leader of the northern Franks, and brother of the French king, Hugh left from south Lyon. His forces were captured at Constantinople because they did not anticipate the size of the Turkish Muslims:

> Hugh the Great, brother of Philip, King of France. The first of the heroes crossing the sea, he landed at the city of Durazzo in Bulgaria with his own men, but having imprudently departed with a scant army, he was seized by the citizens there and brought to the Emperor of Constantinople, where he was detained for a considerable time not altogether free.[25]

Bohemond of Taranto led the second band of Frank warriors. He was the son of Robert Guiscaro, the founder of the Norman kingdom of Naples. A wealthy man who was snobbish, Bohemond was aided by Tancred du Hauteville, who offset Bohemond's sullen disposition with a vibrant personality. Together, they commanded one hundred thousand mounted and twenty thousand foot soldiers.[26]

Godfrey of Bouillon, along with his two brothers, led another large troop movement to Constantinople, tracing the exact steps of the common crusaders. His group was large enough, however, to stave off any attacks, and they arrived at the city in the winter of 1096.

Of all the chieftains, the least qualified to lead a brigade was Robert of Normandy. Nicknamed "short-hose"[27] and "the fat," Robert was the son of William the Conqueror, and came to his position by birthright. His battalion consisted of servants of his estate, whom he sold as mercenaries to the desperate pope for ten thousand silver marks.[28]

Raymond of Toulouse led the men of Languedoc. He was the most notoriously opulent and haughty of the chieftains, but also the most experienced. As a knight under Cid of Spain, he had fought bravely against the Muslims from Spain, known as the Moors. His one hundred thousand troops were also led by the spiritual head of the Crusades, Adhemar of Puy.[29] Adhemar incited the troops by preaching that they were the fulfillment of the millennium peace promised in Isaiah.

The various troops set out during the summer months, and all journeyed toward the city of Nicea. Fulcher writes:

> So, with such a great band proceeding from western parts, gradually from day to day on the way there grew armies of innumerable people coming together from everywhere. Thus a countless multitude speaking many languages and coming from many regions was to be seen. However, all were not assembled into one army until we all arrived at the city of Nicea.[30]

Godfrey traveled through Hungary, and met with Alexis. A wise diplomat, Godfrey signed a peace treaty with the Hungarians to avoid attacks from non-Muslim, but usually antagonistic, forces. When he learned that Count Hugh, another nobleman, had been captured, Godfrey destroyed a town and began to burn villages until Alexis, his new partner, negotiated for Hugh's release.

Raymond attempted to guide his troops through northern Italy, around the Adriatic Sea and through the mountains. However, the cold temperatures and snow slowed their progress. Robert of Normandy took his troops through southern Italy, and stopped there in the warm waters for the winter. His men relaxed in the sun, and once the spring came, did not want to leave their resort. Even Raymond lost his desire to crusade, and his men did not even leave for the battle until Easter 1097.

Begin the Battle with Nicea (May 15, 1097)

The first objective of the conquest was Nicea, a city sacred in the memories of the church leaders as the site of the first ecumenical council of the Christian Church.[31] A few survivors from Peter's troops, including Peter himself, met the warriors outside the city. Haggard, bloody, and starving, the weary commoners inspired the regiment of the chieftains to battle. On May 15, 1097, they united and began the siege.

The crusading knights were clad in the hauberk, which consisted of a coat of mail made of rings of steel. All soldiers wore the casque around their chests, covered in iron for the common soldiers, steel for the knights, and silver for the princes. Helmets of steel or chain hoods covered the head, and the weapons of battle were heavy. Each soldier carried a lance tipped in steel, a sword, an ax, a club, a sling, and a crossbow of steel. These weapons were said to be unstoppable if brandished properly.[32]

The horses were all hooded with metal, and saddle-plated with steel. The troops carried siege engines such as battering rams, catapults, and moveable towers complete with crossing bridges. When the siege began in Nicea, the crusaders were well prepared for any circumstance.

Against the weighty armor of the crusaders, the Turks were much more agile. Their horses were more slender and much faster. Their weapons were bows and axes. They had iron shields covered with leather, and carried sacks full of arrows and turbans to shield them from the sun.[33]

At the battlefield, the Christian forces numbered a quarter of a million men. About one hundred thousand Turks were behind the city walls. Two walls surrounded Nicea, and 370 towers were spaced around the parameters. A deep moat also surrounded the city, and high mountains shielded the eastern border. The Christian troops built nineteen camps, and attacked the fortified city on three sides. After seven weeks of intense fighting, it seemed the crusaders were on the verge of victory. It was at this crucial moment that Alexis, the eastern emperor who had issued the call to Urban II for help, surprised the crusaders and sent a detachment of his troops to help the Turks.

The Battle for Jerusalem (June 13, 1099)

Enraged by Alexis's deception, the crusaders demolished the city, and made their next conquest at Antioch a quick one. After the crusaders seized Antioch, they traveled south to Jerusalem. Arriving on March 7, 1099, the troops waited approximately three months to attack. On June 13, the battle commenced. It was nothing short of unbridled carnage. The Turks, overwhelmed by the onslaught, became confused, and one chronicler described the scene in a harrowing manner, using apocalyptic language and imagery:

> Some of our men . . . cut off the heads of their enemies; others shot them with arrows, so that they fell from towers; others tortured them longer by casting them into flames. . . . It was necessary to pick one's way over the bodies of men and horses. But these were small matters compared to what happened at the Temple of Solomon. . . . Men rode in blood up to their knees and bridle reins. Indeed it was a just and splendid judgment of God that this place should be filled with the blood of the unbelievers, since it had suffered so long from their blasphemies. At nightfall, the Crusaders' hands were still bloody when they folded them in prayer and knelt at the Church of the Holy Sepulchre, sobbing for excess joy.[34]

In the end, the First Crusade was the only successful expedition during the three centuries of battle over the Holy Land. Euphoria surrounding this achievement was palatable. The dismal failure of the troops under Peter the Hermit had heightened awareness of the ability of the Seljuk Turks. When the city eventually returned to the Islamic powers, the Christians were well aware of the advanced proficiency of the Muslim forces. Yet for well over three hundred years, the Vicars of Rome continued to send men, women, and even children, to their demise.

Coming chapters will seek further understanding of answers to central questions: What were the motives for the First Crusade, for both those who mandated the excursion, and those who sacrificed themselves during the journey? How did Urban motivate a quarter million people to offer their lives for the conquest of a land they had never seen? Untold thousands of lives were sacrificed on Middle Eastern soil, and the number of troops willing to make the sacrifice was rarely depleted. How was Urban II able to order the Crusade in the first place and how did he justify the first aggressive assault by Christian forces since Jesus Christ was on the earth?

We will continue to explore these critical questions in the coming chapters.

Notes

1. August C. Krey, *The First Crusade: The Accounts of Eye-Witnesses and Participants* (Princeton, N.J.: Princeton University Press, 1921), 103.
2. L. E. Browne, *The Eclipse of Christianity* (Cambridge, England: Cambridge University Press, 1932), 55–61. The life of Urban is often overlooked by those more intent on the events that surround the instigation of the Crusade. See also Pierre Mansthal, *The Writings of Urban II* (New York: University of New York Press, 1861), 110–15.
3. Mansthal, *Writings of Urban II,* 112.
4. J. N. D. Kelly, *The Oxford Dictionary of the Popes* (Oxford: Oxford University Press, 1986), 158. Also noteworthy is the contention that Urban "sold" the papacy for the land. In effect, Gunther Bornkamm (*Christian Experience* [New York: Harper and Row, 1971], 22); and Robert Stewart (*Charlemagne and On* [New York: Firebird, 1964], 35), contend that Urban traded power for land.
5. James Brundage, *The Crusades: A Documentary Survey* (Milwaukee, Wis.: Marquette University Press, 1962), 8–9.
6. Ibid., 10.

7. Ibid. The letter was dated December 7, 1074.

8. Oliver J. Thatcher and Edgar Holmes McNeal, eds., *A Source Book for Medieval History* (New York: Scribners, 1905), 417–18.

9. Dana C. Munro, *Urban and the Crusaders* (Philadelphia: University of Pennsylvania Press, 1896), 5–8. Emphasis added. Munro translated freely from *Recueil des historiens des croisades, Historiens occidentaux,* 5 vols. (Paris: Biblioteque, 1844–1895), 3:26–28.

10. Ibid., 6–7.

11. *Recueil des historiens des croisades,* 4:210

12. Augustine of Hippo, *Contra Faustum,* in *The Nicene and Post-Nicene Fathers* (New York: Christian Literature, 1887), 6:442.

13. Guibert, Abbot of Nogent, *Historia quae dicitur Gesta Dei per Francos,* in *Recueil des historiens des croisades,* vol. 4. Author's translation.

14. Pierre Mansthal, *Writings of Guibert* (New York: Pantheon, 1862), 82.

15. Frances Rita Ryan, trans., *Fulcher of Chartres' A History of the Expedition to Jerusalem, 1095–1127* (Knoxville, Tenn.: University of Tennessee Press, 1927), 26.

16. For a detailed study on the life of Peter the Hermit and his band of nomadic preachers, see Daniel Goodsell, *Peter the Hermit* (Cincinnati: Jennings, 1906).

17. Ibid., 63.

18. Munro, *Urban and the Crusaders,* 20.

19. *Recueil des historiens des croisades,* 4:211. Author's translation.

20. It is a fallacious assumption that all the crusaders were male. As Finucane notes, "Women followed the pilgrimage routes of medieval Europe as avidly as men. Women suffered while on ordinary pilgrimage to the Holy Land, and they could hardly expect lighter treatment on the Crusades." Ronald C. Finucane, *Soldiers of Faith: Crusaders and Moslems at War* (New York: St. Martin's, 1983), 38. One such female warrior was Margaret of Beverly, who put a cooking pot on her head as a helmet and carried water to the men on the walls of Jerusalem.

21. A. C. Krey, *Gesta francorum et aliorum Hierosolymitanorum: The Deeds of the Franks,* 141.

22. Ibid.

23. Ibid., 73.

24. Ibid.

25. Ryan, *Fulcher of Chartres' A History of the Expedition to Jerusalem, 1095–1127,* 32.

26. Henry Ameoroz, *The Eclipse of the Abbasid Caliphate: Original Chronicles of the Fourth Islamic Century* (Oxford: Oxford University Press, 1920), 4:110. Ameoroz uses the estimates of the Turks who served as sentries in Jerusalem.

27. Literally "Robert Curthose." This was a term of derision, used without Robert's knowledge. See Letienne Brehier, trans., *Histoire anonyme de la première croisade* (Paris: Champion, 1924), 122.

28. Ibid.

29. Armand Maurer, *Medieval Philosophy* (New York: Random House, 1962), 204.

30. Ryan, *Fulcher of Chartres' A History of the Expedition to Jerusalem, 1095–1127,* 31.

31. This took place in 325. See Philip Schaff, *The Creeds of Christendom* (New York: Harper and Row, 1931), 1:57–61.

32. Anna Comnena, *The Alexiad* (Chicago: University of Chicago Press, 1926), 212. As a later chronicler, Comnena is cited as a primary source in Walter Walbank, *Civilization Past and Present* (New York: Scott, 1942), 335; and Zoe Oldenbourg, *The Early Crusaders* (New York: Pantheon, 1964), 191.

33. Nowhere was the Medieval Islamic ideal of warfare more detailed than in the writings of Saladin (1138–1193). Though he would become the Muslim leader approximately ninety years later, he often spoke of the historic practice of Islamic warfare. See Gertrude Slaughter, *Saladin* (New York: Exhibition Press, 1955), 178.

34. Brehier, *Histoire anonyme de la première croisade,* 241. Author's translation.

Chapter 5

Sanctified Slaughter

When the Body of Christ Became the Army of God

Though the First Crusade ended in victory, it represented a quantum shift in the theology, thought, and ethics of the Christian community. For the first time in history, an army was gathered under the aegis of the cross of Jesus Christ, sanctified by the pope to kill in the name of the Lord. Indeed, the pontiff himself was the titular commander of the forces, as well as the financier of the expeditions. One thousand years of history—complete with persecution, pacifism, reluctant participation, and Just War parameters—was swept aside, and the "Army of God" conquered the Muslim forces in Acre, Antioch, and finally Jerusalem.

Losses had been heavy, and the actions of many of the soldiers were shocking even to the faithful chroniclers who had been sent by the Vatican to record this great spiritual event. Certainly it would take much time to repair the damage which had been inflicted from the warmongers.

Yet the very fact that Pope Urban II was able to marshal the forces, motivate the troops, and send them out for such an excursion raises more questions. How was the Church at Rome able to rally the warriors, gather the leaders, and then justify the slaughter? How did the papacy justify the first "Christian army" in history? How was the pope able to declare and legitimize a "Christian jihad"?

This chapter will be an attempt at outlining the motivations that made such a profound impact on the believers and soldiers that it merited actually spilling the blood of those they were forsworn to reach with the gospel. While these motivations may seem weak and paltry to the modern reader, please remember that they were more than enough to assemble the largest military force of West Europeans in history.

Religious Motivation: Martyrdom Guarantees Forgiveness

The most deeply disturbing motivation for the majority of the soldiers was the explicit promise of salvation for martyrdom. Indeed, Pope Urban was so generous with this offer that the mere enlistment in battle, regardless of outcome, was enough to earn salvation. As we shall see, he was not the first Roman Catholic pope to attempt to offer such a promise, but he was the first to do so successfully.

Life at the dawning of the second millennium was less than genial for the average serf. Poverty, hard work for little return, and epidemic diseases that ravished the populace all contributed to a hopeless existence for lower-class Europeans. Daily survival was difficult enough. Few ever had any hope of education, advancement, or personal fulfillment.

Enter the Pope.

In his speech at the Council of Clermont in the winter of 1095, Urban II offered an elusive prize that must have seemed too good to be true. By calling for the Crusade, and extending "crusader privileges," he offered that which had eluded them their entire miserable lives—purpose and assurance. In effect, he was saying, "You, my forlorn Christian brother, you have a purpose in life. You are called to a task greater than yourself. You can serve your Lord and Savior by rescuing that which is most precious to him—the Holy Land."

God almighty himself needs and is calling them for this task. An injustice must be righted, and fellow believers require help. He instills in these potential soldiers their high calling:

> Although, O sons of God, you have promised more firmly
> than ever to keep the peace among yourselves and to preserve

the rights of the church, there remains still an important work for you to do. Freshly quickened by the divine correction, you must apply the strength of your righteousness to another matter that concerns you as well as God. For your brethren who live in the east are in urgent need of your help, and you must hasten to give them the aid that has often been promised them. For, as the most of you have heard, the Turks and Arabs have attacked them and have conquered the territory of Romania [the Greek empire] as far west as the shore of the Mediterranean and the Hellespont, which is called the Arm of St. George. They have occupied more and more of the lands of those Christians, and have overcome them in seven battles. They have killed and captured many, and have destroyed the churches and devastated the empire. If you permit them to continue thus for awhile with impurity, the faithful of God will be much more widely attacked by them. On this account I, or rather the Lord, beseech you as Christ's heralds to publish this everywhere and to persuade all people of whatever rank, foot-soldiers and knights, poor and rich, to carry aid promptly to those Christians and to destroy that vile race from the lands of our friends. I say this to those who are present, it is meant also for those who are absent. Moreover, Christ commands it.[1]

Notice Urban's "logic" at this point—abandon the petty issues which divide us, and let us unite for a task far more worthy of our attention. This "vile race" of Muslims has killed many of our brethren, and has conquered the land of our Lord. This is a high point on our history, and now, "Christ commands" you to battle.

In the modern context, one can hear the echoes of Pope Urban's voice in the voices of Usamah bin Ladin and Saddam Hussein. Each leader calling his people to bloodshed has used the same general tactics of speech and logic to encourage enlistment:

1. We are under attack by an evil, outside force.

2. Our lands have been taken, and our brothers have been killed by this force.
3. The one you say you worship is calling you to battle. To refuse is damnation and sin, and to enlist is to be led by the Creator himself.
4. You are desperately needed if we are to succeed.

Any who are offended by this comparison of bin Ladin to Pope Urban can stand with us, for we are offended as well. We are offended that the institutional representation of Christianity stooped to such a level of evil enterprise. As will be argued in Appendix A, it is one thing to have Christians in the army, serving under a secular power. Because we live in a fallen world where injustice must be stopped and life must be defended, Christians can serve in the military and remain a godly influence and moral agent. The entire concept of *Just War* is built on this premise. It is another thing altogether, however, to field a Christian army to kill the enemy in the name of Jesus Christ.

Add to this corporate motivation an intensely personal one for the soldier. Not only does the soldier identify with a great purpose as part of a force led by God, but the soldier who fights is promised salvation. He is given assurance. In a religious system where salvation is only promised for the faithful who accomplish all the steps from infant baptism to last rites, absolute assurance is a rare commodity.

Yet Urban offers precisely that which eluded nominal Christians of his time: an absolute guarantee that they would inherit heaven. According to the chronicler, in his very next sentence Urban offered the warranty of salvation, based upon his ability as "vicar of Christ": "All who die by the way, whether by land or by sea, or in battle against the pagans, shall have immediate remission of sins. This I grant them through the power of God with which I am invested."[2]

Again, a painful comparison across time must be made. There is no difference between the offer of eternal forgiveness in the speech of Pope Urban II in 1095 and the declaration of jihad by Usamah bin Ladin in 1998. We show this in Appendix B.

This attempt to barter salvation for blood was not new. Two

centuries prior to Urban, Pope Leo IV (847–855) made a similar pledge to the Frank soldiers who would help fight the Muslims:

> Now we hope that none of you will be slain, but we wish you to know that the kingdom of heaven will be given as a reward to those who shall be killed in this war. For the Omnipotent knows that they lost their lives fighting for the truth of the faith, for the preservation of their country, and the defense of Christians. And therefore God will give them, the reward which we have named.[3]

A generation after Leo IV, Pope John VIII also offered salvation for the Christian martyrs, as long as they were engaged in battle "for Christ." In 878, he wrote to King Louis II, who was also known as "The Stammerer":

> We confidently reply that those who, out of love to the Christian religion, shall die in battle fighting bravely against pagans or unbelievers, shall receive eternal life. For the Lord has said through his prophet: "In whatever hour a sinner shall be converted, I will remember his sins no longer." By the intercession of St. Peter, who has the power of binding and loosing in heaven and on the earth, we absolve, as far as is permissible, all such and commend them by our prayers to the Lord.[4]

If Urban was not the first to make such an offer, he was the first to successfully enact the pledge, declaring a Christian holy war (*Bellum Sacrum*). This paradigm shift in Christian theology did much damage, perhaps irreparable, to the Christian witness.

The Territorial Motivation: Repel the Muslims from Jerusalem

In the first week of March 1095, a full eighteen months prior to the Council of Clermont, a separate council of bishops from France, Italy, and Germany met in Piacenza. In attendance at the council was an ambassador representing the Byzantine emperor Alexius I Comnenus. His one purpose for the journey was to appeal to Pope Urban for aid in their darkest hour. The Turkish army had conquered everything in their path through Asia Minor, and they were nearing Constantinople. Furthermore, the Christians living in Jerusalem had been subjected to unspeakable horrors. The Byzantine Church needed help.

The second motivation for Urban's call to Crusade was the onslaught of the aggressive Muslims. It was not that the Muslims had suddenly begun to inhabit Jerusalem. As noted above, they had ruled the land for centuries. However, the new Muslim rulers had intensified persecution of Christians to an unprecedented degree and with impunity. As one author writes, "The caliphs of Cairo, who had taken advantage of the transient conquests of the Greeks to extend their empire, at first treated the Christians as allies and auxiliaries."[5] By the beginning of the ninth century Islam had emerged as a formidable force. It had conquered much of the Middle East, North Africa, Spain, and southern Italy. The presence of the Muslims, however, stirred more than just territorial conflict; it was a cultural conflict as well. As Lewis notes:

> The Arab conquerors brought their own religion and created their own state; much of the conflict of early Islamic times arises from the [cultural] clash between the two. All the Arab warriors shared . . . in the tribute of the conquered lands. Many of them were tribesmen in search of pasturage, oasis-dwellers looking for estates, and Meccan merchants avid to exploit the rich commerce of great cities.[6]

The problem in the eleventh century began in earnest when the third Fatimite caliph, Hakim, began a wholesale persecution of the Christian community just south of the Holy Land. Michaud writes:

> When the caliph Hakim had once given the signal for persecution, he found himself at no loss for executioners. At first, they who abused their power were the objects of pursuit; the

Christian religion became the next crime, and the most pious among the faithful were deemed the most guilty. The blood of Christians flowed in all the cities of Egypt and Syria.[7]

It was only a matter of time until the onslaught reached the Holy Land. When word of the torment reached Urban following the Piacenza, his travels enabled him to validate the horrific stories. In his sermon at Clermont, Urban's most vivid language was spared for his description of the abuse suffered by the Christians of Jerusalem:

> They have led away a part of the captives into their own coun-
> try, and a part they have destroyed by cruel tortures; [Islam]
> has either entirely destroyed the churches of God or appro-
> priated them for the rites of its own religion. They destroy the
> altars, after having defiled them with their uncleanness. They
> circumcise the Christians, and the blood of the circumcision
> they either spread upon the altars or pour into the vases of
> the baptismal font. When they wish to torture the people by a
> base death, they perforate their navels, and dragging forth the
> extremity of the intestines, bind it to a stake; then with flog-
> ging they lead the victim around until the viscera having
> gushed forth the victim falls prostrate upon the ground. Oth-
> ers they bind to a post and pierce with arrows. Others they
> compel to extend their necks and then, attacking them with
> naked swords, attempt to cut through the neck with a single
> blow. What shall I say of the abominable rape of the women?
> To speak of it is to be worse than to be silent.[8]

Baldric of Dol, who referred to the Muslim soldiers as "The pollu-
tion of paganism,"[9] includes intense language as well, focusing on the psychological effects of the persecution. He writes,

> More suffering of our brethren and devastation of churches
> remains than we can speak of one by one, for we are oppressed
> by tears and groans, sighs and sobs. We weep and wail, breth-

ren, alas, like the Psalmist, in our inmost heart! We are
wretched and unhappy.[10]

Amazingly, though most modern commentators are aware of the
tragic fate many of these Christians faced, few are willing to mention
the rescue motif as a cause for the Crusade. In one specific example,
Justo Gonzalez lists eight causes for the First Crusade, none of which
include the terrors of the Islamic onslaught.[11]

Was Urban justified in his depiction of Islam as an adversarial force?
Were the Muslim caliphs in fact oppressing the Christians in Jerusalem? Was there a valid justification for crusade, if in fact the caliphs
were imperiously torturing the Christian pilgrims?

The plight of the indigenous and pilgrim Christians in the Holy
Land was considered worse following the most recent occupation by
the Muslims than at previous times. Rumors of wholesale slaughter of
Christians in the Holy Land contributed to a blood frenzy that went
far beyond whatever brutalities the Muslims had committed against
Christians.

Fearing both the exponential growth of Islam and its theocratic
form of government, Urban's fears mounted. If the Muslims could
conquer the Holy Land, one of the most fortified cities in civilized
history, what would stop them from attacking Rome? Note the im-
plicit suggestion in Urban's words as recorded by Baldric:

Holy men do not possess those cities; nay, base and bastard
Turks hold sway over our brothers. The blessed Peter first presided as Bishop at Antioch; behold, in his own church the
Gentiles have established their superstitions, and the Christian religion, which they ought rather to cherish, they have
basely shut out from the hall dedicated to God! The estates
given for the support of the saints and the patrimony of nobles
set aside for the sustenance of the poor are subject to pagan
tyranny, while cruel masters abuse for their own purposes the
returns of the lands. The priesthood of God has been ground
down into dust. The sanctuary of God (unspeakable shame!)

is everywhere profaned. Whatever Christians still remain in hiding there are sought out with unheard of tortures.[12]

Parallels between Rome and Jerusalem were more than just coincidental: Jerusalem's priesthood was ground to dust; Rome's priesthood could be endangered. Jerusalem's estates had fallen into disarray; Rome's vast estates could be reduced to rubble. Jerusalem's sanctuaries had been profaned; Rome's opulent sanctuaries could as easily be laid to waste. Urban's intimation could not have been clearer: *It could happen here. If we do not stop the pagans in Jerusalem, they might storm our shores.*[13]

Concurrent with those fears was the alleged threat of forced Islamic worship. Fulcher, who not only participated in the First Crusade but also lived in Jerusalem for a quarter of a century, continued to relate tales that the Muslims used to pray to an idol made in the name of "Mahumet" at the Dome of the Rock.[14]

Pope Urban's Motivation: Regain the Glory of the Papacy

The final motivation we will discuss was the motivation of Urban himself. Why would he want to enter such an endeavor so obviously fraught with complications, expense, and danger? In his mind, the very existence of the Roman papacy was at stake. If the Muslims could travel north and conquer Rome, then the rule of St. Peter would be vanquished. If, however, he could lead the forces of Jesus Christ to conquer the Muslims, then he would forever solidify the legitimacy of Rome as the protector of Christianity.

The bothersome presence of the antipope (Clement III) weakened the authority of the Roman pontiff. Subjects in the land were split. Which pope would they recognize as authentic? Urban needed to reestablish himself as the sole voice of God to the Christian people.

In Fulcher's version of Urban's Clermont speech, it is evident that Urban immediately declares himself the only Vicar of Christ:

One after another, [Urban] beseechingly exhorted them all, with renewed faith, to spur themselves in great earnestness to overcome the Devil's devices and to try to restore the Holy Church, most unmercifully weakened by the wicked, to its former honorable status. . . . "Most beloved brethren," he said, "by God's permission placed over the whole world with the papal crown, I, Urban, as the messenger of divine admonition, have been compelled by an unavoidable occasion to come here to you servants of God. I desired those whom I judged to be stewards of God's ministries to be true stewards and faithful, with all hypocrisy rejected.[15]

To restore the "Holy Church . . . to its former honorable status,"[16] Urban unites the Church under the protection of his newly formed forces. Following a brief description of the world situation without the crusading forces, Urban commands a three-pronged method of defense:

Especially establish ecclesiastical affairs firm in their own right, so that no simoniac heresy will take root among you. Take care lest vendors and moneychangers, flayed by the scourges of the Lord, be miserably driven into the narrow streets of destruction. Uphold the Church in its own ranks altogether free from all secular power. See that the tithes of all those who cultivate the earth are given faithfully to God; let them not be sold or held back. Let him who has seized a bishop be considered an outlaw. Let him who has seized or robbed monks, clerics, nuns and their servants, pilgrims, or merchants, be excommunicated. Let the robbers and burners of homes and their accomplices, banished from the Church, be smitten with excommunication.[17]

Urban's attack on the corrupt clergy ("establish ecclesiastical affairs firm") would preserve the integrity of the priestly offices. His admonition against "all secular power" was his desire to see the purity of the Church maintained. His threat to excommunicate all those who attacked the clergy was not just an empty pledge; he wanted to protect the leaders and servants of the Church.

No person involved in the controversy was spared from Urban's piercing gaze. Fulcher, who has already established himself as an advocate for Urban, spent eleven paragraphs detailing the contention between Urban and Clement:

> But the Devil, who always persists in the detriment of man and goes about like a lion seeking to devour him, stirred up, to the confusion of the people, a certain man stimulated by pride, by the name of Wilbert [Clement III], Urban's adversary. Recently supported by the impudence of the aforementioned emperor of the Bavarians, while Urban's predecessor, Gregory, who was Hildebrand, was held on the throne rightly, this man began to usurp the papal office after that same Gregory was excluded from the threshold of Saint Peter's Church.[18]

Fulcher includes a note of sarcasm in his description of Henry IV. Though his domain stretched north to the Saxons and south to the Germans, Fulcher simply calls him the "emperor of the Bavarians." This could be due to the revolt against Henry's rule in those outlying areas at the time, though this is uncertain. His inclusion of Gregory as the rightful seat on the throne clearly displays his allegiance with the reformed clerical movement.

Urban convinced the majority of the Church leaders that he alone deserved to be pope, though a vocal minority still marked a movement within the region. This group succeeded in getting Urban exiled briefly, though the expulsion did not defeat him; rather, it compelled him to action. Fulcher continues:

> Because he acted thus perversely, the better people did not wish to recognize him. When Urban was lawfully elected and consecrated by the bishops and cardinals after the death of Hildebrand, the greater and more pious part of the people

favored obedience to him. But Wilbert, spurred by the support of the emperor and by the encouragement of most of the Roman citizens, forced Urban to become an exile from the monastery of Saint Peter's as long as he could. While Urban was thus separated from the Church, in going through the provinces, he united with God those people who had wandered somewhat astray.[19]

As Urban traveled throughout the provinces, he quickly won the hearts of the common peasants as well as the local princes. One such advocate was Countess Mathilda of Tuscany. The chronicler notes that she was instrumental in reinstating Urban to the Roman See:

> Wilbert, puffed up because of his preeminence in the Church, was inclined to favor sinners, and exercising the office of the Apostolate among his sympathizers, although unjustly, he disparaged the acts of Urban as vain. However, in that year when the first Franks going to Jerusalem passed through Rome, Urban obtained the entire papal power with the aid of a certain noble matron by the name of Mathilda, who was then powerfully active in Rome.[20]

With two men claiming absolute authority over the Church and living in the same city, how was the average citizen of the Empire to know which to follow? Fulcher cites the criterion as holiness: "Wilbert was then in Germany. So two popes were over Rome; but whom to obey, or from whom to seek advice, or who cured illnesses was a question to many. Some favored this one; some, the other. But it is evident to the minds of men that Urban was the more just; for he who subdues his passions as he would his enemies, must rightly be considered the better man."[21]

In summary, Fulcher reflects on the negative effects of the papal schism on the Christian world. It is clear that he felt the preceding power struggle contributed to the need for a unifying enterprise: the Crusade to Jerusalem. He concludes:

[It is not] surprising that the whole world was disquieted and disturbed. When the Roman Church, from which all Christendom must obtain correction, is in disorder, it happens that all of the subordinate members, being affected by the diseased fibers of the head, become weakened. To be sure, the Church, our mother, on whose milk we were reared, by whose example instructed, and by whose prudence protected, was violently struck by that proud Wilbert. Whenever the head was so bruised, at once the members of the body are hurt. If the head ail, the rest of the members suffer pain. The head was thus hurt, and already the members languished with pain, since in all parts of Europe, peace, goodness, and faith were forcibly trod upon by both the high and the low within the churches and without. But when all these evils had been renounced because of the warning of Pope Urban, it was necessary to substitute war against the pagans for wars between Christians.[22]

If the struggle against the antipope was a negative issue that motivated Urban to call for the Crusade, then a potential "blessing" from the Crusade would be the end of strife among the Christian kingdoms. These supposedly Christian monarchs were waging constant war with one another, and it was virtually impossible to call a truce between them. Urban's repugnance for this civil war is evident in Baldric's version of his plea:

What are we saying? Listen and learn! You, girt about with the badge of knighthood, are arrogant with great pride; you rage against your brothers and cut each other in pieces. This is not the [true] soldiery of Christ which rends asunder the sheepfold of the Redeemer. The Holy Church has reserved a soldiery for herself to help her people, but you debase her wickedly to her hurt. Let us confess the truth, whose heralds we ought to be; truly, you are not holding to the way that leads to life. You, the oppressors of children, plunderers of widows; you, guilty of homicide, of sacrilege, robbers of another's rights; you who await the pay of thieves for the shedding of Christian blood— as vultures smell fetid corpses, so do you sense battles from afar and rush to them eagerly.[23]

He does not simply urge them to lay down their arms against one another; Urban threatens these soldiers in his next breath:

If, forsooth, you wish to be mindful of your souls, either lay down the girdle of such knighthood, or advance boldly, as knights of Christ, and rush as quickly as you can to the defense of the Eastern Church. For she it is from whom the joys of your whole salvation have come forth.[24]

For the warriors concerned about eternity, who were "mindful of [their] souls," the choice was clear. The defense of the Eastern Church was the key to eternal salvation. The end of civil war among Christians was the door through which the sinner, guilty of spilling *Christian* blood, would enter.

Once the threat was issued, Urban turned to the positive effects of such a union of forces. Note again what Fulcher reports:

"Let those," he said, "who are accustomed to wage private wars wastefully even against Believers, go forth against the Infidels in a battle worthy to be undertaken now and to be finished in victory. Now, let those, who until recently existed as plunderers, be soldiers of Christ; now, let those, who formerly contended against brothers and relations, rightly fight barbarians; now, let those, who recently were hired for a few pieces of silver, win their eternal reward. Let those, who wearied themselves to the detriment of body and soul, labor for a twofold honor. Nay, more the sorrowful here will be glad there, the poor here will be rich there, and the enemies of the Lord here will be his friends there."[25]

Apparently, Urban's admonition was effective. In a letter written on September 11, 1098, the princes united to report back to Urban that they sent "greetings as faithful servants and sons to their spiritual father."[26] In Antioch, Fulcher noted:

> Who ever heard of such a mixture of languages in one army, since there were French, Flemings, Frisians, Gauls, Allobroges, Lotharingians, Allemani, Bavarians, Normans, English, Scots, Aquitanians, Italians, Dacians, Apulians, Iberians, Bretons, Greeks and Armenians? If any Breton or Teuton wished to question me, I could neither understand nor answer. But we who were diverse in languages, nevertheless seemed to be brothers in the love of God and very close to being of one mind.[27]

Urban pounced on the opportunity to exploit the inherent xenophobia that had saturated much of Western Europe for four centuries. Give these warring countries a common enemy, Urban reasoned, and Rome will have a formidable army.

Therefore, Urban's desire to accomplish the seemingly impossible unification of the Christian kingdoms for a common goal was realized before the crusaders ever reached Jerusalem. The risk of the Crusade was great, but the benefits from a potential victory, in Urban's mind, far outweighed the dangers involved. The Christian soldiers were satisfied, since they were either going to find victory in Jesus Christ's service in battle, or they were assured heaven as their next destination. If Jerusalem remained in the hands of the Islamic forces after this expedition, then at least the Crusade would forestall any Muslim assault on Rome. Finally, even if the Crusade was a failure, Urban reasserted his position as the only leader of the Church, since he was able to unite most of Western Europe in the expedition.

The shortsightedness of Urban's strategy, however, was tragic. He did not foresee the potential dangers of success. The recapture of Jerusalem brought more difficulty. The means by which the crusaders were victorious breached all boundaries of Christian ethics. It was their brutality that became legend, and subsequent generations of Europeans would assume that victory was perpetual.

It was not.

Notes

1. Oliver J. Thatcher and Edgar Holmes McNeal, eds., *A Source Book for Medieval History* (New York: Scribners, 1905), 513–17.
2. Ibid.
3. Ibid., 511–12.
4. Ibid., 512.
5. Joseph Francois Michaud, *The History of the Crusades* (New York: A. C. Armstrong, 1895), 1:16.
6. Bernard Lewis, *Islam in History* (Chicago: Open Court, 1993), 295.
7. Michaud, *History of the Crusades,* 1:17.
8. Dana C. Munro, *Urban and the Crusaders* (Philadelphia: University of Pennsylvania Press, 1896), 26–28.
9. A. C. Krey, trans. *Baldric of Dol Version.* In *The First Crusade: The Accounts of Eye-Witnesses and Participants* (Princeton, N.J.: Princeton University Press, 1921), 36.
10. Ibid.
11. Justo L. Gonzalez, *The Crusades: Piety Misguided* (Nashville: Graded Press, 1988), 5–13. Gonzalez lists the lure of romantic adventure, social factors, economic factors, unity of the masses, the unity to the cause, corporate expiation, the code of chivalry, and the vow of the doomed. Gonzalez concludes that the concept of the Crusades "meant that the violence, pillage, and outright murder . . . were often seen as acts of virtue in the context of the Crusades." He never mentions the horrors suffered at the hands of the caliphs. See also, *The Challenge of Peace: A Pastoral Letter on War and Peace by the National Conference of Catholic Bishops* (Washington, D.C.: United States Catholic Conference, 1983), 99. Gonzalez's statement is a reinterpretation of the medieval Roman Catholic position, and interestingly ignores the Medieval Canon Law in view of Augustine's Just War criterion.
12. Krey, *Baldric of Dol*, 33–36.

13. John La Monte, *Feudal Monarchy in the Latin Kingdom of Jerusalem: 1100–1291* (Cambridge, Mass.: Medieval Academy of America, 1932). La Monte posits some interesting scenarios of Islamic world dominance. The political relationships between the various monarchs would lend themselves to a complete dominance by the theocrat. Monarchs, according to La Monte, are intrinsically weak, and the Sultans reigned with little internal trouble. Thus, Islamic domination in Rome would have been a final stumbling block in the way of complete world command.

14. Frances Rita Ryan, trans., *Fulcher of Chartres' A History of the Expedition to Jerusalem, 1095–1127* (Knoxville: University of Tennessee Press, 1927), 210; republished with H. S. Fink by University of Tennessee Press, 1969.

15. Ibid., 24.

16. Ibid.

17. Ibid., 28.

18. Ibid., 29

19. Ibid.

20. Ibid.

21. Ibid., 31.

22. Ibid., 34–35.

23. Krey, *Baldric of Dol*, 35.

24. Ibid.

25. Ryan, *Fulcher of Chartres' A History of the Expedition to Jerusalem, 1095–1127*, 37.

26. Ibid., 65.

27. Ibid., 49.

Chapter 6

"Pyrrhic Victory"

*The Disintegration of Crusades into Defeat
(1099–1291)*

Pyrrhic Victory: A victory which comes at such a great price that it ends up becoming a defeat. The term comes from Pyrrhus (318–272 B.C.), the king of Epirus in the Greek empire. He tried to form a kingdom of lower Italy and the island of Sicily in 281 B.C., but he lost so many men and invested so much money in the battle against Rome that he was forced to withdraw from Italy altogether.

The aftermath of the First Crusade saw the Roman Church once again in possession of Jerusalem and the sacred places, but it also brought about an entirely new litany of problems that would prove to be almost fatal. The victory of 1099 came at an exceedingly high cost. The Christian community lost stature as the reasonable voice of peace in the midst of conflict. They also abandoned perspective as a holy band working toward the kingdom of Jesus Christ.

The victory caused the leadership of the Church at Rome to become increasingly inebriated with power. Tragically, when victory comes at such an excruciating cost, it can rarely be duplicated. The subsequent Crusades, lasting until the beginning of the fourteenth century, illustrated the increasing desperation of the Church, as well as the horrific consequences of attempting to use the sword to convert. This chapter will briefly detail the disintegration of successive defeats of the crusading forces.

The Second Crusade:
Crusading for Fun and Profit (1147–1148)

If the First Crusade achieved its goals because the Muslim forces were scattered and the Christian forces were united in the common endeavor, then the Second Crusade failed for precisely the same reasons—in reverse. By the end of the Second Crusade in July 1148, the Christian armies were horribly divided, and the Muslim armies were gathering once again.

Following the Crusade, the Church established Latin states throughout the Middle East, each with a king or ruler who was loyal to the Pope. In the summer of 1144, the Muslim armies attacked Edessa, a Latin state east of Jerusalem. The leader of the Islamic forces was Prince Zengi, a formidable and capable general, who circled the city and began to attack the walls surrounding it. William of Tyre reports that Edessa was defenseless because they did not have the manpower to stand against the army:

> Towers, walls, and earthworks are of little value to a city unless there are defenders to man them. Zengi found the town bereft of defenders and was much encouraged. He encircled the town with his forces, assigned the officers of his legions to appropriate stations, and dug in. The catapults and siege engines weakened the fortifications; the continual shooting of arrows tormented the citizens incessantly; and the besieged were given no respite. It was announced, meanwhile, and the news was also spread by rumor, that the city of Edessa, a city faithful to God, was suffering the agonies of a siege at the hands of the enemy of the faith and the foe of the Christian name.[1]

Immediately the city fathers sent word to neighboring Latin states that they were under attack. The result, however, was not brotherly love. Instead, these other Latin states, supposedly Christian brothers, rejoiced at Edessa's misfortune. During the forty-four years since the end of the First Crusade, the Christian regents assigned to the various states had been more interested in personal gain and fortune than in Christian unity or common endeavor. Indeed, even the Count of Edessa no longer lived in the city itself. He had taken up residence at a resort region, according to William, "due to his own laziness." William continues to lament this lack of aid from neighboring Antioch:

> There was, as we have said before, bad feeling between Count Joscelyn and the Prince of Antioch—a feeling that was not hidden, but rather had become an open hatred. For this reason, each of them took little or no care if the other were attacked or suffered misfortune. Rather they rejoiced at the other's catastrophes and were made glad by the other's mishaps.[2]

The result of the lack of help and the incessant bombardment of the walls of the city was an inevitable breach in the wall and death for the inhabitants. William gives the gruesome details:

> Their forces rushed together into the city. They slew with their swords the citizens whom they encountered, sparing neither age, condition, nor sex. Of them it might be said: "They murder the widow and the stranger, they slay the orphan, the youth, and the virgin, together with the old man." The city, therefore, was captured and delivered to the swords of the enemy. The more prudent or more experienced citizens rushed to the citadel which, as we have said, was in the city. This they did so that they might at least preserve their lives, their children, and their wives, if only for a short time. At the gate there was such a crush of people trying to enter that, because of the press of the crowd, many were suffocated and died miserably. Among these was the most reverend Hugh, the Archbishop of the city. He is said to have expired in this fashion together

with several of his clerics. Some of those who were present would blame his miserable end on the Archbishop himself, for he is said to have collected a vast sum of money. Had he used this for soldiers, it would have been helpful to the city, but he preferred to heap up his treasure like a miser rather than to consider his dying people. Thus it happened that he received the reward of his greed by perishing with his people.[3]

In the summer of the next year, 1145, Eugenius II ascended to the throne of Rome, and by the fall, he called for a crusade against the new occupants of the city. He called on King Louis VII and the Gauls to lead the Crusade:

> We exhort therefore all of you in God, we ask and command, and, for the remission of sins enjoin: that those who are of God, and, above all, the greater men and the nobles do manfully gird themselves; and that you strive so to oppose the multitude of the infidels, who rejoice at the time in a victory gained over us, and so to defend the oriental church—freed from their tyranny by so great an outpouring of the blood of your fathers, as we have said,—and to snatch many thousands of your captive brothers from their hands,—that the dignity of the Christian name may be increased in your time, and that your valour which is praised throughout the whole world, may remain intact and unshaken.[4]

Once again, salvation is promised to the soldiers of God, and once again, the defense of Jesus Christ's lands is invoked. This time, however, the king did not rush to crusade. King Louis VII was ambivalent at best, and no action was taken.

Infuriated, Eugenius called on Bernard of Clairvaux (1090–1153) to inspire Christians to fight in Jesus' name. Beginning in the spring of 1146, Bernard, an abbot of immense influence, urged Christians to battle. At a council at Vezelay, Bernard pleaded for soldiers; this time both kings and peasants responded. The people of Sicily, Germany, and Hungary joined in the Christian forces. However, the princes in this campaign had personal reasons for joining, which proved to be the fatal flaw of the enterprise. King Conrad of Germany, King Roger of Sicily, and King Geza of Hungary all wanted to increase their own wealth, and they remembered the plunder of Acre and Antioch in Urban's Crusade.

The armies were not motivated by any sense of divine purpose, even the salvation offered by the pope, so self-serving divisions quickly rent the troops. They paid the penalty in a resounding defeat at Damascus. In a letter to Eugenius, Bernard tried to explain why the children of God could not stand against the infidels:

> I remember, most Holy Father Eugene, my promises [to give you an explanation] made to you long ago, and at long last I shall acquit myself. The delay, were I aware that it proceeded from carelessness or contempt, should cause me shame. It is not thus, however. As you know, we have fallen upon grave times, which seemed about to bring to an end not only my studies but my very life, for the Lord, provoked by our sins, gave the appearance of having judged the world . . . with justice, indeed, but forgetful of his mercy. He spared neither his people nor his name. Do not the heathen say: "Where is their God?" Nor do I wonder, for the sons of the Church, those who bear the label, "Christian," have been laid low in the desert and have either been slain by the sword or consumed by famine.[5]

It was a solemn note for the Christian leaders. They had felt they were invincible. They were not.

Jerusalem Lost: The Third Crusade (1189–1192)

In 1187, the unthinkable happened. The Muslim forces, united under the leadership of a strong battlefield general, once again captured Jerusalem. At the helm of the Islamic armies was Saladin, the sultan of Egypt and ruler of Damascus. Saladin called for a jihad against the Christians living in Jerusalem, which he saw as a Muslim holy site.

Cutting a swath across the Latin states through the summer of 1187, Saladin's forces finally reached the walls of Jerusalem in the early fall.

> The Holy City of Jerusalem was besieged on September 20. It was surrounded on every side by unbelievers, who shot arrows everywhere into the air. They were accompanied by frightening armaments and, with a great clamor of trumpets, they shrieked and wailed, "Hai, hai." The city was aroused by the noise and tumult of the barbarians and, for a time, they all cried out: "True and Holy Cross! Sepulchre of Jesus Christ's resurrection! Save the city of Jerusalem and its dwellers!"[6]

For two weeks a fierce battle ensued, with Saladin's men firing weapons that reached the walls from the Mount of Olives. Christians within the walls of the city slowly lost heart. Finally, the Christians sent a delegation of surrender to Saladin, and he negotiated a ransom for the inhabitants. If they were willing to surrender the city and pay the ransom, they would be allowed to live. The chronicler who recorded the scene was aghast:

> Saladin had taken counsel and laid down these ransom terms for the inhabitants of Jerusalem: each male, ten years old and over, was to pay ten besants for his ransom; females, five besants; boys, seven years old and under, one. Those who wished would be freed on these terms and could leave securely with their possessions. The inhabitants of Jerusalem who would not accept these terms, or those who did not have ten besants, were to become booty, to be slain by the army's swords. This agreement pleased the lord Patriarch and the others who had money. . . . On Friday, October 2, this agreement was read out through the streets of Jerusalem, so that everyone might within forty days provide for himself and pay to Saladin the tribute as aforesaid for his freedom. When they heard these

arrangements, the crowds throughout the city wailed in sorrowful tones: "Woe, woe to us miserable people! We have no gold! What are we to do? . . ." Who would ever have thought that such wickedness would be perpetrated by Christians?[7]

Obviously, this was seen as a betrayal by the Christian leaders of the city. They were wealthy enough to purchase their freedom, so they quickly accepted the terms, but the vast majority of Jerusalem's inhabitants could not, as they did not have such money. The subsequent scene, however, even left the historian disheartened. Remorsefully, he wrote:

> But, alas, by the hands of wicked Christians Jerusalem was turned over to the wicked. The gates were closed and guards were posted. The *fakihs* and *kadis,* [judges] the ministers of the wicked error, who are considered bishops and priests by the Saracens came for prayer and religious purposes first to the Temple of the Lord, which they call Beithhalla and in which they have great faith for salvation. They believed they were cleansing it and with unclean and horrible bellows they defiled the Temple by shouting with polluted lips the Muslim precept: *"Allahu akbar! Allahu akbar!..."* Our people held the city of Jerusalem for some eighty-nine years.... Within a short time, Saladin had conquered almost the whole Kingdom of Jerusalem. He exalted the grandeur of Mohammed's law and showed that, in the event, its might exceeded that of the Christian religion.[8]

News of the capture of Jerusalem quickly reached Rome. Pope Alexander III called upon Emperor Frederick I, called Barbarossa, to enter into the Crusade. His army numbered in the tens of thousands, and as an aged veteran of the Second Crusade, Frederick was an able warrior. As his forces passed through the Byzantine empire on their way to Jerusalem, Frederick formed an alliance with the Byzantine Emperor, Isaac Angelos.

Yet there was intrigue and deceit in this confederation. Emperor

Angelos had entered into a secret agreement with Saladin. He was to stall Frederick, giving Saladin time to garner a strategy to defeat Frederick. Now, even supposed Christian brothers were betraying one another.

Frederick discovered this deceit in a letter from Sibylla, the former Queen of the Christians in Jerusalem. She wrote:

> I, your most humble maidservant as I said above am compelled to tell your highness and supreme excellency of the grief of the whole city and of the disgrace of the sacred Christians. For the emperor of Constantinople, the persecutor of the church of God, has entered into a conspiracy with Saladin, the seducer and destroyer of the holy Name, against the name of our Lord Jesus Christ. I tell this, which I am indeed not able to say without tears. Saladin, the aforesaid enemy of Christ, has sent to the Grecian emperor and the persecutor of the holy Name many presents very pleasing to mortals, in order to make a compact and agreement. And for the slaughter and destruction of the Christians wishing to exalt the name of God, he sent 600 measures of poisoned grain and added a very large vase of wine, filled with such a malignant poison that when he wanted to try its efficacy he called a man who was killed by the odor alone when the vase was opened. Along with the rest I am compelled to tell my lord another thing: the aforesaid emperor, in order to increase our misfortunes and magnify the destruction of the Christians, does not permit wheat or other necessary victuals to be carried from his country to Jerusalem. Wherefore, the wheat which might be sent by himself and others, is also shut up in the city of Constantinople.[9]

Though Frederick would defeat the Turks at Iconium and thwart the conspiracy, he drowned in Armenia shortly thereafter. The crusaders had another leader, however, King Richard I of England, who was to be remembered as Richard the Lionheart.

Through the winter of 1191 and the spring of 1192, Richard laid siege to Acre, a city where the Muslims were purported to be hiding the "true cross of Christ." Finally, in July 1192, the Muslims surrendered and promised to return the True Cross, two hundred thousand gold pieces and two thousand Christian prisoners, in return for their lives. The only problem was, they did not have any of these.

It was at this juncture, however, that the armies of God once again descended to levels unforeseen by the Christian community of history. King Richard brought twenty-seven hundred Muslim men outside the city walls, and proceeded to have them slaughtered, one by one. A Muslim historian recorded the horror:

> The king of England, seeing all the delays interposed by the Sultan [Saladin] to the execution of the treaty, acted perfidiously as regards his Musulinan prisoners. On their yielding the town he had engaged to grant their life, adding that if the Sultan carried out the bargain he would give them freedom and [allow] them to carry off their children and wives; if the Sultan did not fulfill his engagements they were to be made slaves. Now the king *broke his promises to them* and made open display of what he had till now kept hidden in his heart, by carrying out what he had intended to do after he had received the money and the Frank prisoners. It is thus that people of his nation ultimately admitted.
>
> In the afternoon of Tuesday, 27 Rajab, [August 20] about four o'clock, he came out on horseback with all the Frankish army, . . . [King Richard] ordered all the Muslim prisoners, whose martyrdom God had decreed for this day, to be brought before him. They . . . were all bound with ropes. The Franks then flung themselves upon them all at once and massacred them with sword and lance in cold blood. . . . On the morrow morning our people gathered at the spot and found the Muslims stretched out upon the ground as martyrs for the faith. They even recognized some of the dead, and the sight was a great affliction to them. The enemy had only spared the prisoners of note and such as were strong enough to work.[10]

Not only did the Christian forces not get to Jerusalem, but they earned the everlasting mistrust of the Muslims, who believed King Richard when he promised to allow them to live. It was becoming difficult to distinguish between Christian and non-Christian forces, as each were reaching new heights in brutality and deceit.

Disintegration: The Children's Crusade of 1212

The three subsequent Crusades accomplished nothing more than the further blurring of the original purposes for which the Crusades were called and any distinction between Christian and nonbeliever. In the Fourth Crusade (1200–1204), the Roman forces actually attacked Byzantine Christians at Constantinople, rather than engage the Muslim forces. Yet the darkest hour in Christian history could have been 1212, when Rome allowed the launch of the Children's Crusade.

In a small village near Vendome, France, a twelve-year-old boy named Stephen believed he received a vision. Jesus Christ was calling the children of the Christian empire to launch a Crusade. Surely, he reasoned, if the adult men were incapable of conquest, the children—the pure of heart—could achieve with faith what the men could not do with might. In Cologne, Germany, another young boy named Nicholas had the same inspiration.

Distressingly, Rome did nothing to stop the movement. Thousands of young children and teenagers from northern France and western Germany united, for what can only be called one of the darkest chapters in Christian history. Against the pleadings of their parents, these children set out en masse.

The result was horrifying.

As many as fifty thousand were sold into slavery. Many died of starvation. Still others were defeated in their vain attempts to fight. One author recorded:

> About the time of Easter and Pentecost, . . . many thousands of boys, ranging in age from six years to full maturity, left the plows or carts which they were driving, the flocks which they were

pasturing, and anything else which they were doing. This they did despite the wishes of their parents, relatives, and friends who sought to make them draw back. Suddenly one ran after another to take the cross. Thus, by groups of twenty, or fifty, or a hundred, they put up banners and began to journey to Jerusalem. They were asked by many people on whose advice or at whose urging they had set out upon this path. They were asked especially since only a few years ago many kings, a great many dukes, and innumerable people in powerful companies had gone there and had returned with the business unfinished. The present groups, moreover, were still of tender years and were neither strong enough nor powerful enough to do anything. Everyone, therefore, accounted them foolish and imprudent for trying to do this. They briefly replied that they were equal to the Divine will in this matter and that, whatever God might wish to do with them, they would accept it willingly and with humble spirit. They thus made some little progress on their journey. Some were turned back at Metz, others at Piacenza, and others even at Rome. Still others got to Marseilles, but whether they crossed to the Holy Land or what their end was is uncertain. One thing is sure: that of the many thousands who rose up, only very few returned.[11]

The Crusades began with a shout of "God wills it!" and ended with a whimper of defeat. The concept of converting the world by the sword and fighting as an army of Jesus Christ had led to three hundred years of strife and bloodshed. Armies were regularly gathering under the banner of Christianity and confronting the enemy with swords, rather than the gospel. More grievously, these soldiers marched to their death under the assumption that Christ had called them to kill in his Name and the promise that if they died in battle they would be admitted to heaven because of their commitment to this warfare. Christianity had fallen on the sword of jihad.

Jews were particular victims of the swords of the Christian crusaders. In the First Crusade, one chronicler wrote:

The slaughter of Jews was first done by citizens of Cologne. These suddenly fell upon a small band of Jews and severely wounded and killed many; they destroyed the houses and synagogues of the Jews and divided among themselves a very large amount of money. When the Jews saw this cruelty, about two hundred in the silence of the night began flight by boat to Neuss. The pilgrims and crusaders discovered them, and after taking away their possessions, inflicted on them similar slaughter, leaving not even one alive.[12]

It would not be the last time we engaged in a form of theocratic jihad. At later junctures in our history, we even inflicted it upon our own people. Perhaps the victory of the First Crusade was a pyrrhic victory, for it seemed that though we had gained the whole world, we had lost our souls.

Notes

1. James Brundage, *The Crusades: A Documentary History* (Milwaukee, Wis.: Marquette University Press, 1962), 79–82.

2. Ibid.

3. Ibid.

4. Ernest F. Henderson, *Select Historical Documents of the Middle Ages* (London: George Bell and Sons, 1910), 133–36.

5. Ibid., 115–21.

6. Ibid.

7. Ibid., 159–63.

8. Ibid.

9. Dana C. Munro, "Letters of the Crusaders," in *Translations and Reprints from the Original Sources of European History*, vol. 1:4 (Philadelphia: University of Pennsylvania Press, 1896), 20–22.

10. Beha-ed-Din, a member of Saladin's court, as recorded in eyewitnesstohistory.com/lionheart.htm. Accessed November 12, 2003.

11. Brundage, *The Crusades*, 213.

12. Albert of Aix and Ekkehard of Aura, in Brundage, *The Crusades*, 172.

Chapter 7

Ask and You Shall Receive

The Inquisition of the Middle Ages

This sentence having been pronounced, they were led out to punishment. They went with gladness and in great haste, their leader, namely, Gerard, going before them, singing, "Blessed are ye," says the Lord, "when men shall hate you, for my sake." They were then, according to the rigor of the sentence, branded on their foreheads, their leader receiving a double brand, one on his forehead, the other on his chin, as a sign that he was their leader.

Thereupon their upper garments, to the waist, were cut from their bodies, and they were publicly scourged, and cast out of the city. But it being a bitter cold winter, and no one showing them the least mercy, they miserably perished by the intense cold, which they were unable to bear on their naked bodies.[1]

—Thieleman J. van Braght, Dutch martyrologist,
writing in 1660

In 1161, as King Henry II ruled England, thirty German Evangelicals, known as Petrobusians after their founder Peter de Bruys, crossed the English Channel in order to spread their faith with the commoners of England. The papal legates quickly apprehended the outlaws and their leader Gerard. As one contemporary papal account explained, these Petrobusians were regarded as "illiterate idiots, a very low and boorish class of people . . . [that] belonged to a strange sect."[2]

King Henry, not wanting to hastily punish the foreigners without due process, requested that Gerard be examined by theological inquisitors. When asked about his orthodoxy, Gerard assured the examiners that the group was entirely Christian "regard[ing] the doctrine of the apostles." After hours of investigation, it was clear that these thirty men and women pledged their sole allegiance to the Bible, and not to the tradition and authority of the Roman Catholic Church. The charges, signifying the differences, were thereby brought as follows:

> That their belief concerning the sacraments, of baptism and the Supper, as well as respecting marriage, was different from what had been decreed by the Roman church, whom they called the whore of Babylon, because she had forsaken the true faith in Christ; they said that she was like the barren fig-tree which our Lord Jesus Christ cursed. They also said that the pope and the bishops must not be obeyed when they command anything that is contrary to the Word of God; also, that monachism was a stinking carrion, also, that all monastic vows are vain and useless, yea, that they foster lasciviousness; also, that all the orders and degrees of the priestly dignity are marks of the great beast; also, that purgatory, masses, church consecrations, worship of the saints, anniversaries for the dead, etc., are genuine inventions of the devil.[3]

Now it was clear to King Henry and all Catholics that the Petrobusians must be punished. The chilling sentence was carried out without delay. Gradually each one of them perished in the cold winter snow of England as starvation, frostbite, and illness ripped through their bodies. The hatred for their heresy was seen in the absence of any aid from the community.

What is ironic of such a story is not the uniqueness of the persecution, for this harassment was common in countries that looked to Rome for centuries. Rather, the irony rested in two facts. First, persecuted groups, notwithstanding the severity of how they were treated, tended to survive and indeed thrive. Second, though Roman Catholics had intensely questioned groups such as these Evangelicals, they did not know from whence they came. In the above case, the Catholics readily admitted their ignorance in the matter, only speculating that the group might be traced to the Waldensians (Poor Men of Lyons), Petrobusians (Evangelicals), or Berengarians (Italian Mystics).

"You People All Look Alike": The Problem with Finding Heretics among the Christian People

Large movements such as the Waldensians and the Cathars, the latter of which we shall examine more closely in chapter nine, were almost eradicated from their respective cities through called crusades. Nevertheless, the Roman Church was unable to remove heresy from within Christian Europe. It seemed each time one soul was purged from the world, three more heretics immediately reared their ugly heads. As one group faded from popularity, another group quickly rose to prominence. The Crusades were highly successful in their appointed task of getting rid of particular heretical people and groups, but they did not have the wherewithal to handle the enormity of the problem of religious protest that encapsulated Europe.

The problem, of course, was that, unlike Jews and Muslims, dissenting Christians were not required to wear special clothing, did not hold to different religious tenets that were obvious in the public arena, and believed in mostly the same things as the organized Church. Moreover, they did not build grand structures of worship, but preferred instead to meet in each other's homes. In lieu of prestigious celebrations they opted for quiet meditation in thankfulness of God's blessings. This is not to say that their faith was private. Dissenters usually shared their faith openly, despite the dangers to which such boldness exposed them. They carried out missionary journeys throughout much of the continent and beyond.

But the Crusade programs were intended to remove sects as a group, not as individuals. Like a conventional army in guerilla-style warfare, they were ill-prepared to handle individual threats. As one author pointed out, "The crusade . . . was a very blunt instrument, capable of dealing with heretics *en masse* but less useful in coping with them once they responded to defeat by going underground."[4]

Hence, another stage of Christian jihad evolved out of ecclesiastical necessity. The Inquisition, officially begun by Pope Gregory IX in the thirteenth century, enlisted two corps of volunteers: the Franciscan and Dominican Friars. These warriors were to be much more meticulous in their endeavor than had been their crusading predecessors, for they were sniffing out underground heretics from among their own. It was their job, once the traitor was exposed, to either cleanse the heresy from an individual or to remove the spiritual cancer from the body of Christ by any means necessary. This epoch in Roman Catholic history spanned over six centuries. In India, Portuguese priests carried out their orders in the town of Goa. Across the Atlantic Ocean, Spanish inquisitors conducted trials in what is now Mexico and Peru.[5] The New World was, for the most part, still the Old World.

The Founding Fathers: Papal Bulls and Priestly Warriors

"All in the Family": Uncle and Nephew Solidify the Inquisition

Although Thomas Torquemada is most closely associated with the Inquisitions, the movement commenced more than two centuries before the Grand Inquisitor's name became synonymous with the era. The true father of the movement was, without question, Pope Gregory IX (Ugolino de Segni, 1227–1241), the nephew of Innocent III.

Presiding over the Fourth Lateran Council (1215), Innocent provided the theological foundation for his nephew, as the Council obligated every adult to make confession to their parish priests and receive Holy Communion at least once a year. Reiterating previous decrees, the Council also sanctioned confiscation of property, removal from public office, and excommunication for lapsed heretics. Ominously, Innocent declared that heretics should be given over to the secular authorities for proper punishment. Taking the process one step further, the pope even called for the removal of priests who failed to protect the flock from heretics.[6]

Thus, when Gregory IX assumed the pontifical throne, he was able to build on a grand heritage. A passionate Catholic who viewed himself as a pastor, he dedicated himself to the destruction of splinter groups who divorced themselves from the Holy Mother Church. Only two years after assuming the role of pontiff, Gregory, at the Council of Toulouse, set up a permanent court to try cases of heresy.[7]

In February 1231, the major shift in purpose and power occurred when Gregory issued his new constitution, entitled *Excommunicamus*. This systematic legislation provided

1. burning at the stake by the proper secular authorities as the appropriate punishment for unrepentent heresy;
2. excommunication of heretics (e.g., Cathars and Waldensians) and of all who would defend them, sympathize with them, or even refuse to denounce them;
3. officially labeling as "heretic," without trial, those who eluded the inquisitors for over a year;
4. life imprisonment as punishment for all impenitent heretics;
5. exhumation of the bodies of unpunished heretics for burning at the stake;
6. demolition of the homes of convicted heretics.[8]

Judges instantly had clear and concise law with which to work. Now, they needed only circumstantial evidence of the crime.

Men in Black: Marching Orders for Dominicans (and Franciscans)

Already eighty-four years of age when he was given the keys of St. Peter, Pope Gregory was personal friends with both St. Dominic and St. Francis, founders of two mendicant ("begging") orders of the Church. In fact, at the request of Francis, who considered Gregory "the bishop of the whole world and the father of all nations,"[9] Gregory served as the first cardinal protector of the Franciscans.

It made perfect sense to choose priests from both of these two orders. They were men who took vows of poverty and hence were less
prone to bribery. Moreover, being men without parishes, they could
give their full attention to the search for heretics without any pastoral
distractions. Previously, inquisitors were usually local bishops who
had to spend much of their time with the faithful, and thus could
spend less time fighting the heretical. Although the local bishops were
jealous at the loss of their powers, Gregory knew this dedicated move
would pay off in the long term.[10]

Yet of these two orders requested to lead in the Inquisition, it was the
Dominicans who were primarily chosen to march into battle against
the enemies of the cross. Thereby, the order known for their black rega-
lia became feared throughout the Empire. When people saw the men in
black coming, fear pervaded the town, for they were not there to give
Mass or celebrate a special holiday, but to hunt down the wicked or
those who sympathized with the devilish hoard. By the time of the Reformation, the reputation of the Dominican Order, especially among
those who dissented from the Church, was as dark as their robes.

Double Trouble: The Inquisition Through
the Eyes of Two Inquisitors

> Therefore you, or any of you, wherever you may happen to
> preach, are empowered, unless they [other priests] desist from
> such defense [of heretics] on admonition, to deprive clerks of
> their benefices forever, and to proceed against them and all
> others, without appeal, calling in the aid of the secular arm, if
> necessary, and coercing opposition, if requisite, with the cen-
> sures of the Church, without appeal.[11]
>
> —Gregory IX, granting Dominicans
> absolute power, even over other priests

Gregory was so resolute in expunging dissent from Christian Europe that, as seen in the above quote, he invested inquisitor monks
with unequivocal power. Those who complained about any excesses

against their parishioners were subjected to unrestricted harassment and judgment. The inquisitors only answered to the Holy See and thus were unchecked in their authority. Once they entered a jurisdiction, they were judge and jury and had the secular powers at their disposal.

Quickly recognizing the dangers of such blunt legislation, Gregory began honing the procedures of inquisition. Hence, the inquisitors had a permanent organization but no standardized policies at the start. Over time, through trial and error, inquisition was perfected to work in the most efficient way to gain the most desired results. Therefore, the best way to view this gradual development is through the eyes of the inquisitors themselves, who were responsible for molding a practical framework around their ideals.

Conrad of Marburg: The Prototype of the Inquisitor

One of the earliest inquisitors, Conrad, already had an impressive résumé after suppressing the Cathars in Innocent III's Albigensian Crusade early in the thirteenth century. He had gained notoriety for the bloody massacres that occurred under his leadership. A few years later Gregory IX turned to Conrad to remove the Waldensian sect from parts of the Rhineland. With ruthless zealotry, Conrad, who accused the group of devil-worship, stalked the disciples of the sect. When other bishops complained to Pope Gregory that Conrad had coerced innocent people to confess under the threat of being burned at the stake, Gregory wholeheartedly defended Conrad. He was the right man for the hour.[12]

Conrad was the first to hold the title of "Inquisitor into Heretical Depravity." He was a poster child for the formative Inquisition, the bridge between the Crusades and the Inquisitions, for he had a foot in either camp. While crusading fever was in decline and inquisitorial fervor was rising, Conrad imbued the developing movement with the principles and passion that had sustained the previous one. Yet, unlike the Crusades, which proved an utter failure, the Inquisitions would succeed against a helpless—though persistent—enemy.

For two years Conrad combed the cities and countryside of

Germany searching out the Waldensians with unabated pleasure. He enlisted Dominicans and Franciscans to assist in his endeavor, which they did without reservation. But Conrad did not waste his time with cumbersome trials, moving ahead with the swift and savage punishment he believed was deserving of such theological criminals. According to one author, "He burned heretics with such frenzy that contemporary chroniclers say that even the king and bishops of the Rhineland feared for their lives while he was at work."[13]

With Conrad's absolute sovereignty, those in power had good reason to fear. In fact, Conrad did attempt, without success, to place guilt on one nobleman in particular, Count Henry of Sayn. But in 1233, the council appropriated innocence to the count, a decision unacceptable to the inquisitor. His authority had been questioned and his supremacy was restrained. Seeking reprisal for the abuse of their beloved count, anonymous henchmen assassinated the inquisitor five days later.[14] No trial was necessary.

Bernard Gui: The Parliamentarian of the Inquisition

Bernard Gui, the Dominican monk who led the Inquisition between 1307 and 1323, inherited a system of persecution known for its fervor but not for its efficiency. Gui recognized that the movement needed a methodical, systematic, and disciplined approach to dealing with the arrest, trial, and punishment of heretics, strictly regulating the work and replacing its random subjectivity with strict regulations. This reform was not only intended to deal with the heretics more resourcefully, but also to assist novice examiners who were ill prepared to deal with the sly sophistry of biblically literate heretics. Gui wrote in one of his manuals, "When a heretic is first brought up for examination, he assumes a confident air, as though secure in his innocence. I ask him why he has been brought before me. He replies, smiling and courteous, 'Sir, I would be glad to learn the cause from you.'"[15]

Gui thus provided talking points for other inquisitors, a somewhat rudimentary apologetic handbook against the cunning and sarcastic tactics of dissenters. Through example, Gui passed down to his inheritors an illustrative guide to train inquisitors in properly handling interrogations of those with the "untutored shrewdness of the peasant struggling to save his life and his conscience."[16]

In Socratic fashion, the inquisitor was intellectually trained to ask the proper questions in order to coerce the desired answers. Further, they were duly warned to recognize the reverse logic used by dissenters who sought to turn the tables on the inquisitors. Note the following intellectual exchange in Gui's manual:

I: Will you then swear that you have never learned anything contrary to the faith which we hold to be true?

A: (Growing pale) If I ought to swear, I will willing swear.

I: I don't ask whether you ought, but whether you will swear.

A: If you order me to swear, I will swear.

I: I don't force you to swear, because as you believe oaths to be unlawful, you will transfer the sin to me who forced you; but if you will swear, I will hear it.

A: Why should I swear if you do not order me to?

I: So that you may remove the suspicion of being a heretic.

A: Sir, I do not know how unless you teach me.[17]

Gui cautioned inquisitors not to be worked over by the baffling techniques of the dissenters, but to "proceed firmly till he makes these people confess their error, or at least publicly abjure heresy, so that if they are subsequently found to have sworn falsely, he can, without further hearing, abandon them to the secular arm."

The problem with training inquisitors to ask such probing, if not trick, questions is that all people, whether they disagree with the

Catholic Church or not, were at risk of giving the wrong answers and failing the orthodoxy test. The war against protest had many casualties of friendly fire among those ignorant that their answers were not suitable to the proper scholastic theology of the age.[18]

Consequently, the desire of Gui to systematize the examination was perhaps helpful, yet it demonstrated the frustration of inquisitors who were not able to retrieve proper responses from subjects considered ignorant fools and theological simpletons. One can readily see why harsh tortures accompanied many examinations, as disconcerted monks transferred their exasperations to the bodies of their helpless victims.

Calm Before the Storm:
The Inquisition Goes into Hibernation

The strength of the Inquisition was directly proportional to the supremacy of the pope. Most historians acknowledge that Innocent III (1198–1216) represented the height of papal power and prestige. Likewise, the thirteenth century popes held significant sway over political affairs, manipulating secular rulers with the power of the Holy See. However, when Boniface VIII was elected pope in 1294, the world had changed, and the papacy went into decline. Nationalism had emerged victorious over the feudal systems. Countries such as France and Germany had no desire to listen to dictates from a man who did not have the best interests of their country in mind.

Philip IV, King of France, best signified this shift in power when, in battling Pope Boniface over the taxation of French clergy to pay for the war against England, the king went against the orders of the pontiff to remove the tax, thereby risking certain excommunication. Instead of worrying over the state of his own soul, Philip declared Boniface an immoral heretic, had him arrested, and brought the papacy into utter humiliation. Though finally rescued from his confinement, Boniface died a beaten man, a legacy he passed down to future pontiffs for the next two hundred years.[19]

With the subjugation of the papacy to secular potentates, the Inquisitions took a backseat to local and national affairs. This is not to say that the Inquisitions faded away completely as the fourteenth century saw its share of persecuted Christians. However, secular rulers were less interested in theology and more interested in politics. Police were no longer consumed with assisting in the suppression of heresy. The rampant fear of inquisitors once so pervasive was gone as the Inquisition devolved into an unorganized and sporadic tool used against the most wayward of sects. Those who were able to spread their faith secretly usually went unnoticed by the authorities.

"Give Me That Old Time Religion!" Grand Inquisitor Torquemada Revives the Work

> Torquemada's name, with clouds o'ercast,
> Looms in the distant landscape of the past.
> Like a burnt tower upon a blackened heath,
> Lit by the fires of burning woods beneath.[20]
> —Longfellow

Never had such a blessed union turned a nation into such a bloody theatre. In 1479, five years after Queen Isabella was enthroned in Castile, her husband Ferdinand ascended the throne of Aragon, thus creating one of the most powerful empires in Europe. This merger also held the optimistic hope of restoring the entirety of Spain to what many Roman Catholic Spanish believed was its rightful place as a Christian nation. This respect had not been seen in the region since Muslim invaders had conquered much of the land nearly eight hundred years before.

But for such a unification of religion and state to succeed, all heretics on the Iberian Peninsula—whether Jews, Muslims (Moors), dissenting Christians, or pagans (witches)—would have to be forcibly converted or removed. With two devout Roman Catholics on the throne, this dream soon became a realistic possibility. In fact, Isabella's closest confidant was a priest whose name is now tantamount with the Spanish Inquisition, Thomas Torquemada (1420–1498). The Dominican friar strongly influenced the policies of Isabella and convinced her to grant him the power to eradicate all known heresy. In 1483, with the approval of Pope Sixtus IV and later on Innocent VIII, Torquemada was appointed Inquisitor-General, making him the most powerful nonroyal in Spain.

What happened next has given the term *Inquisition* its infamous designation. The enormity of the task gladly undertaken by Torquemada was quite difficult, as Spain was known for its pluralistic society. The Jews, long regarded as some of the most brilliant tradesmen in Europe, had the greatest prosperity within the Iberian Peninsula. The measure of their success is all the more impressive, given the cycles of persecution that had befallen the religious group. Most persisted in the face of opposition, while some outwardly converted to Christianity in order to keep their lives intact.

Yet, these Jewish converts to Catholic Christianity were identified with suspicion as "New Christians" and were subject to more severe persecution due to their pseudoconversion. Once baptized, they were subject to the Church and its decrees. If the authorities suspected that their conversion was insincere or that they had lapsed into their old faith, they faced perpetual imprisonment, confiscation of property, or worse. Sometimes sentences were more lenient on those who turned over other heretics, but many met a cruel end at the stake, whatever they did to save themselves.

Nearly ten years after the organized hunt began, Ferdinand and Isabella attacked Grenada, the last stronghold of the Moors. In a last attempt to secure their citizenship, the Jews promised to give the sovereigns thirty thousand pieces of silver to finance the war. The king and queen seriously considered the option until Torquemada reproved the couple saying, "Judas sold his master for thirty pieces of silver, your highnesses are about to do the same for thirty thousand."[21] Thus, the fate of the Jews was sealed.

The Jews were commanded to leave Spain no later than July 31, 1492. They were forced to sell their property for nearly nothing as one chronicler described, "The Jews gave a house for a donkey, and a vineyard for a small quantity of cloth or linen." That year eight hundred thousand Jews were exiled and had to begin new lives in foreign lands.

Usually the people in their new environments showed them no more hospitality than did the Spaniards.[22]

While they bore the brunt of Torquemada's religious intolerance, Jews were not alone in their pain. Between Christians who settled in the New World and Muslims forced to immigrate to Africa, Ferdinand and Isabella expelled more than two million of their subjects. However, those who were banished at least escaped with their lives. Within the sixteen years of his administration, Torquemada arrested more than 105,000 people, burning thousands of Jews, Moors, Christians, and pagans. When he died at the end of the fifteenth century, the Dominican handed down to future generations of priests the rights and regulations of trial, torture, and death. The Spanish Inquisition itself lasted over three hundred years, with more than 300,000 arrests and 32,000 burned at the stake. The permanent tribunal empowered by the pope and supported by royalty was finally abolished after the Revolution of 1820.[23]

Crime and Punishment: Terrible Lessons in Trial and Torture

What made the Inquisition such a horrific spectacle was not merely the numbers of those executed or brutalized, but the sheer and savage process that accompanied the examinations. Such popular punishments as burning at the stake or the torture rack are more notorious, so that few know the precise details of arrest, trial, torture, and sentencing. The procedures of an inquisition, usually carried out in Dominican monasteries, large churches, or bishops' palaces, were methodically governed to gain optimum results.[24]

The Secret Police: Arresting Heretics

What made citizens so fearful was that anyone could accuse a person of heresy. The charge was always believed by the inquisitors and almost impossible to disprove. Thereby, the secular authorities were empowered to arrest an accused heretic without any evidence beyond hearsay and without the accused having any knowledge of the accusation before arrest. Turning in neighbors was encouraged by inquisitors, who promised mercy if the accused gave specific names and locales of other apostates. Refusal to name another suspect was further proof that heresy still resided within the soul.[25]

In fact, trepidation did not elude the young; males by the age of fourteen and females as early as twelve were said to have reached the age of intelligibility and thus must answer for their beliefs. Even in societies where teenagers were protected by civil laws, inquisitors skirted the legislation by appointing a curator, under whose authority the adolescent could be tried, tortured, and punished.[26]

Furthermore, arrest need not even take place for a trial to ensue. If a heretic somehow escaped the long arm of the law, his guilt increased as he was supposed to be running from both God and the Church. Accordingly, it was the responsibility of the heretic to discredit theological charges brought against him. Many dissenters were already under the censure of their local parish and were deemed *truands,* a Latin term which connoted any person absent from the Mass and other sacraments.[27] As one author explained, "Enduring excommunication for a year without seeking its removal was evidence of heresy as to the sacraments and the power of the keys."[28] Consequently, dissenting Christians who never attended Mass or answered charges of unorthodoxy, were already found guilty and could be punished at once following their capture.

Law and Disorder: The Trial of an Accused Heretic

> They dug up that Galvan and took him from the cemetery of the Villeneuve where he had been buried, then in great procession dragged his body through the town and burned it in the common field outside the town. This was done in praise of our Lord Jesus Christ and the Blessed Dominic and to the honor of the Roman and Catholic Church, our mother, in the year of the Lord 1231.[29]
>
> —Testimony of Dominican inquisitor William Pelhisson

It goes without saying that if a dead man cannot escape the wrath of the Church, a living specimen's fortunes are probably not too great either. It was common during the Middle Ages to exhume corpses of those who had been so rude as to escape punishment by dying. The most prominent example of this involved the body of John Wycliffe, the beloved fourteenth-century English professor of theology, preacher, and translator of the Bible into English. Decades after his death, his bones were dug up, burned, and the ashes scattered in the river by order of the Council of Constance.

The typical trial of a suspect began as the inquisitor drew up formal charges, based on the depositions given by those who, under oath, swore to have witnessed unorthodox behavior or signs of heretical belief. These formal declarations were entered into the official record as the trial got underway. The tribunal, made up of clergymen and lawyers, judged the veracity of the information while the informants were sworn to secrecy. The words of the documents were scrupulously studied by scholastic theologians who almost always proclaimed theological censure on the accused. Finally, the accused was arrested and placed in a secret prison.[30]

The trial then officially commenced. The tribunal recommended to the suspect that he or she openly admit error and, in so doing, earn the tribunal's mercy. Otherwise, the inquisitor felt no ethical constraint. But the suspect did not have the advantage of knowing what particular accusations had been brought against him, only that he or she had somehow offended the Catholic Church or the Inquisition. After inquisitors searched the accused's family records to find out if heresy had been passed down from ancestors, the suspect was asked to recite the Apostles' Creed or an official dogma of the Church.

Moving on, the charges were publicly read as though they were already proven. In addition, the charges brought were multiplied by varying the statements subtly so that one accusation seemed like five or more. With such indictment, any admission on the part of the accused, whether true or not, appeared partial at best. As a result, the soul must be cleansed through punishment of the body.[31]

Coercing a Confession: The Role of Torture

Since suffering was believed to lead to repentance, more acute suffering proportionately could lead to greater repentance. Therefore, putting heretics under psychological or physical torture was not cruel, but actually kind treatment that led to the salvation of their souls from the eternal flames of hell.

Anecdotal evidence proved as much. In one instance, a wayward priest was captured and placed under the supervision and care of Nider, a priest who taught at the University of Vienna. Even under duress, the priest was obstinate in his sin and fully able to defend his beliefs against the most eminent of theologians. The heretical priest was ordered bound to a pillar with tightly fitted cords, a punishment which slowly tore away at his flesh. The pain was so intense that the priest begged to be burned at the stake, a request refused by the inquisitors. In time, the priest was broken, humbly recanted his doctrines, and returned to the monastery, where it was said he lived an assiduous and virtuous life.[32]

Torture led to the desired result, saved the soul from eternal damnation, and kept heresy from creeping into the community. Thereby, it should not be shocking that different torture techniques were invented or perfected to secure the needed confession. Many of these methods relied on mental anguish, rather than physical torment. The following list gives a brief outline of some of the methods employed:

1. *Reverse Psychology.* After enduring harsh conditions in a dungeon, the heretic was given luxurious accommodations in the hope that the change in atmosphere might lead to a change of heart.

2. *Solitude.* The prisoner was isolated from all society for a period that could last for years, eventually bringing about despair and hopelessness.

3. *Family.* The suspect was allowed to see his wife and children, who begged him to recant so that he might come home.[33]

However, many sectarians were mentally able to endure the worst hardships. If punishing the mind proved futile, punishing the body was requisite to secure the confession. In all, six major forms of physical torture were administered:

1. *Ordeal of Water.* The prisoner was forced to drink vast quantities of water through a funnel or by soaking a piece of silk or linen that was jammed into the throat. In time, blood vessels began bursting.
2. *Ordeal of Fire.* The soles or entire feet were placed over a fire and fried until a confession was given.
3. *Pulley Torture (Strappado).* With hands tied behind his back and ankles bound, the prisoner was hoisted by the wrists into the air six feet or higher. If unrepentant, the prisoner was dropped, dislocating joints when the rope came taut.
4. *The Wheel.* The suspect was tied to a cartwheel and beaten with hammers, bars, or clubs.
5. *The Rack.* Probably the most notorious instrument, this ladder-like mechanism attached the victim's ankles and wrists to rollers at opposite ends of the rack. The body was then stretched as much as thirty centimeters.
6. *Stivaletto.* Four thick boards were attached—two to each leg—with tightly placed rope. Other wedges were then driven between the boards, crushing the bones.[34]

With such brutal examinations, it is hard to imagine how the ultimate sentence could be worse. Yet many men and women withstood such pain yet did not make the proper confession. For these, the most tenacious and intractable, removal became the only option.

Martyr or Menace: Sentencing the Heretic

For those not considered a danger to society or ultimately heretical in belief, different levels of penance were required. Simple penance included prayers, pilgrimages to major sites such as Rome, fasting, regular church attendance, and monetary fines. If the penance was not completed, the person was deemed a relapsed heretic and handed over to the authorities for more extreme measures.

One such measure, designed to utterly humiliate the offender, mandated that the penitent wear a special yellow cross on the shoulder, publicly displaying to all that the person had been found guilty of heresy. In many cases, this punishment led to the unemployment of the criminal, making life harder on the entire family.

Financial retribution handed down by the tribunal included confiscating property, imposing overwhelming fines on the convicted, or demolishing homes with the condition that they could never be rebuilt. Thereby, the punishment passed to the future generations.

Finally, long, if not irrevocable, prison sentences were pronounced on repentant heretics whose crimes were regarded as particularly offensive. While some prisons offered acceptable conditions and social interaction, others were more or less dungeons meant to subdue those whose confessions were incomplete or who attempted to escape. For the vilest of prisoners, the super dungeon was retained in which the prisoner, chained by hands and feet, was placed in absolute solitude from the outside world. Food was passed through a minute slit in the cell wall.[35]

The ultimate sentence was the stake, set aside for those who relapsed into heresy. This public execution, preceded by a sermon, was a spectacle of sorts, intended to discourage any further outburst of unorthodoxy. The execution itself was designed by the inquisitors to draw as many people as possible to demonstrate that heretics had no place in Christian Europe. Frequently this grave exhibition gave dissenters an audience to which to preach, and earned the sympathies and admiration of curious onlookers.[36]

Answering One Final Question: Vatican II Extinguishes the Flames of the Inquisition

In 1808, when Napoleon Bonaparte entered Spain, the Inquisition was finally abolished. Despite sporadic attempts to renew the pro-

ceedings, the Inquisition was forbidden in 1834, and religious tolerance was demanded in the new Spanish Constitution of 1869.

Yet the Vatican only begrudgingly entered modernity, forced by
political revolutions that left its temporal authority vastly weakened.
Although the office of "Secretary of the Inquisition" continued to exist, its power was confined to verbal denunciations. However, even
this polemical power diminished in time. In 1966, the *Index of Prohibited Books,* a list of anathematized books which, if read, could lead to
excommunication, was formally discarded.[37]

Most astonishingly, Vatican II (1962–65), the most recent Roman
Catholic council, proclaimed the right of the individual to hold to
beliefs in accord with personal conscience. In part, it declared:

> This Vatican Council declares that the human person has a
> right to religious freedom. This freedom means that all men
> are to be immune from coercion on the part of individuals or
> of social groups and of any human power, in such wise that
> no one is to be forced to act in a manner contrary to his own
> beliefs, whether privately or publicly, whether alone or in as-
> sociation with others, within due limits.
>
> The council further declares that the right to religious free-
> dom has its foundation in the very dignity of the human person
> as this dignity is known through the revealed word of God and
> by reason itself. This right of the human person to religious free-
> dom is to be recognized in the constitutional law whereby soci-
> ety is governed and thus it is to become a civil right.[38]

Arguing in a manner strangely similar to Protestants and Enlightenment philosophers, the Vatican, with one stroke of the pen, inciner-
ated over seven centuries of Inquisitions. The final verdict was given.

Notes

1. Thieleman J. van Braght, *The Bloody Theater or Martyr's Mirror of the
Defenseless Christians,* trans. by Joseph F. Sohm from the 1660 Dutch

edition, 295–300, at homecomers.org/mirror/martyrs040.htm. Accessed December 29, 2003.

2. Ibid., 295.

3. Ibid.

4. "Dealing with Differences: Heresies and Inquisitions," at majbill.vt.edu/history/burr/3324/Heresy1.htm. Accessed December 29, 2003.

5. Church History Institute, "February 6, 1481: First auto da fe in Spain," *What Happened This Day in Church History,* at gospelcom.net/chi/DAILYF/2002/02/daily-02-06-2002.shtml. Accessed December 31, 2003.

6. Edward Burman, *The Inquisition: The Hammer of Heresy* (New York: Dorset, 1984), 29.

7. Ibid., 32–33.

8. Ibid., 33.

9. The quote originates from *The Catholic Encyclopedia* of 1917. See Newadvent.org/cathen/06796a.htm. Accessed December 29, 2003.

10. Burman, *The Inquisition,* 34. See also Bernard Hamilton, *The Medieval Inquisition* (New York: Holmes and Meier, 1981).

11. Henry Charles Lea, *The Inquisition of the Middle Ages* (New York: Citadel, 1954), 25.

12. Burman, *The Inquisition,* 35.

13. Ibid., 36.

14. Ibid.

15. Lea, *Inquisition of the Middle Ages,* 107.

16. Ibid.

17. Ibid., 109. "I" = inquisitor; "A" = answer.

18. Ibid., 110–11.

19. For further information, see Phillip Schaff, *History of the Christian Church,* at ccel.org/s/schaff/history/6_ch07.htm. Accessed January 1, 2004.

20. Henry W. Longfellow, quoted in Schaff, *History of the Christian Church,* at ccel.org/s/schaff/history/6_ch07.htm. Accessed January 1, 2004.

21. Juan Antonio Llorente, *A Critical History of the Inquisition of Spain* (Williamstown, Mass.: John Lilburne, 1967), 54.

22. Ibid., 54–55. Burman approximates that between 165,000 and 400,000 were exiled.

23. Ibid., 578. Also see Church History Institute, "February 6, 1481."

24. Burman, *The Inquisition,* 56.

25. Llorente, *Critical History of the Inquisition of Spain,* 35. Burman, *The Inquisition,* 59.

26. Lea, *Inquisition of the Middle Ages,* 97–99.

27. Leonard Verduin, *The Reformers and Their Stepchildren* (Sarasota, Fla.: Christian Hymnary, 1991), 74.

28. Ibid., 100.

29. Burman, *The Inquisition,* 60.

30. Llorente, *Critical History of the Inquisition of Spain,* 60–62.

31. Ibid., 63–64.

32. Lea, *Inquisition of the Middle Ages,* 114.

33. Ibid., 114–15.

34. Burman, *The Inquisition,* 62–65.

35. Ibid., 66–70.

36. Ibid., 72–74.

37. Ibid., 206–7, 213.

38. "Declaration on Religious Freedom," at vatican.va/archive/hist_councils/ ii_vatican_council/documents/vat-ii_decl_19651207_dignitatis-humanae_en.html. Accessed January 1, 2004.

Chapter 8

ꟽAGISTERIAL ꟽAyHEꟽ

When a State-Run Church Leads to Blood-Filled Streets

Theological Treason

Michael Sattler shall be given into the hands of the executioner. The latter shall take him to the square and there cut out his tongue, then forge him fast to a wagon and with glowing iron tongs twice tear pieces from his body, then on the way to the site of the execution five times more as above, then burn his body to powder as a heretic.[1]

On May 21, 1527, former Benedictine monk turned Anabaptist[2] evangelist Michael Sattler (1490–1527) was gruesomely executed for the crime of theological heresy. The charges brought against the thirty-seven-year-old newlywed were nine-fold, mostly doctrinal in nature. Sattler was guilty of treasonous acts, including "believ[ing] that infant baptism does not conduce to salvation, . . . despis[ing] and condemn[ing] the mother of God and the saints, . . . and reject[ing] the sacrament of extreme unction."[3] Though many citizens openly expressed their disgust at the upcoming execution, the authorities, under the direction of Roman Catholic King Ferdinand, demanded the harshest sentence.

Sattler himself argued against the right of any court to hold hearings and decide the fate of anyone regarded as a heretic. He explained, "You servants of God, we are not sent to defend the Word of God in court. We are sent to testify to it. We cannot therefore approve of this as a legal trial."[4] Yet, the judges were convinced of their authority. After all, magistrates within European courts had passed sentence on heretics for over a millennium. History supported their cause and licensed their power. No young radical was going to uproot an institution which found its origins within the great Roman Empire.

Hence, on a calm Tuesday morning in the city of Rottenburg, Germany, Sattler, along with nine other men and eight other women of the Anabaptists—including his faithful wife Margaret—finally witnessed their faith with their own blood. Sattler was put to death by civil authorities on charges of ecclesiastical heresy. Worried that he might break under the torture, Sattler promised his disciples that he would give a clear signal if the pain were bearable.

The executioners joyously carried out the orders with meticulous measure and painful precision. They cut out a part of his tongue, yet he was still heard praying for his inquisitors. They then began mutilating his body with red-hot tongs, tearing pieces from his flesh as if he were a mere animal. On the mile-long journey to the place of his execution, the persecutors five times more ripped pieces of flesh from his worn and tattered person. Sattler, however, stayed courageous as well as compassionate. He pleaded with his persecutors to repent of their sins against God and place their faith in Jesus Christ as "the way and the truth."

In the midst of the excruciating pain, Sattler, intent on demonstrating the power of God in the most trying of times, did not forget his pledge. After being tied to a stake, the fire was lighted and burned through the ropes which were tying his hands. Free from the hindrance, Sattler, bloodied but bold, raised his two forefingers to heaven indicating the strength given by God in the cruelest of persecutions. He had paid the ultimate price for an unending faith.

Still, the irony of such a circumstance cannot elude the student of history. Here was a minister of God who at one time had been accorded power to forgive sins, placed under the political and spiritual judgment of temporal rulers. Furthermore, these rulers were not of another faith, but were self-acclaimed Christians who had much in common with the "heretic." They both worshiped the same God and believed in the same authority—the Bible. Nevertheless, the deadly combination of church and state, found within the history of Christianity but not within the pages of the Scripture, found its illustrative apex that auspicious day when Sattler was slaughtered.

The Free Church in an Enslaved Society

Sattler was representative of a group sometimes known as the Radicals or Anabaptists. These men and women were not political revolutionaries engaging in anarchy and rebellion. They were simple peasants for the most part who, basing their faith in the Bible, believed that each local church should be made up of believers in Jesus Christ who had publicly professed their faith in believer's baptism, and voluntarily placed themselves under the authority of the congregation.

With such a strong New Testament definition of the church, they could not hold to a church entwined with the state, an idea the apostle Paul would have deemed ridiculous. The state Church was involuntary as every citizen born in that territory was automatically a member of the local assembly. Furthermore, it was the town council or princes who authorized the acceptance of the church in that region, a power never given to the state in the New Testament. In essence, only God had the right to govern someone's soul—not the state or a group of individuals.

Nonetheless, the magistrates and their religious leaders feared this decentralizing and depoliticizing of Christianity. A citizen was one who was baptized as an infant and thereby counted as one of the brethren in the community. In addition, the unity of the community was based on a common, state-sanctioned religion. To advocate another reason for baptism would be the equivalent of asking for a new constitution for the government. Hence, in a way, the Anabaptists were radicals, not because they wanted to throw away government, but because they wanted government to act according to the mandate of the New Testament—as a supporter of peace and enforcer of civil laws.

The government was not the church, and the church was not the government. They were separate entities that had entirely different purposes. One was sent to keep peace; the other was to herald the Prince of Peace. One was sent to bring fear to lawbreakers; the other was to bring hope to sinners. One was sent to wield the sword against those who would harm citizens in society; the other was to wield the sword of the Word of God, proclaiming the good news of Jesus Christ that brings about a new citizenship in heaven. The Anabaptists wanted to restore the purity of both organizations.

But the magisterial reformers, who merged church and state, had one strong argument on their side: tradition. History recorded that the last one thousand years was filled with this marriage between two strange bedfellows. Now the Anabaptists wanted a divorce between the couple which had seen many anniversaries come and go. Indeed, the minister who performed the wedding was none other than an emperor who lived in the fourth century, Constantine the Great. Constantine has sometimes been regarded as one of the great heroes of the faith, creating a union that lasted longer than any other empire in the history of the world. Alternatively, he is one of the greatest corrupters of the faith, creating a marriage that should never have been, a union leading to the slaughter of countless thousands by joining the two swords of church and state. In this case, the church—the Bride of Christ—became a whore for the state, her beauty and purity defiled.

Jihad Against the Pagans: Constantine's Sullied Stain on the Saints

Since the establishment of Christianity at the incarnation of Jesus Christ, believers were persecuted, sporadically and sometimes locally while at other times universally. Before the conversion of Constantine to the faith, the persecutors of Christians were almost always Roman pagans who wished to bring back the glory days of polytheism and eliminate the ever expanding "cult" of Christianity. One needs to look no further than the gruesome exercises of emperors Nero (54–68),[5] Decius (249–251), and Diocletian (284–305) to observe Christians being thrown to the lions, hung as living candles, or decapitated.

However, a new era dawned on Europe the moment Emperor Caesar Flavius Constantine (312–337) converted to the faith his predecessors had so vehemently endeavored to destroy. The days of matchless bravery by those who suffered in the Roman persecutions were over. In its place was the growing recognition of Christianity as an authentic religion by society and the blanket recognition by most European states.

Indeed, the means by which Constantine was convinced of Christianity says volumes of the way he wanted to institute the religion and how Christianity was going to thrive in the future under the privilege of the state. When vying for the Roman throne against archrival Maxentius, Constantine turned to the Christian God for assistance. In a magnificent dream, Constantine caught sight of a cross in the sky and the words, "In this sign conquer." Constantine's strategy proved successful as he captured Rome and earned the title of Caesar. The city once known as the center of Roman paganism became the new capital of Christianity. Once feared and persecuted, Christianity now became favored and pampered.[6]

Eusebius of Caesarea, known as the first Church historian, illustrates the enthusiasm many Christians felt for the new emperor and the new era:

> Thus the pious emperor, glorying in the confession of the victorious cross, proclaimed the Son of God to the Romans with great boldness of testimony. And the inhabitants of the city, one and all, senate and people, reviving, as it were, from the pressure of a bitter and tyrannical domination, seemed to enjoy purer rays of light, and to be born again into a fresh and new life. All the nations, too, as far as the limit of the western ocean, being set free from the calamities which had heretofore beset them, and gladdened by joyous festivals, ceased not to praise him as the victorious, the pious, the common benefactor: all, indeed, with one voice and one mouth, declared that Constantine had appeared by the grace of God as a general blessing to mankind.[7]

The combination of church and state seemed harmless at first. On balance, the changes made by Constantine were tremendously favorable to Christians. Though Constantine continued to hold his pagan title of *Pontifex Maximus*, denoting him as head of the Roman religion, he clearly gave preferential treatment to Christianity and reared his own children as Christians.

The overwhelming change in church polity and theological principles cannot be overestimated. The emperor, once the fiercest enemy of Christianity, became its greatest supporter and promoter. Not only were churches that had been destroyed by government forces rebuilt, but new edifices were constructed. Older buildings were opulently remodeled. Christian bishops now accompanied Constantine to war, praying for his success and guarding his soul. In 325, Constantine, knowing that the Roman Empire could be unified only if Christianity was unified, called and presided over a church council. The Council of Nicea debated how to handle the heresy of Arianism, a movement named after the bishop Arius, who stated that Jesus Christ was created by God and was not of the same substance as God the Father. Though church leaders deliberated and bestowed the final verdict, it must be noted that it was Constantine himself who gave them the authority to do so, authority he did not truly have in the first place.

But religious liberty was not the policy of Constantine. Instead, he granted Christians the right to worship freely while withholding that same right from other faiths. Eusebius noted the infringement in his biography on Constantine:

> After this the emperor continued to address himself to matters of high importance, and first he sent governors to the several provinces, mostly such as were devoted to the saving faith; and if any appeared inclined to adhere to Gentile worship, he forbade them to offer sacrifice. This law applied also to those who surpassed the provincial governors in rank and dignity, and even to those who occupied the highest station. . . . If they were Christians, they were free to act consistently with

their profession; if otherwise, the law required them to abstain from idolatrous sacrifices.[8]

Now that they were no longer harmed by such guidelines, Christian leaders supported them. The persecuted became the persecutors. The powerless gained power. Many of them took joy in the fact that Constantine was enthusiastically endorsing Christianity while demolishing pagan religions. The power of God shifted from the church to the state. Constantine was the high priest.

Setting the Stage for Internal Jihad: The Civil War Between Established Church and Dissenting Church

Soon traditional Roman paganism was moved from the center to the fringes of society. Yet, Christendom had its own problems and needed solutions. A student of Church history must always remember that there were extensive dissenting groups, popularly known as "sects" and "heretics," who disagreed substantially on issues of church-state relations with the organized and accepted Church of the Roman Empire. Hence, belief in a monolithic church, accepted by so many Christians, has always been a myth.

With the defiled marriage of church and state, the state-backed church gained authority over groups not endorsed by emperors or governors. In particular, Donatism, a movement sprung out of the Constantinian merger of state with church, was targeted by the Roman church. Named after the North African bishop Donatus (313–355), this dissenting group, also known as the Separatist Church of North Africa, maintained that the true church was made up of those who publicly professed their faith. On the other hand, the organized church asserted that the church included everyone in an entire locality.

Moreover, Donatists viewed the merger of church and state as demonic, led by "evil priests working hand in glove with the kings of earth, men who by their conduct show that they have no king but Caesar."[9] Considered insubordinate against both state and church, these separatists were viewed as rebellious revolutionaries to be stopped by any means.

The greatest opponent of the Donatists was Augustine (354–430), the most influential theologian in the history of the church. Author of perhaps the best known book in the first thousand years of Christian writings, *The City of God*, Augustine's theological legacy on both Protestants and Roman Catholics may only be matched by his ecclesiological legacy. Though first not convinced that the Donatists should be suppressed, Augustine came to realize that some Christians must be compelled to faith. Justifying persecution through analogy, Augustine argues, "For both the physician is irksome to the raging madman, and a father to his undisciplined son,—the former because of the restraint, the latter because of the chastisement which he inflicts; yet both are acting in love. But if they were to neglect their charge, and allow them to perish, this mistaken kindness would more truly be accounted cruelty."[10]

With the validation of political persecution on theological grounds, the state was granted unfettered permission to hunt any and all villains, defined as anyone who disagreed with the policies of church or state. It was better to relentlessly and ruthlessly torture someone than to allow them to wallow in their sin, which would lead to eternal reprobation. The state was now fully enthralled in not only ensuring civil order, but in repairing someone's soul.

Carrying the Torch: Magisterial Reformers of the Sixteenth Century

In many ways, the Anabaptists of the sixteenth century were similar to the Donatists of the fourth and fifth centuries. Indeed, they were given the nickname Donatists as a term of derision by those who hated them most. Like the Donatists of old, the Anabaptists held to a believer's church made up of regenerate church members who had publicly professed their faith, followed by baptism. Like their counterparts, Anabaptists believed the combination of church and state was wholly destructive on both divinely ordained institutions. Finally, like the Donatists, the Anabaptists too were hunted as heretics and rebellious anarchists of the worst sort.

Thus, the Anabaptists, along with many groups during the interim twelve hundred years before the Reformation, were the inheritors of Donatist theology and practice. Therefore, when the Reformation came to pass in the sixteenth century, a battle was already raging over the issue of church-state association.

As the Anabaptists mirrored the Donatists, Martin Luther (1483–1546) emulated Augustine. It must be remembered that Luther never intended to leave the Roman Catholic Church, of which he was an Augustinian monk; rather, it was his desire to reform the church's doctrine of salvation, bringing it back to the emphasis on grace (*Sola Gratia*). Similar to Augustine, Luther emphasized the doctrines of human depravity, predestination, justification, and eternal security. Also akin to Augustine, Luther aligned himself with the magistrates, those German princes who protected Luther from the Roman Catholic hoards who wanted the "wild boar" captive or dead.

However, Luther's experience with potential persecution did not sway his conviction that other groups should be harassed for their troublesome doctrines. The reason behind this conviction demonstrates the power of accepted tradition: Luther was taught and believed that anyone who challenged church-state relations was a political nihilist. For example, he wrote, "The Donatists condemned the secular rule which we must allow to remain."[11] Though it is obvious the Donatists only desired separation of church and state, and not destruction of state, Luther viewed any attempt at unraveling the partnership as mayhem.

Consequently, Luther wrote several tracts condemning the Free Church movement of the Anabaptists. Believing it was the responsibility of the magistrate to "keep [subjects in church] with recourse to force if need be and to frighten them away from error,"[12] Luther advocated the most radical measures to ensure the extermination of all Anabaptists. He declared:

> [Anabaptists] are in no case to be tolerated. . . . These are thieves and murderers of whom Christ spoke in John 7, persons who invade another man's parish and who usurp an-

other man's office. . . . They must neither be tolerated nor lis-
tened to, even though they seek to teach the pure Gospel, yes,
even if they are angelic and simon-pure Gabriels from
heaven. . . . If he refuses [to keep his mouth shut]. . . consign
the scamp into the hands of his proper master.[13]

Luther, then, advocated that Anabaptists be hung for heresy, the
only proper punishment for a treasonous wretch. There was no other
option for the radicals for they were a threat not only to society, but to
Christianity in general.

Legalizing Persecution: The Diet of Speyer

As persecution of Anabaptists increased, many of the radicals fled
to safer arenas in southern Germany and Austria. But due to the leadership of Luther in Germany and Catholic Charles V in the Holy Roman Empire itself, the future was not any brighter in these locations
for these brave believers. In fact, in 1529, German princes, many of
whom followed the tenets of Luther, were summoned to an imperial
diet, convened to decide how to eradicate the threat of the Anabaptists.
Charles V, the Holy Roman Emperor, declared the following mandate
upon all his territory:

Whereas it is ordered and provided in *common law* that no
man, having once been baptized according to Christian order, shall let himself be baptized again or for the second time,
nor shall he baptize any such, and especially is it forbidden in
the *imperial law* to do such on pain of death. . . . This old sect
of Anabaptism, condemned and forbidden many centuries
ago, day by day makes greater inroads and is getting the upper hand. In order to prevent such evil and what may proceed
from it, . . . every Anabaptist and rebaptized man and woman
of the age of reason shall be condemned and brought from
natural life into death by fire, sword, and like.[14]

Amazingly, Lutherans and Roman Catholics, who slaughtered thousands of one another's people in religious wars, found common cause in their hatred for the Free Church. Not only were they intimidated by the growing number of converts from their ranks, they worried that this expanding movement could lead to the downfall of their own religious movements, as sustained by government. They even appealed to common tradition, referring to the Justinian Code of the sixth century, to justify applying the death penalty to all Anabaptists.

Hence, police were hired to handle the "problem." In Inquisition fashion, law enforcement roamed from city to city hunting down the radical reformers. In fact, so many Anabaptists popped up that Charles V had to increase his force tenfold to carry out the inquisitor's task.

The Blood Runs South: Ulrich Zwingli, Protestant Leader in Switzerland

Though few Christians recognize the name Ulrich Zwingli (1484–1531), his leadership in the Protestant Reformation was powerful. Pastor of the Grossmunster Church in Zurich, Switzerland, for more than a decade, Zwingli's legacy was diminished by his death on the battlefield at the Second Battle of Kappel in 1531.

Zwingli, known for his love of expositional preaching and teaching, was the most intimately involved with those who later became Anabaptists. By 1521, Zwingli was training Conrad Grebel (1498–1526), Felix Manz (1498–1527), and George Blaurock (1491–1529), the three formative leaders of the early Anabaptist movement. But these young three musketeers went too far when they campaigned for a believer's church through believer's baptism.

On January 21, 1525, Conrad Grebel baptized George Blaurock at the home of Felix Manz. Unnoticed by most of the Zurich community, that baptism launched a tidal wave throughout Christendom that still can be felt. Disengaging the state from the church, these men placed their heads on a platter when they put themselves under the water. Needless to say, Zwingli was not happy. The young men to whom he endeared himself became felonious lawbreakers, committing crimes deserving of death. Zwingli took the responsibility of confronting the threat of these revolutionaries. He immediately banished them from the community and demanded that they stop preaching publicly.

But Grebel, Manz, and Blaurock were far too passionate about their views to adhere to Zwingli's edict. They were, however, fully aware that their outspoken stance would lead to severe repercussions. Conrad Grebel, the father of the movement, was dead within twenty months of his baptism. Accused of sedition, Grebel was promptly arrested and imprisoned for months. Although he did escape, Grebel, weak from his confinement, contracted the plague and died in August 1526. He left behind his wife and three children between the ages of one and three.

Blaurock, known as the Hercules of the Anabaptists due to his fiery temperament, met a more brutal fate than that of Grebel. In 1527, he was arrested by Zwingli, stripped, and beaten severely. He was then banished from the town, and never allowed to return. In 1529, arrested by Austrian authorities in Innsbruck, he was placed under sentence of death by the decrees of the Diet of Speyer. Catholic authorities, desiring to make a mockery out of him, submitted Blaurock to vicious torture before burning him at the stake. In his final words, known as his death hymn, Blaurock illustrates his faith in the Lord and the pain he was going through: "All my body quaked before false teaching and coercion. . . . You, Lord, did have mercy, and by your grace and power helped me, your poor son, and made me victorious."[15] He died with the same valor by which he lived.

Yet, the death of Felix Manz is the most notable of the group. It is not surprising to most students of church history to read about Roman Catholic persecutions, as they are common in the history of medieval Christianity. But it was Zwingli, a thorough-going Reformed Protestant, who is directly responsible for the death of a man who had been his student and an intimate friend.

On Saturday, January 5, 1527, after the town council passed a sentence of drowning upon the Anabaptist, Manz was removed from his prison cell in the Wellenberg Tower and paraded through the streets of Zurich. His final destination was the bottom of the Limmat River, which ran through the center of the bourgeoning city. As he proceeded down the main street, past the fish market and to the boat dock, he dedicatedly witnessed to all who would listen about the loving grace of Jesus Christ, who wished to save all who would believe.

The crowd that gathered that cold winter day was full of naysayers and antagonists. Many wished to argue with Manz about baptism even during his final hour. But in the midst of that harsh crowd, young Manz heard the familiar voice of his mother, Anna, herself baptized by his friend Conrad. She was encouraging her son to stay true to the faith once for all delivered to the saints. He did. Once at the edge of the waters, Manz was ushered into the middle of the river via boat, arms and legs bound, and thrust into the freezing waters. At 3 o'clock in the afternoon, Manz was baptized one last time, and then entered into his eternal rest.

Murdering Souls Before They Infect: Rationalizing the Massacre of Innocents

God raises up the magistracy against heretics, faction-makers, and schismatics in the Christian Church in order that Hagar may be flogged by Sarah. The Donatists murder men's souls, make them go to eternal death; and then they complain when men punish them with temporal death. Therefore a Christian magistrate must make it his first concern to keep the Christian religion pure. . . . All who know history will know what has been done in this matter by such men as Constantine, . . . Theodosius, Charlemagne, and others.[16]
    —Urbanus Rhegius, an associate of Martin Luther

How could Luther and Zwingli accept such horrendous acts? What justification could they possibly give that would rationalize this behavior? The answer is found in the above quote. As pastors of the flock of God, the Reformers of the state churches believed they were protecting the souls of those who were given to them. As a matter of fact, for these Reformers to stand idly by as Anabaptists and other radicals moved in their cities was in their minds analogous to watching wolves devour helpless sheep without a fight from the responsible shepherd.

Hence, any cruelty inflicted upon an individual was for the good of the community. With such justification, one can see why Sattler was assaulted so severely. The greater the punishment, the greater the deterrent, so sects would not raise their wicked heads again. In Protestant thought, the point of inquisition is not the purging of the heretic; rather, it is to purge the heretic *from the society*.

It must be noted, though, that the Magisterial Reformers presumptuously assumed the government's role in the fight. It seems, thus, that they were skirting their responsibility by handing the obligation of trial and punishment to the civil authorities. The religious leaders merely pointed out the so-called heresy and watched as the town council or princes deliberated the doom of the poor soul in question. Luther, Zwingli, and John Calvin all placed their stamps of approval on the sealed sentence.

Perhaps the prime example, and the most notorious trial of a heretic in early Reformation folklore, is that of Michael Servetus (1511–1553), the famed anti-Trinitarian lawyer who argued so vehemently against John Calvin (1509–1564). In this case, unlike that of the evangelical Anabaptists, the accused denied the foundation of the faith of all Christians, Roman Catholic and Protestant. Servetus, consumed with a blend of rationalism with faith, did not believe the Trinity could be explained. Consequently, as he wrote in his work *Errors of the Trinity*, the theology of the said doctrine must be rejected outright.

Servetus was a medical practitioner from Spain who traveled throughout Europe, and was a wanted criminal everywhere. Condemned first by Catholics during the French Inquisition, Servetus escaped before he could be executed. He decided, quite illogically, to travel through Geneva, home of his archrival Calvin, leader of the Reformed Protestants and author of the most influential work of all the Reformation, *Institutes of the Christian Religion*. Servetus had carried on a correspondence with Calvin and he was attacked by name in *Institutes*. The fugitive was almost immediately noticed when he reached Geneva and was captured and imprisoned. Calvin was appointed theological prosecutor by the city governors, and he drew up a list of thirty-eight accusations of heresy. Calvin argued that Servetus should be beheaded, the mode of execution given to those who upset the social order. According to the old Roman Justinian Code, "Heresy shall be construed to be an offense against the civil order."[17] The Genevan Council of Twenty-five would not accept Calvin's ruling that Servetus was engaged in political treason. They demanded that he be burned at the stake, an execution worthy of religious sedition.

Calvin was largely liable for the death of Servetus. He was not merely a bystander without any authority; he was the religious leader of the town who wholeheartedly accepted the merger of state and church. As a matter of record, Servetus posed no immediate threat to the city of Geneva. He was just passing through. As one author wrote:

> Servetus started no parades, made no speeches, carried no placards, had no political ambitions. He did have some erratic ideas touching the doctrine of the Trinity; and he entertained some deviating notions concerning baptism, especially infant baptism. . . . But he was not a revolutionary in the political sense. . . . Only in a [church-state] climate would men deal in such a way with such a man.[18]

Simply put, Servetus was sent to his grave as a spiritual murderer and as a religious harlot.

Even though Servetus was not a citizen of Geneva, Calvin nonetheless demanded the rationalist's execution, thus expanding the principle of Christian jihad to anyone within the grasp of a Christian city-state. Calvin, substantiating his actions, argued:

> This law [Deuteronomy 13] at first sight appears to be too severe. For merely having spoken should one be so punished? But if anybody slanders a mortal man he is punished and shall we permit a blasphemer of the living God to go unscathed? If a prince is injured, death appears to be insufficient for vengeance. And now when God, the sovereign emperor, is reviled

by a word, is nothing to be done? God's glory and our salvation are so conjoined that a traitor to God is also an enemy of the human race and worse than a murderer because he brings poor souls to perdition. . . . But we muzzle dogs, and shall we leave men free to open their mouths as they please? Those who object are like dogs and swine. They murmur that they will go to America where nobody will bother them.[19]

A state-run church, as exemplified above, is the antithesis to a free society. One cannot coexist alongside the other without compromise, corruption, and collusion. In such a closed society, people are forcibly fenced in by orthodoxy as defined by the state and enforced by the religious leaders.

Yet, forced orthodoxy cannot biblically or logically lead to genuine adoration. God never forced anyone to love him. Anyone attempting this procedure is doomed to fail, as it stands in direct opposition to God's plan and human purpose. Worship must be voluntary if it is to be true worship in the same sense that love must be voluntary for the union between man and woman to be authentic and unadulterated. In the long run, continually attempting to force orthodoxy through the state will lead to the destruction of Christianity in that same region. This is most evident across the hills and valleys of Europe today. What was once the heart of Christianity now stands as a mere museum of days gone by.

A Continuing Legacy: Christian Jihad Passed Down Through the Generations

Luther, Zwingli, and Calvin died within thirty years of each other. Each passed down their belief in the state church to their successors, Luther to Philip Melanchthon (1497–1560), Zwingli to Heinrich Bullinger (1504–1575),[20] and Calvin to Theodore Beza (1519–1605). Though the persecutions subsided when there was a popular outcry, they continued to exist, and indeed thrive, through the Reformation and well into the seventeenth century.

Indeed, the second generation of the Reformation was stricter than the first in adhering to the theological system that was developing. Demonstrating this notion well, Beza took the hunting of heretics to a level unseen by Calvin or even Constantine. Criticizing the apparent effeminacy of Constantine, Beza declared:

> Will not Constantine be judged to be guilty in this matter? He would have been wiser if he had defended more sternly the majesty of Christ so wickedly and stubbornly attacked. . . . . While the imperial protection was still a novel thing in the Church it is really no wonder that the more lenient use of it as the first pleased both emperor and bishop.[21]

Hence, the argument of Beza was one of progressive development. The more mature the church became, the harsher the persecution that would follow. Imagine, therefore, what today's church would be like if Beza's legacy were the norm. Envision not only the amount of slaughter justified, but the types of executions allowed.

Only twenty-five years after Beza's death, Puritans began arriving in the New World. As they crossed over the Atlantic into unchartered territory, they carried their church-state baggage with them. Puritans in New England were known to harass those not connected with the official church, forbidding dissenters to preach in public or perform ministerial duties such as weddings. Their dream of the new "city set on a hill" was much like Geneva. They were the new Israelites capturing the new Promised Land from the pagan Canaanites. Furthermore, as Israel had to weed out heresy externally and internally, so too did the Puritans. Thus, the Salem Witch Trials, although overplayed by historians and milder than similar episodes of violence in Europe, were inevitable in the theological climate of the Puritans.

Though it took several centuries to completely remove church-state association and allow each to perform their functions properly, it did happen. Vestiges of state-supported churches and the exclusion of dissenters from general religious rights finally ended. Much blood was shed, but not in vain. The men and women who gave their lives for the faith have not only been rewarded in heaven by the heavenly Father, they also gave us a gift which is priceless as well.

The Last Laugh: A Lasting Legacy from an Unending Battle

Today's New World has less to do with the attitudes of the Puritans and more to do with the separation of the Anabaptists. America is a free nation that heralds the four key freedoms: religion, speech, assembly, and press. But one must remember that those who defend truth must be eternally vigilant. Christians, and citizens in general, must persistently keep watch that the church's freedom is not impeded by the state. To be clear, the state has no right to place its authority over the church.

The converse is also true. Though Christians have every right to participate in government and bring their faith to that political table, Christians do not have the right to make their faith "official" as the preferred faith or desire that their cause be otherwise pampered. Though cliché, it is still true—an open Bible and an open mind will make a Christian every time. The Christian should not fear the arena of ideas found within a religiously open society. Truth may be suppressed, but it will rise from the dead. Furthermore, to advocate a religiously free society is not an admission of equality within all faiths, only a level playing field. One must hold to the exclusivity of salvation in Jesus Christ while at the same time believing that everyone has a right to accept *or reject* that doctrine.

Lest We Forget: Speaking Volumes Without Saying a Word

In the cold winter of 1573, Maeyken Wens, a young Belgium mother and wife, was arrested for the treasonous act of rebaptism. A few weeks later, her sentence was passed to her: she was to be burned at the stake. Moreover, it was ordered she have a tongue screw imbedded in her mouth to prevent her from sharing her faith with the crowd. Her family was notified by other Anabaptists and warned not to attend the execution lest they too be arrested.

But nothing could have restrained Adrian, the young son, from seeing his mother one last time. He could not fully understand why the authorities had chosen to kill someone who had never hurt anyone. On the night before the execution, Adrian crawled under the quilt his mother had made and read the last letter she had written him. It explained:

> Oh, my dear son, though I will soon be taken from you, begin now in your youth to fear God. Then you shall have your mother again in the New Jerusalem, where we will never have to part again. My dear son, I hope now to go before you. Follow me in this if you value your soul, for besides this you can find no other way of salvation.
>
> Love one another all the days of your life. Take little Hans in your arms now and then for me. And if your father should be taken from you, care for one another. My dear children, kiss one another once for me, for remembrance.
>
> Good-bye, my dear children, all of you.
>
> My dear son, do not be afraid of this suffering. It is nothing compared to the suffering which endures forever. The Lord has taken away all my fear. I cannot fully thank my God for the grace which he has shown me.
>
> Good-bye once more, my dear son, Adrian.[22]

Adrian arrived early in the public square the next morning, anxiously awaiting the sight of his mother. In a little while, his mother emerged with a crowd surrounding her. Blood flowed down her mouth from the tongue screw, staining her dress. They placed his mother at the stake, chained her to it, as she quietly stood by with her eyes shut, as if in prayer.

Adrian, overwhelmed by the incident, fainted. When he awoke, the execution was over. All that remained in front of the youth was the ashes of his mother. Adrian waded through the ashes and found the tongue screw the authorities had used to muffle his mother. Putting the item in his handkerchief, he quietly realized the purpose in life through the martyrdom of his mother. He whispered, "Mama, I want you to know . . . I, too, will fear God and follow his Word with my whole heart. You have shown me the way."[23]

Notes

1. John Allen Moore, *Anabaptist Portraits* (Scottdale, Pa.: Herald, 1984), 118. This was taken from an eyewitness account and can also be found in Thieleman J. van Braght, *The Martyrs Mirror of Defenseless Christians* (Scottdale, Pa.: Herald, 1950).

2. From the Latin for re-baptizer, this derogatory name was given by the opponents of men and women who believed that a person had to make a profession of faith in Jesus Christ before being baptized. Therefore, the candidate, who had most likely been baptized as a baby by the Roman Catholic Church, was baptized a second time.

3. van Braght, *Martyrs Mirror of Defenseless Christians,* 416.

4. Moore, *Anabaptist Portraits,* 117.

5. The dates given for emperors in this chapter are the years of their reigns.

6. Bruce Shelley, *Church History in Plain Language* (Waco, Tex.: Word, 1982), 105–10.

7. Eusebius of Caesarea, *The Life of the Blessed Constantine,* in *Internet Medieval Sourcebook,* ed. Paul Halsall, at fordham.edu/halsall/basis/vita-constantine.html. Accessed December 12, 2003.

8. Ibid.

9. Leonard Verduin, *The Reformers and Their Stepchildren* (Sarasota, Fla.: Christian Hymnary, 1991), 33.

10. Augustine of Hippo, *A Treatise Concerning the Correction of the Donatists,* at fordham.edu/halsall/sbook2.html#fathers2. Accessed December 13, 2003.

11. Verduin, *Reformers and Their Stepchildren,* 48.

12. Ibid., 74.

13. Ibid., 184–85.

14. George Hunston Williams, *The Radical Reformation,* 3d ed. (Kirksville, Mo.: Sixteenth Century Journal, 1992), 359.

15. Moore, *Anabaptist Portraits,* 92–93.

16. Verduin, *Reformers and Their Stepchildren,* 50.

17. Ibid., 52.

18. Ibid.

19. Translated from John Calvin, *Defensio orthodoxae fideide sacra Trinitae, contra prodigiosis errores Michaelis Serveti Hispani* (1554).

20. Of the three successors, Bullinger stands out as the most empathetic toward Anabaptists, which may largely be due to the fact that his cousin had joined their ranks. Bullinger most definitely struggled with the idea of punishing "heretics," agreeing with the execution of Servetus but not allowing executions in Zurich.

21. Theodore Beza, quoted by Verduin, *Reformers and Their Stepchildren,* 83.

22. Dave and Neta Jackson, *On Fire for Christ* (Scottdale, Pa.: Herald, 1989), 53.

23. Ibid., 56.

Chapter 9

LET THE HEATHEN WORSHIP!

A Struggle from Within

I am really distressed that these poor people [Anabaptists] should be so pitifully murdered, burned, and horribly put to death. Everyone should be allowed to believe what he likes. If he is wrong, he will be punished enough in hell fire.[1]

—Martin Luther

On October 31, 1517, when Martin Luther nailed his *Ninety-five Theses* on the door of the Wittenberg Castle, the history of Christianity was forever changed. The young Augustinian monk, desiring to reform the Roman Catholic Church from within, hoped his brief yet harsh criticism would remove the abuses of the Church, especially in regards to the heinous doctrine of indulgence—that wayward practice of promising heaven for a deceased relative of someone who gave money to the Church. Across the continent of Europe, in countless churches in rural villages and vast cities, Catholics were promised by John Tetzel, that famous Catholic fundraiser for St. Peter's Basilica in Rome, "As a coin in the coffer rings, a soul from Purgatory springs!"

Hence, the Protestant Reformation, aptly named, is synonymous with Martin Luther. His desire was to bring back the glory days of the Church that found its epiphany with the Church father Augustine (A.D. 354–430). However, Augustine, who emphasized salvation by grace alone and the importance of Scriptural authority, did not consider religious liberty a foundational tenet of the faith. Indeed, when Luther himself was called before the Diet of Worms to give an account of his doctrines, he did not argue that the Catholic Church had no right to question or even persecute him. Rather, he asserted that his beliefs came from the Scripture itself, and therefore he should not be punished for standing on the Word of God.

Conversely, though Luther struggled with the doctrine of persecution at times, as can be seen in the quotation introducing this chapter, the Reformer eventually gave his stamp of approval to persecute those who he believed went against the Word of God. He stipulated, "Although it may seem cruel to punish them with the sword, it must be recognized that they damn the ministry of the Word, possess no true teaching themselves, and suppress that which is true." In the end, persecuting those who were wrong was the responsibility of those who were right.

The Pen Is Mightier Than the Sword

> The Inquisitors are the biggest heretics of all since against the teaching and example of Christ they have condemned heretics to the flames and before the time of the harvest root up the wheat together with the tares.[2]
>
> —Balthasar Hubmaier

As the hammer that nailed those *Theses* has continually reverberated through the pages of Christian history, a quiet pen that beckoned an ecclesiastical revolution has gone unnoticed by the vast majority of those who fondly study the past. Yet, it can be argued convincingly that the pen of Balthasar Hubmaier (1480–1528), the first and foremost theologian of the Anabaptist (Free Church) movement of the sixteenth century, has influenced more people than even that of Luther. Whereas Luther's writings changed a Church, Hubmaier's writings—in due time—helped change the world.

In his brief thirty-six-point thesis titled *On Heretics and Those*

Who Burn Them (1524), Hubmaier, once a Catholic priest who ex-iled the Jews from his parish and demolished their synagogue, be-came the first to advocate complete religious liberty during the Protestant Reformation. Years before his time, Hubmaier not only argued for the religious liberty of dissenting Christians, but also stated that Muslims should be allowed to practice their religion with-out fear of persecution. In fact, to punish those of a different reli-gion was antithetical to winning them to the Christian faith. He explained that Muslims "cannot be overcome by our doing, neither by sword nor by fire, but alone with patience and supplication, whereby we patiently await divine judgment."[3]

Obviously, this system of thought was not welcome by most of those in power. After escaping the tortuous punishment of Protestant re-former Ulrich Zwingli in Zurich, Hubmaier was invited to pastor a Baptist church in Nikolsburg, Moravia (modern-day Mikulov, Czech Republic). Within fourteen months of his arrival, the pastor-theolo-gian had baptized between six and twelve thousand candidates who voluntarily professed their faith in Jesus Christ and desired member-ship within the local body of believers. In essence, Hubmaier proved his belief in an open society true. Nikolsburg, led by the Lichtenstein nobility, was known for its religious freedom within the borders of the town. Catholics, Lutherans, Anabaptists, and other groups all co-existed peacefully.

The Roman Catholic hierarchy had seen enough as King Ferdinand called for the prompt arrest of the arch-heretic. If the Lichtenstein family did not comply, they would be removed from power and lose any hope of continuing some vestige of religious toleration. They thus acquiesced to the request and handed Hubmaier over to the Austrian authorities. His end was inevitable.

Repeatedly placed on the torture rack, Hubmaier never gave in to recantation, but instead, as an eyewitness expressed, was "fixed like an immovable rock in his heresy."[4] On March 10, 1528, Hubmaier was brought to the place of execution where he was to be burned at the stake. While his wife of three years, Elsbeth, encouraged her husband to stand firm, Hubmaier was stripped of his clothes and his beard was laden with sulphur and gunpowder. The fire was lighted, his beard and hair was set ablaze, and he died.

Hubmaier was put to death on the formal charges of heresy and sedition. The former charge had to do with his repudiation of Roman Catholic doctrine, the latter with his supposed rejection of civil authority. But Hubmaier unquestionably believed in the right of the state to defend itself and the right of Christians to serve in positions of political prominence, as can be seen in his work *On the Sword,* published the same year as his arrest. However, Hubmaier denied that the state has any right to interfere in religious matters. To the Catholics in power, this one lapse was seen as a referendum on the entire constitution of the Empire and therefore must be publicly suppressed. Hubmaier paid the ultimate price for a belief that today is considered foundational to much of Western society. The road of religious liberty was largely paved through a small town on the Austrian-Czech border by a little-known theological giant.

"Give Me Liberty or Give Me Death": Religious Toleration Versus Religious Liberty

Littered throughout the annals of Western history are documents that provide minority groups with freedoms not given to them previously. Usually the acts are considered favorable by contemporaries as people were given more freedoms in the future than they were accustomed to in the past. Though a government should always be commended for granting people more rights, the applause should only be as loud as people are free.

To be sure, there is an incredible difference between religious liberty and religious toleration. The former grants all worshipers of every faith complete and equal treatment and allows each person and group total freedom to worship how they choose without any fetters, biases, or coercion from the government. The latter is quite an arrogant rule, stipulating that government will put up with what it considers inferior, inadequate, or incorrect practices—but only to a certain point.

Actually, the former recognizes that it is the government's role to remove itself from the business of a religious organization while the latter believes that the government must act as a loving father to the true religion, however that is proven, and make sure that only a true beneficiary, and not a bastard child, receives the inheritance justly earned. The first puts the power of judgment solely in the hands of God, while the second believes God has empowered them to do his work of judgment.

The Act of Toleration, passed in 1689 after the Glorious Revolution installed Anglicans William and Mary to power in England, is considered the benchmark legislation for the modern arrival of religious freedoms. A closer look, though, removes the idealistic optimism of the bill and replaces it with cautious realism. It is unquestionable that the act was good for some, including Baptists, Presbyterians, and Quakers, all of whom were finally allowed to worship freely after years of persecution at the hands of both Anglicans and Catholics. But the document was not as tolerant as its title generically describes. Consider the following:

1. Older dogmatic legislation, including the Five-Mile Act (by which ministers of dissenting groups were forbidden to come within five miles of cities), and the Conventicle Act (denying the right for five or more people to gather in an unsanctioned religious meeting), were never repealed. Anglican dogma was still officialized, but particular groups were exempted from specific doctrines. Anabaptists were not forced to adhere to infant baptism, for example.
2. Catholics and Unitarians were not protected under the Act of Toleration since they were considered detrimental to the unity of England.
3. Nonconformists still could not hold public office or receive university degrees.[5]

Ultimately, the act had great historical value, as it was the bridge between the religious wars and inquisitions of the past and the religious liberties of the next three centuries. Yet, as a unique document, it is not that impressive.

One of the founders of religious liberty in the United States, John Locke, was also not satisfied with the Act of Toleration. He wrote, "It is not what you would wish, but it is something."[6] In fact, while England and France went through their own political and religious transformations, America stands out as the example of religious freedom in the West, in large part due to the work of Locke and those who agreed with him. But freedom did not come overnight. Many dissenters, who stood against Congregationalists in the Northeast and Anglicans in the Middle and Southern colonies, paid a high price for the freedoms today enjoyed by Americans. The following is a brief reminder of the struggles faced by dissenting colonialists:

1. All citizens within the Northeast were forced to pay taxes to support Congregational ministers, even if they did not attend the official church. This tax was not phased out in Massachusetts until 1833.
2. In Virginia, laws required attendance in the local Anglican Church. If a person disobeyed, he was subject to whippings, fines, and bodily mutilation.
3. Many colonies required a state license in order to preach, which of course was only given to those of the official denomination. In fact, Virginia had passed a law which restricted admission of clergy into the colony only to Anglican ministers.[7]

Today, freedom of religion is granted to each person within the United States. However, religious liberty must always be heralded against creeping and incremental political incursions which are attempting to destroy the foundation of liberty and replace it with tolerance. Any law that relegates government as the enforcer of accepted doctrine is unacceptable.

To move back now toward toleration and away from liberty is to cross that bridge back to the past and move again toward the religious wars and inquisitions of history. It is unconscionable for a nation which has been given such immense freedom to chain itself in religious slavery, owned by the politically correct dogma of the age. If God is the judge of the soul and faith is voluntary for each individual to choose, then those who advocate any form of tolerance over liberty are acting as God to others, a form of political idolatry.

"Lest We Forget": Lessons from the Past

Spiritual Cannibalism: Christians Killing Other Christians

> The King's Guards did commit outrages upon the lives and fortunes of the Protestant Nobles and Gentlemen, even of those that were their family members, and well known to them. . . . For the streets and ways did resound with the noise of those that flocked to the slaughter and plunder, and the complaints and doleful outcries of dying men, and those that were nigh to danger were everywhere heard. The carkasses of the slain were thrown down from the windows, the Courts and chambers of houses were full of dead men, their dead bodies rolled in dirt were dragged through the streets, blood did flow in such abundance through the channels of the streets, that full streams of blood did run down into the River: The number of the slain men, women, even those that were great with child, and children also, was innumerable.[8]
>
> —Eyewitness Account of the
> St. Bartholomew's Day Massacre

The account described above is not an exaggerated or fictitious legend within Reformation folklore, but an actual eyewitness account of one of the bloodiest weeks in human history. Within four days in August 1572, between thirty thousand and seventy thousand French Calvinists called Huguenots were slaughtered by Roman Catholic mobs with government sanction. The Protestant movement was never again viable in France. Though obviously met with disgust throughout the Protestant world, many Roman Catholics cheered the murderers, hoping the momentum of the Reformation had swung back toward their favor. Indeed, Pope Gregory XIII even minted a new coin to commemorate the event.

This was the beginning of the religious conflicts that culminated in the Thirty Years War (1618–1648) between Lutherans and their Calvinist allies and Catholics. This series of wars was more the result of nationalism and the grab for land and power in the new geopolitical realities of Europe, but it had much impetus from the battle between Roman Catholics and Protestants for the soul of modern Europe. Several million soldiers perished in those three decades, and millions more died of starvation or disease. Whole towns were looted and destroyed by enemy soldiers seeking selfish gain or survival. In the end, the population of the Holy Roman Empire was depleted by nearly a third. Germany, the land where Reformation began, was devastated.

What had begun as an internal spiritual reform of the Roman Catholic Church became the most brutal spectacle of savagery Europe had witnessed up to that time. Though politics played a significant part in the war, one cannot overlook the primary responsibility taken by those who wished to enforce their form of religion on those of a different ilk.

But even this stage of brutality was not considered uncommon in the history of Europe. For centuries, thousands had died at the hands of the Roman Catholic hierarchy. Severe brutality was at least necessary, if not at times welcome, in order to keep Christian Europe doctrinally pure and politically unified. France, it seemed, was the breeding ground of dissent, and had no lack of protestant groups in the Middle Ages.

Though the vast amount of energy during the Crusades was focused on victory against Muslim forces, Catholics, when given time and opportunity, also turned their attention west toward the likes of Albi, France, headquarters of the Cathars (from the Greek, meaning "cleansed"). This group of men and women, also known as the Albigensians, was considered heretical by the Roman Catholic Church. They did not hold to apostolic succession and were accused of denying the divinity of Jesus Christ. However, scholars such as

Leonard Verduin point out that though some were most definitely heretical in their beliefs, the group as a whole was basically ortho-dox in their faith.[9]

Whatever the conclusion of the group's orthodoxy, the Catholic jihad is still inexcusable and is a reminder to the reader that not all Christians participated in the Crusades against the Muslims. In fact, the Cathars advocated pacifism and believed it was sinful to partake in any war. According to the Church, they were not only theological malfeasants, but political anarchists as well. It was feared that their pacifism, if it caught on with the majority of Europeans, would be the downfall of Christian Europe. Therefore, it seemed imperative to stop them.

At the beginning of the thirteenth century, Pope Innocent III de-clared a crusade on all Cathars. As imperative as it was to halt the onslaught of Muslim invaders, it was important as well to make sure the Christian Empire did not fold from internal ramblings. In 1209, Arnold Amaury, abbot of Citeaux, called for the collective slaughter of all Cathars in the town of Beziers. His motto, which has carried forth into modern expression, stated, "Kill them all, the Lord knows those who are his." Only a small minority of the town, perhaps five hundred, was made up of Cathars, but all the city paid the price for guilt by association. Twenty thousand were killed.

Thus began the wholesale slaughter of thousands of Cathars in the thirteenth century.

These examples of Christian jihad, only a sampling of the count-less stories within the pages of history, serve to illustrate how devas-tating the results can be when an official church rules a region or nation. When the spiritual sword is merged with the political sword, both are dealt a death blow. As the Crusades led to the shameless slaughter of thousands of Muslims and Jews, it is forgotten that thousands of Chris-tians perished as well.

The result of this spiritual cannibalism was prophesied by Jesus Christ himself, who warned his disciples that if anyone attempts to uproot tares (unbelievers) which are in the field with wheat (believers), the wheat will be harmed as well (Matthew 13:24–30).

The reasons are at least threefold. First, the tares, really weeds, look identical to wheat until the time of harvest. Moreover, the tares, unnoticed from the surface, entwine themselves to the root of the wheat. Hence, the desire to uproot evil will cost the lives of the righteous. Second, God has an appointed time to remove the tares, a time that should not be shortened by those bothered by the effects the tares have on the wheat. Third and most important, Jesus Christ asserted that only he has the right to judge. He and he alone will give heretics their due punishment.

Theological Holocaust: Replacing the Chosen People with the Church

In some provinces a difference in dress distinguishes the Jews or Muslims from the Christians, but in certain others such a confusion has grown up that they cannot be distinguished by any difference. Thus it happens at times that through error Christians have relations with the women of Jews or Muslims, and Jews and Muslims with Christian women. Therefore, that they may not, under pretext of error of this sort, excuse themselves in the future for the excesses of such prohibited intercourse, we decree that such Jews and Muslims of both sexes in every Christian province and at all times shall be marked off in the eyes of the public from other peoples through the character of their dress. Particularly, since it may be read in the writings of Moses [Numbers 15:37–41], that this very law has been enjoined upon them.

Moreover, during the last three days before Easter and especially on Good Friday, they shall not go forth in public at all, for the reason that some of them on these very days, as we hear, do not blush to go forth better dressed and are not afraid to mock the Christians who maintain the memory of the most holy Passion by wearing signs of mourning.

This, however, we forbid most severely, that any one should

presume at all to break forth in insult to the Redeemer. And since we ought not to ignore any insult to him who blotted out our disgraceful deeds, we command that such impudent fellows be checked by the secular princes by imposing them proper punishment so that they shall not at all presume to blaspheme him who was crucified for us.[10]
　　　　—Canon 68 of the Fourth Lateran Council (1215)

In addition to crusading against Muslims and Cathar Christians, Pope Innocent III vehemently attacked the Jewish people. Innocent presided over the Fourth Lateran Council, one of the most powerful tribunals in the history of the Roman Catholic Church, which legitimized much of Catholic doctrine for the next eight centuries. Drawing on ancient Roman laws, the pope demanded that Jews meet three requirements in order to live under Christian jurisdiction. First, fearing intermarriage of Jews and Christians, the Council stipulated that Jews must wear special clothing. To add to the insult, Jews, when seen in public, were required to wear a badge in the form of a ring. Of course this regulation would become eerily familiar to Jews seven hundred years later in Nazi Germany.

Second, Jews were forced to stay in their houses during the final three days of the Passion Week. Though the canon argued that Jews mocked Christians during this sacred time, it is clearly seen that Jews were merely not celebrating the death of Jesus Christ but going about their business as any normal day. To the Catholic officials, this was highly offensive and, in essence, mocking the very sacrifice of Jesus Christ.

Third, Catholics outlawed any offensive words said of Jesus Christ from Jews or Muslims. In fact, the statement's arrogance is most clearly seen in the final phrase, "To blaspheme him who was crucified *for us*" (emphasis added). Note the pride that accompanies the wording, as if Jesus Christ did not die for all sinners—only for a select group of saints.

Removing God's Blessings:
Anti-Semitic Roots in the Church

This prejudice toward the Jewish people did not occur instantaneously; rather, Jews were accustomed to persecution from Christians. Two hundred years after the death of Jesus Christ, Christians began antagonizing Jews, blaming them for the Crucifixion. Furthermore, since the Jews rejected the sacrifice of Jesus, they were replaced in God's plan of redemption with the Church. God had forsaken his chosen people, given all rights and privileges of the Jews to the Church, and damned them to eternal exile due to their idolatry. He would never again call the Jews back to himself. Origen of Alexandria, one of the fathers of the early church, explained, "The Jewish nation was driven from its country, and another people were called by God to the blessed election."[11]

Once the organized Church accepted God's final and complete judgment on Israel, practical persecution was only an afterthought. In the centuries that followed, Jews, declared "murderers of the Lord, assassins of the prophets, rebels and detesters of God, . . . companions of the devil, . . . [and] enemies of all that is beautiful,"[12] were subject to the worst treatment from those who were supposed to follow the Golden Rule. They were at best secondary citizens whose rights were conditional upon proper behavior. At worst, they were scapegoats for the bloodthirsty outcry of crusaders, inquisitors, knights, and politicians.

The following list is a rudimentary outline of some of the harassment Jews endured at the hands of state-sponsored Christians. Though Roman rule must be blamed in part, justification for the persecution lays squarely at the feet of the organized church.

388　　In the town of Callinicum, located on the Euphrates River, a mob of Christians, instigated by their local bishop, burn the Jewish synagogue. When Emperor Theodosius calls for recompense, St. Ambrose, bishop of Milan, convinces him to rethink his decision. In the end, Theodosius condones the action.

413   A group of Catholic monks sweep through Jerusalem massacring Jews in the town, specifically targeting those Jews praying at the Western Wall.

442   The synagogue in Constantinople is turned into a church.

529   Since Byzantium is a Christian territory, Jews are forbidden from reading the Old Testament in Hebrew in the synagogues. The Mishnah is outlawed in its entirety.

937   Pope Leo VII calls on his bishop in Mainz to expel all Jews who refuse to be baptized.

1096   During the First Crusade, entire Jewish communities are exterminated in several cities, including Cologne and Worms. One crusader asserted, "We desire to go fight God's enemies in the East, but we have before our eyes certain Jews, a race more inimical to God than any other."

1222   Council of Oxford forbids the construction of any new synagogues.

1300s   Jews are expelled from France, Hungary, and many parts of Germany.

1492   Seven hundred Jews are burned at the stake during Spanish Inquisition; the entire community is exiled from Spain.[13]

Yet, the Roman Catholic Church alone cannot take the blame for this harsh treatment. Protestants are guilty as well of heinous acts committed against the Jews. Martin Luther, whose frustration that Jews remained resistant to evangelism developed into a hatred, admonished the German princes to take the following steps against the Jews:

> First to set fire to their synagogues or schools and to bury and cover with dirt whatever will not burn, so that no man will ever again see a stone or cinder of them.
>
> Second, I advise that their houses also be razed and

destroyed. For they pursue in them the same aims as in their synagogues.

Third, I advise that all their prayer books and Talmudic writings, in which such idolatry, lies, cursing and blasphemy are taught, be taken from them.

Fourth, I advise that their rabbis be forbidden to teach henceforth on pain of loss of life and limb.[14]

With both Protestants and Catholics directly opposed to Jewish settlement and security, the succeeding centuries were not any brighter than the previous ones.

Obviously, persecution of the Jews did not fade at the end of the Reformation, when the Age of Enlightenment began pervading European culture. Before the atrocities of German Nazis during World War II, countries such as Poland passed laws making Sunday a compulsory day of rest, attempting to coerce Jews into Christian behavior. Furthermore, when Jews pleaded with the world to return to their homeland of Israel, much of the world balked at the endeavor, not on political grounds, but by religious reasoning. Pope Pius X, after meeting with Zionist leader Theodor Herzl, wrote, "I know, it is disagreeable to see the Turks in possession of our Holy Places. We simply have to put up with it. But to sanction the Jewish wish to occupy these sites, that we cannot do. . . . The Jews have not recognized our Lord, therefore we cannot recognize the Jewish people. . . . If you go to Palestine and your people settle there, you will find us clergy and churches ready to baptize you all."[15]

Thus, along with Hitler's belief in a superior race, the genocidal holocaust of World War II was in part enraged by the theological holocaust of more than a thousand years of anti-Semitic medieval Christian theology. Though it must be noted that some popes and bishops fought for the rights of Jews, organized Christianity in large part was guilty of advocating, or at least accepting, certain prejudicial presuppositions against God's chosen people. Only after the war, when the treatment of the Jews became fully known, did the Church change its tenor. In 2000, Pope John Paul II visited Jerusalem and left the following prayer at the Western Wall:

> God of our fathers,
> you chose Abraham and his descendants
> to bring your Name to the Nations:
> we are deeply saddened
> by the behavior of those
> who in the course of history
> have caused these children of yours to suffer,
> and asking your forgiveness
> we wish to commit ourselves
> to genuine brotherhood
> with the people of the Covenant.[16]

So began another benchmark of history, away from the Inquisitions of the past and toward a more biblical model for the future. Indeed, in the New Testament epistle to the Romans, the apostle Paul explicitly devotes much of his energies in reminding the reader that God has not forgotten his chosen people (Romans 9–11). His heart is poured out for those who share a common bond of heritage, as Paul himself is Jewish. Paul's desire that he be "cursed and cut off from Christ for the sake of my brothers" (Romans 9:3) illustrates the unwavering compassion the apostle had for his Jewish kinsmen.

While much of Israel has rejected Jesus Christ, the Savior does not desire to reject them. The unconditional covenant which God made with Israel (Genesis 12) will one day be restored as Jews recognize the Messiah who died for them. Those who call upon Christ will inherit the kingdom of God (Romans 10:13). The gospel, first given to the Jews (Romans 1:16), will once again be accepted by many Jews (Revelation 7) at the consummation of the age. In the meanwhile, the duty of the Christian is to pray for the Jews, not to persecute them.

Declaring Jihad on the Muslims

[Colonel Vujadin Popovic told me] women had to be deported to Kladanj and the men had to be separated and temporarily

detained. When I asked him what would happen then, he said
that all balija [derogatory name for Muslims] had to be killed.[17]
—Momir Nikolic, a senior Bosnian Serb officer
testifying on the slaughter of Muslims at Srebrenica

Three canes and a crutch were found near a shallow grave hastily
dug by soldiers attempting to cover up an atrocious act committed
against humanity. In July 1995, an all-to-familiar situation surrounded
the small Muslim town of Srebrenica, Bosnia-Herzegovina. While the
United Nations' envoy cowardly stood by and watched, Christian Serbs
rounded up all Muslim males in the supposed U.N. protected "safe
area" and sent them off to their death only a few kilometers away.

One by one or in groups, thousands were efficiently executed—
with only a handful able to escape the horrific scene. In three days,
more than six thousand people perished at the hands of those who
hoped to remove Bosnian Muslim presence from what they believed
should be a Serbian Christian territory. Most of those massacred were
unarmed civilians; some were elderly or crippled men. This was the
scene of Europe's worst case of genocide since the Holocaust of World
War II. And it was committed by those who identified themselves as
Christians.

Muslims have not been immune from the danger and onslaught of
Christian persecution throughout their thirteen-hundred-year history.
As early as the ninth century, popes guaranteed the forgiveness of sin
and the blessedness of heaven for all Christian warriors who battled
the infidels, that is, those who warred against the Roman Catholic
Church. In 847, Pope Leo IV promised Frankish forces, "Now we hope
that none of you will be slain, but we wish you to know that the kingdom of heaven will be given as a reward to those who shall be killed in
this war. For the Omnipotent knows that they lost their lives fighting
for the truth of the faith, for the preservation of their country, and the
defense of Christians."[18]

In essence, Christianity took on a distinctively Islamic flavor,
promising the same heavenly reward as provided in the Qur'an (3:169–
171). This pledge, used against various religious groups, found its

culmination in the Crusades. When Urban II declared "*Deus Volt!*" (God wills it!) at the Council of Clarmont (1095), he began an era of slaughter still considered one of the lowest moments of Roman Catholic history.

In one such case, when thousands of Muslims were captured at the Battle of Acre (1191), the joyous savagery was striking. Led by King Richard the Lionheart of England, Christian troops hoped to take revenge for those slain in battle. When the hostages were procured, the Christian warriors eagerly awaited their opportunity. But the Muslim prisoners were counted as collateral by Richard, hoping to swap them for Christian prisoners.

Richard gave Saladin, the legendary general of the Muslim troops who recaptured Jerusalem, a decisive deadline for the exchange. When Saladin was slow to fulfill his end of the bargain, the Christian soldiers, without any hesitation, carried out the swift decapitation of twenty-seven hundred Muslims. One contemporary document expounded, "King Richard always hoped to overwhelm the Turks completely, to crush their impudent arrogance, to confound the Moslem law, and to vindicate Christianity. On the Friday next after the feast of the Assumption of Blessed Mary . . . he ordered . . . the vanquished Turkish hostages be led out of the city and decapitated. Without delay his assistants rushed up and quickly carried out the order. They gave heartfelt thanks, since with the approval of divine grace, they were taking vengeance in kind for the death of the Christians whom these people had slaughtered with the missiles of their bows and ballistas."[19]

Granted, wars always deal a terrible blow to the losers, but the jubilant ecstasy and expeditious fashion in which the orders were carried out cannot go unnoticed. These warriors gladly and gratefully beheaded these men, believing their commission came from the very mouth of God. Not only was this a gleeful retaliation, but a complete justification of their faith. God was demonstrably on their side guiding their swords.

However, victories against the Muslims were scarce after the First Crusade (1095–1099) as Christians failed to recapture the Holy Land or Eastern lands once dominant in Christian witness. Indeed, in 1453, Turks captured one of the holiest cities in all of Christendom, Constantinople. If God had been on their side during victory, his voice was silent in defeat.

The one triumphal moment for Rome at the end of the Middle Ages was the reconquest of Spain from all vestiges of Moorish rule. For nearly eight centuries, North African Muslims commanded much of the Iberian Peninsula through *Shar²ia* (Islamic) law. Weakened by various political divisions, Muslims were exiled into North Africa at the end of the fifteen century. Those not forced out of the country were baptized. All of Spain was once again a Christian country.

For the next four centuries, Muslims went on the defensive against Western colonialism. Muslim-populated lands were placed under the flags of European nations. Illustrated by the Berlin Conference of 1884, colonial powers divided Africa among themselves. Great Britain claimed most of North Africa while France took the west and equatorial plain. Italy claimed Somalia and Ethiopia while Belgium settled for the Congo. Muslims regard this mark of colonialism as a continuation of the Crusades. Indeed, the disdain of political persecution is still quite palatable in the mouths—and memorable in the minds—of Muslims.

A Modern Outcry: The Removal of Religious Liberty and the Resurgence of Religious Toleration

Many people are surprised to find out that the doctrine of religious liberty in the West is more seriously threatened by governmental sanctions and regulations today than at any point during the past one hundred years. The gravest example in Europe is France, a country which has targeted religious liberty more strenuously than any other Western nation. The 2001 About-Picard legislation, passed in reaction to the 1994 mass suicide of members of the Order of the Solar Temple, places strict yet ambiguous restrictions on religious activities and worship practices.

The International Religious Freedom Report of 2002, published in cooperation with the United States Department of State, gave a synopsis of some of the potential criminal offenses for which members of a religious organization could be charged and tried. It includes "endangering life or the physical or psychological well-being of a person; placing minors at mortal risk; violation of another person's freedom, dignity, or identity; the illegal practice of medicine or pharmacology; false advertising; and fraud or falsifications."[20]

Fearing that persecution was only a matter of time, Christians, Muslims, Jews, and other religious groups banded together to protest the legislation. Sadly, their fears are now being confirmed. Since the law passed, the government has subjected several Jehovah's Witnesses and Christian Science organizations to a 60 percent tax on all received revenue. Local courts are now debating whether Muslim girls may wear their headscarves in public school as a religious expression. France is imposing its antagonism against all religion on those most devout in their faith. The new religion of no religion is suffocating traditional religions.

But France is not alone in its endeavor to curb the freedom of religion within its borders. Note the following list of transgressors against freedom:

- *Belarus:* The government continues to favor the Russian Orthodox Church, forbidding the registration of many religious groups, especially evangelicals. Unregistered bodies may not buy property or conduct religious services. The president of the country, Alexander Lukashenko, declared, "The State has always stayed and will stay beside the [Orthodox] church, which brings good to the people."
- *Spain:* In 1999, the Salvation Army was denied a permit to build a children's center. The local government rejected the permit, stating the organization was a "destructive sect." The national government advised the local officials that their conclusion was wrong, but only because the Army was registered with the government.
- *Australia:* In 2002, the province of Victoria passed the Racial and Religious Tolerance Act, outlawing any speech that would

incite hate against another religious group. Almost immediately, the Islamic Council of Victoria sued Catch the Fire Ministries for derogatory remarks toward Islam made at one of their conferences. At the time of this publication, the case is still pending.[21]

In the situations cited above, the move against religious liberty has been stimulated by religious illiteracy and political correctness. Fewer Westerners now appreciate or understand the profound doctrine of religious liberty since religion is at best peripheral in their lives. To many, fanaticism is a term used to describe anyone who practices their faith devoutly or more negatively stated, excessively.

Regarding political correctness philosophy, cultural taboos are now overriding constitutional rights. The promulgation of tolerance is more important than the possibility of truth. The assumption of the new West is that disagreement will lead to violence. Hence, many Western nations are debating the viability of hate-speech laws. In the fall of 2003, Canada's House of Commons passed a law, sponsored by Svend Robinson, an openly homosexual member of the Canadian Parliament, which criminalizes public expression against homosexuals. The bill, repudiated by both liberal free speech advocates and religious conservatives, could be used to judge the Bible as hate literature. In fact, a Saskatchewan man has already been fined by a provincial tribunal for placing an advertisement in the local paper with references from Scripture to homosexuality.[22]

The Final Word

In the end, freedom of worship may be hindered, but it cannot truly be taken away since it is God who endowed each person with the ability to worship him. This is not to say that God accepts all forms of worship, but all forms of worship arise from a drive instilled by God. There is no license from Scripture to act violently toward others. Rather, Christians are to protect religious freedom as a right from God. Only God as Creator and Sustainer has the prerogative or ability to judge someone's soul.

Religious liberty is not only one of the basic freedoms of human-kind; it is, in fact, *the central freedom.* Without this liberty, all other freedoms will evaporate. John Leland, the eighteenth-century Baptist preacher who led the charge in convincing the American Founding Fathers of the righteousness of religious liberty, may have concluded the matter most poignantly:

> Government has no more to do with the religious opinions of men, than it has with the principles of mathematics. Let every man speak freely without fear, maintain the principles that he believes, worship according to his own faith, either one God, three Gods, no God, or twenty Gods; and let government protect him in so doing.[23]

May a renewed call go out to all nations proclaiming: "Let the heathen worship!"

Notes

1. John Oyer, "The Writings of Luther Against the Anabaptists," *Mennonite Quarterly Review* (April 1953), 30:108.
2. William Estep, *The Anabaptist Story,* 3d ed. (Grand Rapids: Eerdmans, 1996), 85.
3. H. Wayne Pipkin and John H. Yoder, *Balthasar Hubmaier, Theologian of Anabaptism* (Scottdale, Pa.: Herald, 1989), 62.
4. Estep, *Anabaptist Story,* 103.
5. Roland H. Bainton, *The Travail of Religious Liberty* (Philadelphia: Westminster, 1951), 234–35.
6. Ibid., 251.
7. H. Leon McBeth, *The Baptist Heritage* (Nashville: Broadman, 1987), 252–69.
8. Jacques-Auguste de Thou, *The History of the Bloody Massacres of the Protestants in France in the Year of Our Lord, 1572* (London: n.p., 1674), at nationalhistoryday.org/03_educators/2001-2002curbook/new_page_32.htm. Accessed December 26, 2003.

9. See Leonard Verduin, *The Reformers and Their Stepchildren* (Sarasota, Fla.: Christian Hymnary, 1991), 131, where Verduin provides this concise summary: "[The Cathars] blazed a new trail, by repudiating the Constantinian change, by reinstituting the Church of believers with conductal distinctiveness, by driving away the sword function out of the Church, by re-introducing Church discipline in which excommunication was the ultimate penalty."

10. H. J. Schroeder, *Disciplinary Decrees of the General Councils: Text, Translation and Commentary* (St. Louis: B. Herder, 1937), 78–127. The original term for Arab Muslim, *Saracén*, has been replaced with its popular designation.

11. Jerry Darring, "A Catholic Timeline of Events Relating to Jews, Judaism, Anti-Semitism, and the Holocaust from the Third Century to the Beginning of the Third Millennium," at shc.edu/theolibrary/resources/timeline.htm. Accessed December 26, 2003. This Web site is the home of Spring Hill College, Mobile, Alabama, known as the "Jesuit College of the South."

12. Ibid. This statement was made by Gregory of Nyssa, one of the Cappadocian Fathers who defended the deity of Jesus Christ against Arians in the fourth century.

13. Ibid.

14. Martin Luther, *The Jews and Their Lies* (1543), at fordham.edu/halsall/source/luther-jews.html. Accessed December 26, 2003.

15. Darring, "A Catholic Timeline."

16. Ibid.

17. Marlise Simons, "Behind the Srebrenica Massacre," *New York Times* (13 October 2003), at iht.com/articles/113341.html. Accessed December 27, 2003.

18. Oliver J. Thatcher and Edgar Holmes McNeal, eds., *A Source Book for Medieval History* (New York: Scribners, 1905), 511–12.

19. James Brundage, *The Crusades: A Documentary History* (Milwaukee: Marquette University Press, 1962), 183–84.

20. Bureau of Democracy, Human Rights, and Labor, "International Religious Freedom Report 2002," at state.gov/g/drl/rls/irf/2002/13938.htm. Accessed December 27, 2003.

21. Jewel Toppsfield, "Vilification test case heats up," (12 December 2003), at news.com.au/common/story_page/0,4057,7579377%255E1702,00.html. Accessed December 27, 2003.

22. Art Moore, "Bible as hate speech bill passes," 18 September 2003, at worldnetdaily.com/news/article.asp?ARTICLE_ID=346711. Accessed December 27, 2003.

23. McBeth, *Baptist Heritage,* 275.

Chapter 10

THE CALL OF THE CRUSADERS

Learning from History

By military standards, the First Crusade was a successful excursion. Jerusalem, after the fall of the Turks, was established as a feudal kingdom of the Latin Empire, with the cooperation of the participating countries. From a papal viewpoint, the Crusade effectively reestablished the Church at Rome as the primary sovereign in foreign affairs. Yet the question remains: With such a quantum shift in polity and doctrine, and indeed in the very essence of the Christian mission, what are the overriding implications of *holy war?*

As a summary of this epoch in Christian history, the historian may find some positive influences. The classical Greek and Roman cultures were rediscovered by the Latin kingdom, as the Roman Catholic kingdom was inundated with the influences of the Middle Eastern world. This rediscovery of Hellenistic thought helped bring about the Renaissance, as theologians and philosophers began to read Socrates, Plato, Aristotle, and their brethren.

Sadly, however, the negative influence of the Crusade is much worse. Rather than instituting peace between the Eastern and Western Churches (with the West, under Urban, responding to the call from the Eastern Church under Alexis), warfare increased, due to the brutality of the Crusaders and the duplicity of Alexis. Each watched the other with a jaundiced eye, wary of any betrayal.

The Crusade did little to settle the disputes between Muslim and Christian empires. Neither was willing to concede defeat, and the subsequent Crusades were dismal failures, with their nadir in the carnage of the Children's Crusade. Muslims ultimately conquered the Christian bastions established after Godfrey's induction as ruler in Jerusalem.

Deicide and the Blood Libel: The Jews and the Crusading Holocaust

The worst effects of the Crusade were the internal and external ravages caused by the crusading movement. The savagery with which the Christians treated the Jewish population forever scarred Judeo-Christian relations. Crusaders called the Jews "Christ-killers," and sentenced them to death for the crime of *Deicide:* murdering God. As one historian notes, the Jews were given the option: "*Embrace the Cross or die!*" The savagery that followed has scarred the Jewish community to this day:

> [Twelve thousand] Jews in the Rhine Valley alone were killed as the first Crusade passed through. Some Jewish writers re-fer to these events as the "*first holocaust.*" Once the army reached Jerusalem and broke through the city walls, they slaughtered all the inhabitants that they could find (men, women, children, newborns). After locating about 6,000 Jews holed up in the synagogue, they set the building on fire; the Jews were burned alive. The Crusaders found that about 30,000 Muslims had fled to the al Aqsa Mosque. The latter were also slaughtered without mercy.[1]

To further inflame the warriors, the "blood libel myth" was spread. This thesis taught that the Jews committed ritualistic acts of torture on Christians, in order to stem the tide of Jewish conversions to Christianity. During the Crusades, a particularly virulent strain of this myth began an urban legend in Western Europe:

> In 1144, an unfounded rumor began in eastern England, that Jews had kidnapped a Christian child, tied him to a cross,

stabbed his head to simulate Jesus' crown of thorns, killed him, drained his body completely of blood, and mixed the blood into matzos [unleavened bread] at time of Passover. The rumor arose from a former Jew, Theobald, who had become a Christian monk. He said that Jewish representatives gathered each year in Narbonne, France. They decided in which city a Christian child would be sacrificed. The boy became known as St. William of Norwich. Many people made pilgrimages to his tomb and claimed that miracles had resulted from appeals to St. William. The myth shows a complete lack of understanding of Judaism. Aside from the prohibition of killing innocent persons, the Torah specifically forbids the drinking or eating of any form of blood in any quantity. However, reality never has had much of an impact on blood libel myths. This rumor lasted for many centuries; even today it has not completely disappeared.[2]

By the thirteenth century, even the Vatican was issuing such accusations, as found in the example of Pope Innocent IV (ca. 1274) and others:

Holy shrines were erected to honor innocent Christian victims, and well into the twentieth century, churches throughout Europe displayed knives and other instruments that Jews purportedly used for these rituals. Caricatures of hunchbacked Jews with horns and fangs were depicted in works of art and carved into stone decorating bridges. Proclaimed by parish priests to be the gospel truth, each recurrence of the blood libel charge added to its credence, thus prompting yet more accusations.[3]

One of the prevailing themes of the Crusade was the certainty that Christians could be manipulated for both political and economic purposes. Those convinced that the excursion was to result in eternal salvation were often bent on inflicting as much destruction as possible, so as to cement their prominence in the movement. Thus, the butchery often enacted by the soldiers was not only in the *name* of Christianity; it was for the *sake* of eternity, the belief that God would bless such ignominious deeds. Since the Jewish community was perceived as being wealthy, they became an obvious target. Though Pope Urban may not have realized the extent of such a proclamation at the time, the call for Crusade was ultimately little better than the Muslim doctrine of jihad in the name of Jesus Christ.

Romanticized Sacred Violence

It is important to note the influence the summons of the Crusade had on the replication and doctrinal trends in Church history. There has been an enormous bifurcation in opinion, as literature records. As one author writes:

> The results of the Crusades are impressive mainly for their destructiveness. To begin with, there was the enormous expenditure of blood and suffering on all sides. Of the peasant mobs that set out for the Holy Land in 1096, none ever reached their destination: either they despaired and went home; or they were murdered by robbers and bandits; or they died of disease or malnutrition; or if they got as far as Asia Minor, they were massacred by the Turks.[4]

Yet from the other end of the spectrum, authors have a tendency to either ignore the Crusade movement and its effects on society and political order,[5] or to romanticize the era with tales of gallantry and valor. Winston Churchill, in his famous *History of English Speaking Peoples,* wrote:

> The Byzantine Emperor appealed to the West for help, and in 1095 Pope Urban II, who had long dreamt of recovering Jerusalem for Christendom, called on the chivalry of Europe to take the Cross. . . . Western Christendom, so long the victim

of invaders, had at last struck back and won its first great footing in the Eastern world.[6]

Apart from the fray of contemporary ethics, it would be important to investigate the immediate effects of the Crusade on the Church and the political arena. The metamorphosis of the doctrines of the Church eventually led to the apotheosis of the Middle Ages, the Lateran Council of 1215. The Church was perceived to have become a participant in political and military confrontation, rather than a mediator of them.

The Church as Salvific: Mediated Grace

If three of the mottos of the Reformation were *Sola scriptura* (only the Bible), *Sola fide* (only faith), and *Sola gratia* (only grace), then the resulting underlying thesis for all of these themes was *Sola persona* (only the individual). The concept of the priesthood of the believer, and individual responsibility was a foreign one to the crusader. Not only were the masses illiterate, and therefore unable to deduce the implications of Scripture, but they were wholly dependent upon supposedly learned leaders in the Church to care for their souls.

Thus, when Urban stepped to the pulpit and proclaimed that all would be absolved if they took up the cause of reclaiming Jerusalem, the people saw within the claim instantaneous forgiveness in a world in which assurance of salvation had been regarded as impossible. Urban, completely aware of what this promise would mean to those who heard it, noted:

> It is plain that good meditation leads to doing good work and that *good work wins salvation of the soul*. But, if it is good to mean well, it is better, after reflection, to carry out the good intention. So, it is best to win salvation through action worthy of the soul to be saved. Let each and everyone, therefore, reflect upon the good, that he makes better in fulfillment, so that, deserving it, he might finally receive the best, which does not diminish in eternity.[7]

The implication was clear: If one truly meditates upon my offer, then he will clearly submit to the movement. This submission will win salvation through a heart committed to the "cause of Christ."

The response, therefore, was somewhat understandable. In order to gain entrance into heaven, the soldier would not dare abdicate his faith to save his life. Apparently, the logic was clear to many. Fulcher, not normally given to overstatement, became passionate about these terms:

> Oh, how worthy and delightful to all of us who saw those beautiful crosses, either silken or woven of gold, or of any material, which the pilgrims sewed on the shoulders of their woolen cloaks or cassocks by the command of the Pope, after taking the vow to go. To be sure, God's soldiers, who were making themselves ready for battle for his honor, ought to have marked and fortified with the sign of victory. And so by embroidering the symbol of the cross on their clothing in recognition of their faith, in the end they won the True Cross itself. They imprinted the ideal so that they might attain the reality of the ideal.[8]

Even among the priests, the transformation was becoming evident. Their ability to absolve the soldier brought them obvious high regard, and they too were compelled to join in the battle for the sake of the Holy Land. As the spiritual descendants of the Levites, the nobility of their sacrifice would incite the prayers of the highest "servants" in the land. The compulsion was clear.

The Roman Church was able to institute the sacramental and penitential systems within the Church, in order to systematize the steps by which the searching soul would find such salvation. The Church would be the *agent* of salvation. *Penance* through the Roman Church came to be the worthy substitute for repentance.[9]

The Church as Adversary: Jews and Muslims

There was no question of Urban's contempt for those who held the Holy Land hostage. Yet within his speech, another trend was established when he escalated this unified contempt for the Muslims into an armed confrontation. The sins of the Muslim populace were not only aimed at the Christian world, but at Jesus Christ himself. He noted:

> Your own blood-brothers, your companions, your associates (for you are sons of the same Christ and the same Church) are either subjected in their inherited homes to other masters, or are driven from them, or they come as beggars among us; or, which is far worse, they are flogged and exiled as slaves for sale in their own land. Christian blood, redeemed by the blood of Christ, has been shed, and Christian flesh, akin to the flesh of Christ, has been subjected to unspeakable degradation and servitude. Everywhere in those cities there is sorrow, everywhere misery, everywhere groaning (I say it with a sigh). The churches in which divine mysteries were celebrated in olden times are now, to our sorrow, used as stables for the animals of these people! . . . The blessed Peter first presided as Bishop at Antioch. . . . The priesthood of God has been ground down into dust. The sanctuary of God (unspeakable shame!) is everywhere profaned.[10]

The inference was explicit. The sin of the Muslim was not just directed at the living Christian world, but at the holy places of God, and indeed, at Jesus Christ himself. The same blood shed at the hands of the Turks coursed through the veins of Jesus due to his Jewish lineage. Urban called for the crusader to defend Jesus Christ, which could only be viewed as a holy and worthy venture.

Within his admonition, Urban also entreated crusaders to halt the advent of any who stood in the way of their "holy work." His summons signed the death warrant for many Jews. Though Urban makes numerous references to the Old Testament characters and places, those who denied the holiness of Jesus Christ were now herded within one category—the pollution of paganism in Jerusalem. Therefore, a wholesale slaughter of the Jews was instigated, which injures evangelism

among Jews to this day. This anti-Semitism was graphically described
in a detailing of the massacre in one particular battle:

> At the beginning of summer in the same year in which Peter
> and Gottschalk, after collecting an army, had set out, there
> assembled in like fashion a large and innumerable host of
> Christians from diverse kingdoms and lands; namely from
> the realms of France, England, Flanders, and Lorraine. . . . I
> know not whether by a judgment of the Lord, or by some
> error of mind, they rose in a spirit of cruelty against Jewish
> people scattered throughout the cities and slaughtered them
> without mercy, especially in the Kingdom of Lorraine, assert-
> ing it to be the beginning of their expedition and their duty
> against the enemies of the Christian faith. This slaughter of
> Jews was done first by citizens of Cologne. These suddenly
> fell upon a small band of Jews and severely wounded and killed
> many; they destroyed the houses and synagogues of the Jews
> and divided among themselves a very large amount of money.
> When the Jews saw this cruelty, about two hundred in the
> silence of the night began flight by boat to Neuss. The pil-
> grims and crusaders discovered them, and after taking away
> all their possessions, inflicted on them similar slaughter leav-
> ing not even one alive.[11]

Conversely, the Jews and Muslims who had long fought over the
use and claims to Jerusalem now had a common antagonist—the
Christians. Both suffered at the hands of the crusading forces, and
therefore justly developed a mistrust of the Christian community that
continues. The alleged peaceful occupation by Saladin during the Third
Crusade has always been held in comparison to the brutality of the
Christian forces in the First Crusade. Lewis postulates:

> A major accession of strength resulted from the emancipa-
> tion of Jews in central and western Europe and their conse-
> quent entry into the universities. Jewish scholars brought up

the Jewish religion and trained in the Hebrew language found Islam and Arabic far easier to understand than did their Christian colleagues, and were, moreover, even less affected by nostalgia for the Crusades, preoccupation with imperial policy, or the desire to convert the "heathen." Jewish scholars like Gustav Weil, Ignaz Goldziher, and others played a key role in the development of an objective, nonpolemical and positive evaluation of Islamic civilization.[12]

The Church as Ambassador: Christian Jihad

Was the major aim of the First Crusade to seek the conversion of the occupying forces of Islam in Jerusalem? If, as Urban preached at Clermont, this was the chief purpose, then in retrospect this desire was frustrated. Indeed, the subsequent millennium has been irreducibly harmed by the slaughter carried out by alleged Christian warriors.

Certainly the papal forces sometimes sought to convert the heathen, but their methods were flawed. They sought to force conversion by the sword, in a type of Christian jihad. As logic dictates that forced conversion is no conversion at all, one is perplexed by the tragically misguided and brutally vicious crusaders.

Narratives of forced public conversions abound in the Crusade literature. "Mora Zaida," the daughter-in-law of the Muslim leader Seville, was forced into baptism prior to the Crusade launch, and subsequently became a concubine of Alfonso VI.[13] The twelfth-century African Muslim historian Abu Marwan ʿAbd al-Malik adds that many Muslims, including the sister of a Muslim military leader, were forced to convert and be baptized during the siege of Majorca in 1114.[14]

The monks, hermits, and preachers of the Crusades often had an errant if sincere belief that the conquest of occupied Jerusalem would allow for mission among the Islamic community. As an example, the hermit Anastasius traveled to Spain in 1074 to preach, under the direct orders of Pope Gregory VII. Persuaded by Abbot Hugh of Cluny that preaching to the Saracens (Arab Muslims) was profitable, Anastasius returned to Cluny after the Crusades began, noting that bloodshed did not enable proclamation.[15]

The Church as Material Steward: Temporal Obsession

Prior to the Crusade movement, many who sought holiness often retreated from desire for material gain. Peter Damiani (1001–1072) reflected this prominent teaching when he wrote: "The world is so filthy with vices that any holy mind is befouled even by thinking of it."[16] Yet the advent of the Crusade brought about a new obsession with the temporal realm. The Church, now a guardian of real estate, was interested in protecting "holy places," but also in advancing its interests in these places. Both the land and power that came with the land became increasingly important, and thus instituted a new venue for the Church. David Herlihy writes:

> In summoning the first crusade at Clermont in southern France in 1095, Pope Urban II is reported to have told the assembled knights that because they were too many for their narrow land, shut in between the mountains and the sea, they murdered and devoured one another, and therefore should betake themselves to Jerusalem, the navel of the world, and not allow concern for their families or possessions to detain them. The church too was working to turn the gaze of these warriors to the outer world.[17]

The effort to reclaim the land, and therefore temporal power, was not without supporters. Claude Jenkins, the former chaplain to the Archbishop of Canterbury, poignantly noted:

> There is a false antithesis when [one is] told that the sieges and battles and sufferings of the Crusades do not properly find a place in Church history at all, as though the Church were concerned only with men's ends while the means to attain

them and the secular activities amid which they are pursued remained outside their purview.[18]

To Jenkins, a holistic view of humanity and the world stimulated the Crusades. This posed a problem for him, however, when he attempted to rationalize the methods by which the crusader cause was advanced. Crusaders showed a manifest disregard for human life, and the rationalization of their use of force could be stated: "Since these people are obviously pagan, and therefore antagonistic to the things of God, we are therefore justified to use whatever force available to carry out the protection of the cause of Christ." Not only does the end justify the means, but the means are actually instruments by which the end can be furthered.

Such a schematic does have detractors. Paul Tillich, in *The Interpretation of History*, writes:

> Force becomes distorted when the presupposition of meaningful power, the implicit acceptance of the structure of power, has disappeared, and power tries to maintain itself by means of the apparatus of power standing at its disposal. The worst excesses of force are to be found in situations wherein the inner foundation has been taken away from power. When force becomes isolated from power, whose function it is, it soon dissolves, for force thrives on acquiescence to it, even on the part of those who are subjected to it.[19]

For Urban, the force by which the crusaders would expel the Muslim forces was not only necessary (and by inference proper), but the work was actually a fulfillment of prophecy. The crusader was going to carry out the mandate of God to spare the Holy Land. Even liberal theologians, who have little claim to biblical truth, can see through this fallacy.

Such an argument was not lost on the subsequent crusaders and their recruiters. In attempting to garner the troops for the Second Crusade, Bernard of Clairvaux wrote:

Now is the acceptable time, now is the day of abundant salvation. The earth is shaken because the Lord of heaven is losing his land. . . . [A]nd now, for our sins, the enemy of the Cross has begun to lift his sacrilegious head there, and to devastate with the sword that blessed land. . . . [N]ow, O mighty soldiers, O men of war, you have a cause for which you can fight without danger to your souls; a cause in which to conquer is glorious and for which to die is gain.[20]

The obsession with power thus blinded the eyes and motives of the crusaders.

Thus, the implications of the Crusade movement on subsequent generations reached into both the political and ecclesiastical worlds. All arenas of faith and practice were transformed by the paradigm. Along with these radical shifts within Christendom, the crusaders forever changed the interaction between the church and the world.

An Apology Too Late?
The Reconciliation Walk 1996–1998

In 1996, about 150 Christians attempted to build bridges into the lives of Muslims and Jews by tracing the steps of the crusaders and publicly apologizing for the acts of carnage performed in Jesus Christ's name. On Easter Sunday, they arrived at a mosque in Turkey.

The first crusaders set off for Jerusalem in 1096-APR, from the cathedral in Cologne. Exactly 900 years later, on Easter Sunday, about 150 walkers departed from the same cathedral. Their first stop was a Turkish Mosque and teaching center. Their leader explained that the walkers had come to apologize for the atrocities committed in the name of Christ during the Crusades. Then they read a letter of apology in German, Turkish and English. They were "greeted with loud, sustained applause." The Imam responded: "When I heard the nature of your message, I was astonished and filled with hope. I thought to myself, 'whoever had this idea must have had an epiphany, a visit from God himself.' It is my wish that this project should become a very great success."[21]

This unique attempt at reconciliation was greeted with amazement by many Jews and Muslims. The account continues:

Following the ancient routes of the Crusades, one team passed through France, Switzerland, Austria, Italy, Slovenia Croatia, Montenegro, Albania, Macedonia and Greece. A second team set out from Germany and passed through Slovakia, Hungary and Bulgaria. The teams met at Istanbul, Turkey on October 10, 1996. The Deputy Mufti of Istanbul, the Chief Rabbi, the Representative of the Ecumenical Patriarch (head of the Orthodox Church) and the Deputy Mayer welcomed the team with warmth and appreciation. "*In towns and villages, people spilled out of their houses and applauded the team as they passed.*" They visited countless cities, towns, and villages in Turkey during 1996 and 1997.[22]

Over the course of two years, 2,500 Christians from twenty-seven countries participated in this corporate act of repentance. Many wore hats and shirts emblazoned with the words "I apologize" in Arabic and Hebrew.

Was the apology a case of "too little, too late"?

Certainly the Crusade period, and indeed all acts of forced conversion, have done no great service to the fulfillment of the Great Commission. The chronicles in this book have assessed deep chasms of distrust that developed in direct response to some of the most evil acts carried out "in Jesus' name." The authentic Christian cannot defend the Crusades, the Inquisitions, or other horrible movements in Church history. Genuine authenticity demands a clear and unapologetic stance: God never called for a Christian army and Jesus Christ never promised salvation by bloodshed. As the official apology read countless times during the Reconciliation Walk stated:

Nine hundred years ago, our forefathers carried the name of Jesus Christ in battle across the Middle East. Fueled by fear, greed and hatred, they betrayed the name of Christ by conducting themselves in a manner contrary to his wishes and character. The Crusaders lifted the banner of the Cross above your people. By this act they corrupted its true meaning of reconciliation, forgiveness and selfless love.

On the anniversary of the First Crusade we also carry the name of Christ. We wish to retrace the footsteps of the Crusaders in apology for their deeds and in demonstration of the true meaning of the Cross. We deeply regret the atrocities committed in the name of Christ by our predecessors. We renounce greed, hatred and fear, and condemn all violence done in the name of Jesus Christ.

Where they were motivated by hatred and prejudice, we offer love and brotherhood. Jesus the Messiah came to give life. Forgive us for allowing his name to be associated with death. Please accept again the true meaning of the Messiah's words:

"The Spirit of the Lord is upon me, because he has anointed me to bring good news to the poor. He has sent me to proclaim release to the captives and recovery of sight to the blind, to let the oppressed go free, to proclaim the year of the Lord's favor."[23]

Whether the reader would carry a banner or retrace the steps of the crusaders, the apology can resonate throughout Christianity. If we are seriously committed to evangelism, we must learn the lessons from our history. Still, an apology for events that came to pass nearly a millennium ago can deem hollow, especially in regard to granting or obtaining forgiveness.

A Brutality That Justifies: The Cross in Light of History

Let's not forget the primary motivating factor for both Christian and Muslim crusaders. Risking their lives in the Crusades was the guarantee of God's forgiveness if they shed the blood of the infidel—or lost their own lives in the process. God's command to forgive others was usurped and abrogated by the desire to be forgiven. This selfish ambition was unacceptable then—as it should be now.

Nevertheless, hatred, prejudice, and bloodshed will continue sporadically or vociferously if the dilemma of forgiveness is not resolved in each individual. Ironically, forgiveness can come through brutality—but not by blood spilled by ordinary men. Instead, the blood shed by Jesus Christ on the Cross, an event of unequaled violence ordained by God himself, is the only true solution.

Mel Gibson's *The Passion of the Christ,* an admittedly graphic portrayal of the crucifixion based on the gospel of John, was recently released in movie theaters worldwide. Within the mire of reviews on the movie, the most unfounded criticism is that the film is *too* gruesome and bloodthirsty.

When one reads the narrative of the crucifixion from the four gospels within the Christian Scriptures, it becomes apparent that Gibson's version of the crucifixion is honest. If anything, Gibson held back from showing how bad it was.

If someone has a problem with the depictions of violence and bloodshed in *The Passion of the Christ,* they also are struggling with the biblical account—an account far more moving than any visual portrayal can illustrate.

The extent of the descriptions within the Gospels is necessary and intentional. The four writers of the Gospels go into great detail to remind the reader of the incredible sacrifice the Son of God made to pay the penalty of sin and demonstrate God's love toward humanity.

In comparison, the amount of pain suffered by Jesus Christ can be correlated to the extent of forgiveness you and I may receive. A complete sacrifice gives complete forgiveness. But that forgiveness is not obtained by a human work or war or peace, but only through the acceptance of that terrible sacrifice made *by* Jesus Christ *for* each person who will believe in him.

The shedding of more blood isn't required. Jesus Christ's spilled blood is enough. His sacrifice was both justified and justifies.

It is justified to appease the wrath of God.

It also justifies, forgiving men and women of their sins, no matter how gruesome their pasts have been.

May we be more committed than ever to embrace and live out the meaning of that Good News.

Notes

1. Accounts are ubiquitous. Citation from religioustolerance.org/chr_cru1.htm. Accessed on November 11, 2003.
2. M. I. Dimont, *Jews, God and History* (New York: Mentor, 1994), 235, as cited in religioustolerance.org/jud_blib2.htm. Accessed on November 11, 2003.
3. Ibid.
4. Jeffrey Burton Russell, *A History of Medieval Christianity: Prophecy and Order* (Arlington Heights, Ill.: Harlan Davidson, 1968), 159.
5. Pope Duncan, Church historian and author, ignores the Crusades completely in *The Pilgrimage of Christianity* (Nashville: Broadman, 1965). Though Duncan does write of the Medieval period, his discussion dwells mainly on doctrinal shifts within the Roman Church.
6. Winston Churchill, *A History of English Speaking Peoples* (New York: Dodd, Mead, 1958), 179, 181. Churchill does discuss the negative ramifications of the Crusading Movement, but his writing clearly is part of the "means to an end" genre, justifying the excesses as a worthy loss for the footing gained in the lost regions.
7. Frances Rita Ryan, trans., *Fulcher of Chartres' A History of the Expedition to Jerusalem, 1095–1127* (Knoxville, Tenn.: University of Tennessee Press, 1927), 172. Emphasis is the author's.
8. Ibid., 30. Urban did not exclude those incapable of fighting. In fact, one chronicle notes his exemptions: "And we do not command or advise that the old or feeble, or those unfit for bearing arms, undertake this journey; nor ought women to set out at all, without their husbands or brothers or legal guardians. For such are more of a hindrance than aid, more of a burden than advantage. Let the rich aid the needy; and according to their wealth, let them take with them experienced soldiers.

The priests and clerks of any order are not to go without the consent of their bishop; for this journey would profit them nothing if they went without permission of these. Also it is not fitting that laymen should enter upon the pilgrimage without the blessing of their priests." Dana C. Munro, *Urban and the Crusaders* (Philadelphia: University of Pennsylvania Press, 1896), 8.

9. Alister McGraith traces this movement to the Vulgate translation of "the opening words of Jesus' ministry (Matthew 4:17) . . . 'do penance, for the kingdom of heaven is at hand.' This translation suggested that the coming of the kingdom of heaven had a direct connection with the sacrament of penance. . . . In other words, where the Vulgate seemed to refer to an outward practice (the sacrament of penance), Erasmus insisted that the reference was to an inward psychological attitude—that on 'being repentant.' Once more, an important justification of the sacramental system of the medieval church was challenged." Alister McGraith, *Christian Theology: An Introduction* (Oxford: Blackwell, 1994), 53.

10. *Recueil des historiens des croisades, Historiens occidentaux,* 5 vols. (Paris: Biblioteque, 1844–1895), 4:422.

11. Albert of Aix, *Chronicle,* in Edward Peters, ed., *The First Crusade* (Philadelphia: University of Pennsylvania Press, 1971), 102.

12. Martin Kramer, *The Jewish Discovery of Islam* (Tel Aviv: The Moshe Dayan Center, 1999), 2. In citing Bernard Lewis, Kramer also notes, "Jewish scholars were among the first to attempt to present Islam to European readers as Muslims themselves see it and to stress, to recognize, and indeed sometimes to romanticize the merits and achievements of Muslim civilization in its great days." Ibid.

13. Etienne Levi-Provencal, "La 'Mora Zaida,' femme d'Alphonse VI," *Islam d'Occident: Études d'histoire Medievale* (Paris: University, 1948), 137–51.

14. Menendez Pidal, *La Espana del Cid* (Paris: University, 1944), 1:315.

15. Noreen Hunt, *Cluny under Saint Hugh, 1049–1109* (London: Edward Arnold, 1967), 149.

16. As quoted in Alban G. Widgery, *Interpretations of History: Confucius to Toynbee* (London: George Allen & Unwin, 1961), 123.

17. David Herlihy, "Ecological Conditions and Demographic Change," in

One Thousand Years: Western Europe in the Middle Ages, ed. Richard L. DeMolen (Boston: Houghton Mifflin, 1974), 22.

18. Claude Jenkins, "The Religious Contribution of the Middle Ages," in *Medieval Contributions to Modern Civilization: A Series of Lectures Delivered at King's College University of London* (New York: Barnes and Noble, 1921), 46. The crusaders, to Jenkins, were simply human instruments that solved both a religious and political problem. Ibid., 49.

19. Paul Tillich, *The Interpretation of History* (New York: Charles Scribner's Sons, 1936), 193.

20. Bruno Scott James, ed., *The Letters of St. Bernard of Clairvaux* (Chicago: Henry Regnery, 1953), 461–62.

21. Worldwide media covered the event. This account is taken from religioustolerance.org/chr_cru1.htm. Accessed on November 12, 2003.

22. Ibid.

23. Ibid.

Appendix A

The Just War Criteria

Among true worshipers of God those wars are looked on
as peacemaking which are waged neither from aggran-
dizement nor cruelty but with the object of securing peace,
of repressing the evil and supporting the good.[1]

—Thomas Aquinas

So that the reader does not assume that this book is yet another in
a long line of antiviolence, pacifistic tomes, bent upon calling all
men to a polyannic peacefest, the authors have included this appendix as an explanation. While we vigorously refute the claims that the
Crusades were "God's work," we do not hold to a stance of absolute
pacifism. In fact, both of us are on record as supporting the wars in
Afghanistan and Iraq. We believe that President George W. Bush and
the men and women of our armed forces have given our Iraqi kinsmen according to the flesh the opportunity for freedom from oppression. Indeed, many Iraqui men and women now have the opportunity
to be educated and to hear the gospel without fear of being stoned to
death as a consequence.

How does one balance such views? By embracing the Christian
teaching of *Just War* (*bellum justum*).

While the New Testament never allows for a "Christian army" that
receives forgiveness of sin in battle, we believe that Scripture does allow one to be a Christian *in* the army. It is feasible for a believer in

Jesus Christ to defend the innocent and fight injustice, while maintaining his or her faith. This concept of "just war" developed out of just such questions. The purpose of this appendix is to examine the development of the *Just War criteria*.

The major onus in the development of the church's teaching concerning warfare was the development of a normative ethic of warfare, formulated by Augustine and enlarged and systematized by Thomas Aquinas. Less than a century before Augustine, the Christian community had risen from the status of the hunted to the status of the protected. There was now the dilemma of reconciling the teachings of Jesus Christ to warfare. Following Constantine's authorization of Christianity, it had become the national religion. As Swift notes, "It is a truism that the reign of Constantine represents a watershed in the development of Christian attitudes concerning war and military service. In as much as the question is no longer whether participation in war is justified, but what conditions should govern the right to declare war."[2]

The inherent conflict between morality and war was a question as ancient as war itself. The Greek and Roman philosophers suggested many solutions to the issue, and some modern scholars believe that following the particular brutality of the Athenian warriors, Plato countered the basal nature of the brute warrior with the ideal of the philosopher king in *The Republic*.[3]

Ambrose, the bishop of Milan during the formative Christian years of Augustine, provided a foundation to a theory that Augustine would later deepen. Ambrose believed in the right of the civil government in Rome to declare wars, both defensive and punitive. Christians were admonished to submit to secular authority in Romans 13. In presenting his case for a rejoinder for warfare, Ambrose cited both the civic laws of the day and Old Testament illustrations. The clear demarcation for Ambrose (as will be echoed by Augustine) is the *denial of personal vengeance*. Only in corporate endeavor is war justified, for the individual Christian should follow the example of Jesus Christ in turning the other cheek. In emphatic terms, Ambrose also concludes that the priest is forbidden from any combat, as his duties pertain to the soul, not the body.[4]

Augustine lived in a time of barbarian invasion. In fact, as he lay on his deathbed in 430, Vandals were at the gates of Hippo. He concluded that, to be considered just, warfare must have the purpose of vindicating justice. Augustine, though, clearly considers only Christian duties and responsibilities in an army fielded by secular government. It was beyond Augustine's realm of thought that a "Christian" army might be assembled to prosecute warfare.

Augustine addressed the issue of warfare frequently in writings that reflect over thirty years of thought. Many of his references to war are not fully argued because they come in response to issues raised by others in correspondence. For instance, in his letters to bishop of Rome Boniface I (418–422), whose office was evolving into the papacy, Augustine mainly was describing how the Vandal hordes were then sweeping through North Africa. He was not presenting a systematized thesis on the conduct of war.[5]

The Roman philosopher-orator Cicero (106–43 B.C.), whose work was a foundation on which Augustine could build, obviously contributed much to the Christian theologian's thinking. Cicero posited three ethical criteria involved in the waging of just war, which he believed must be used only as a last resort in defense of national security: (1) There must be a formal declaration of war. (2) The aim must be to secure a just peace. (3) Prisoners of war must be treated humanely.[6]

For a Scripture-based ethical construct, Augustine sought to apply Jesus Christ's teachings on the law of love for God and others. His justifications included the end purpose of sociopolitical and economic justice, even for the conquered, within the realm of maintaining peace. He notes, "Just wars are usually defined as those which avenge injuries, when the nation or city against which warlike action is to be directed has neglected either to punish wrongs committed by its own citizens or to restore what has been unjustly taken from it."[7]

The Value of Protection and Justice

The moral doctrine of the just or limited war is founded upon what later popularly came to be called the "Golden Rule" principle: *How we treat our neighbor is indicative of how we shall be treated.* As the church continued to grow in number and influence, the pacifistic response to martyrdom became replaced with the desire to see civil codes enacted to shape social interaction. The key question that led to the formulation of the Just War criteria was: *Is it ever justifiable to defend oneself against attack?* Augustine posited a solution that served Christians for hundreds of years. The doctrine indicated a subtle shift from a complete pacifistic posture to a defensive one.[8]

In *The City of God*, Augustine holds that humankind, immersed in sin, is incapable of true peace. Evil is inherent in the thoughts of men and women and must be restrained. Therefore, warfare is not only understandable, *it is inevitable.* He writes:

> There are some exceptions made by the divine authority to its own law, that men may not be put to death. These exceptions are of two kinds, being justified either by a general law, or by a special commission granted for a time to some individual. And in this latter case, he to whom authority is delegated, and who is but the sword in the hand of him who uses it, is not himself responsible for the death he deals. And, accordingly, they who have waged war in obedience to the divine command, or in conformity with his laws, have represented in their persons the public justice or the wisdom of government, and in this capacity have put to death wicked men; such persons have by no means violated the commandment, "Thou shalt not kill."[9]

The central tenet is that acts of justice and piety negate any sin that might be part of a military action, because the believer (even in warfare) is following God in obedience. Citing biblical examples, Augustine proposes that the death of the heathen is within the will of God. He draws a careful distinction between warfare and murder:

> Abraham indeed was not merely deemed guiltless of cruelty, but was even applauded for his piety, because he was ready to

slay his son in obedience to God, not to his own passion. And
it is reasonably enough made a question, whether we are to
esteem it to have been in compliance with a command of God
that Jephthah killed his daughter, because she met him when
he had vowed that he would sacrifice to God whatever first
met him as he returned victorious from battle. Samson, too,
who drew down the house on himself and his foes together, is
justified only on this ground, that the Spirit who wrought
wonders by him had given him secret instructions to do this.
With the exception, then, of these two classes of cases, which
are justified either by a just law that applies generally, or by a
special intimation from God himself, the fountain of all justice, whoever kills a man, either himself or another, is impli-
cated in the guilt of murder.[10]

Peace and Justice as the Goal of War

Augustine makes a strong effort to depict the inevitable nature of
war as both the product of sin and the weapon to contain sin (injustice). He writes:

Whoever gives even moderate attention to human affairs and
to our common nature, will recognize that if there is no man
who does not wish to be joyful, neither is there any one who
does not wish to have peace. For even they who make war
desire nothing but victory—desire, that is to say, to attain to
peace with glory. For what else is victory than the conquest of
those who resist us? And when this is done there is peace. It is
therefore with the desire for peace that wars are waged, even
by those who take pleasure in exercising their warlike nature
in command and battle. And hence it is obvious that peace is
the end sought for by war. For every man seeks peace by waging war, but no man seeks war by making peace. For even
they who intentionally interrupt the peace in which they are
living have no hatred of peace, but only wish it changed into

a peace that suits them better. They do not, therefore, wish to have no peace, but only one more to their mind.[11]

Therefore, war can be just if it is used to protect the innocent, or to restrain evil. Still, most commentators believe that Augustine was suggesting a defensive, nonaggressive posture, as opposed to one actively seeking injustice.[12] Yielding to the commandment of love, one acts to protect another who is in danger due to the aggression of a fallen warrior bent on injuring or even killing another.

In his allegiance to Cicero, Augustine also agrees that a just war must vindicate injustice. The state not only preserves a measure of order, but must also give protection to its citizens against inequity. He concludes:

> It is therefore agreed that, according to Cicero, a state should engage in war for the safety which preserves the state permanently in existence though its citizens change; as the foliage of an olive or laurel, or any tree of this kind, is perennial, the old leaves being replaced by fresh ones. For death, as he says, is no punishment to individuals, but rather delivers them from all other punishments, but it is a punishment to the state.[13]

The Disposition of War as an Inward Love

Interestingly, Augustine differentiates between killing and a just war by inward criteria. If the warrior's deeds are not for the sake of capricious cruelty, then his actions mirror the chastisement of God on sinners. Though the distinction is a fine one, it is a profound difference, as Augustine argues. He purports:

> If it is supposed that God could not enjoin warfare because in after times it was said by the Lord Jesus Christ, "I say unto you, Resist not evil," then the answer is what is here required is not a bodily action but an inward disposition. Moses in putting to death sinners was not moved by cruelty but by

love. . . . Love does not preclude a benevolent severity . . . [and] love does not exclude wars of mercy waged by the good.[14]

Finally, Augustine argues that a just war must be fought only under the aegis of an established ruling authority. God has given the regent the responsibility to issue the command to warfare. When the Christian soldier obeys even a pagan emperor, the culpability rests on the ruler, rather than the one enlisted to fight.[15]

Thomas Aquinas's Amplification of the Criteria

Before the second Christian millennium began, the Just War criteria had faced the test of Holy Roman Empire under Charlemagne and the onset of the perpetual Christian-Muslim conflict. Thomas Aquinas (1225–1274) revisited the topic of warfare and built upon Augustine's principles to address his times of increased world conflict. He approached four major points of inquiry, which served as a platform for his restatement of the doctrine of a careful approach to warfare.

The first issue was the very nature of warfare. If humankind fights because of sin, is not the participation in war also a sin? While Aquinas does allow that all wars are unlawful, he sets clear parameters for an ethical conflict:

> In order for a war to be just, three things are necessary. First, the authority of the sovereign by whose command the war is to be waged. For it is not the business of a private individual to declare war, because he can seek for redress of his rights from the tribunal of his superior. . . . Secondly, a just cause is required, namely that those who are attacked, should be attacked because they deserve it on account of some fault. Thirdly, it is necessary that the belligerents should have a rightful intention, so that they intend the advancement of good, or the avoidance of evil. For it may happen that the war is declared by the legitimate authority, and for a just cause, and yet be rendered unlawful through a wicked intention.[16]

The second major question Aquinas addresses concerns clerical participation in war. Were bishops, priests, and monks allowed to engage in battle, if they were willing to fulfill all other obligations? To this inquiry Aquinas spoke emphatically against their fighting. Aquinas believed that the ministry was incompatible with the shedding of blood. He noted:

> Now warlike pursuits are altogether incompatible with the duties of a bishop and a cleric, for two reasons. The first reason is a general one, because, to wit, warlike pursuits are full of unrest, so that they hinder the mind very much from the contemplation of Divine things, the praise of God, and prayers for the people, which belong to the duties of a cleric. . . . The second reason is a special one, because, to wit, all the clerical Orders are directed to the ministry of the altar, on which the Passion of Christ is represented sacramentally. Wherefore it is unbecoming for them to slay or shed blood, and it is more fitting that they should be ready to shed their own blood for Christ, so as to imitate in deed what they portray in their ministry.[17]

Many of Aquinas's contemporaries violated his teaching in this regard, traveling with the Crusaders and often participating in battle themselves.

The third issue that Aquinas addressed was the common use of deception in warfare. Was it sinful for a Christian soldier to hide in ambush, deceive the enemy, or use methods of artifice? Was this not a violation of the integrity of a believer? Aquinas answered somewhat vaguely, prohibiting the Christian soldier from telling outright lies, but allowing silence to deceive the enemy if necessary.[18]

Finally, Aquinas addressed the issues related to the *Truce of God*, namely the lawfulness of fighting on the Sabbath. Was the Christian transgressing by shedding blood on the Lord's Day? Could the Christian soldier fight on holy days? Aquinas answered:

The observance of holy days is no hindrance to those things which are ordained to man's safety, even that of his body. Hence Our Lord argued with the Jews, saying (John 7:23): "Are you angry at me because I have healed the whole man on the Sabbath-day?" Hence physicians may lawfully attend to their patients on holy days. . . . Therefore, for the purpose of safeguarding the common [welfare] of the faithful, it is lawful to carry on a war on holy days, provided there be need for doing so: because it would be to tempt God, if notwithstanding such a need, if one were to choose to refrain from fighting. However, as soon as the need ceases, it is no longer lawful to fight on a holy day.[19]

As the Christian community began to implement this formula, a standard emerged. This synopsis was designed to present a restricted and defensive posture for all combat, even with Christian involvement. Rather than presenting a justification for ready combat, the criteria limited wanton bloodshed. Rather than supplying an excuse for arbitrary hostilities, often born from petty and political machinations, these rules severely limited the purposes, means, and methods of warfare. As Atkinson notes, Augustine and Aquinas's classic guidelines for just war can be summarized:

1. The tradition does not offer a justification of all wars. A distinction is to be made between *just war* and the crusading militarism of a *holy war*. The professed aim of just war is peace through the vindication of justice.
2. There are circumstances in which the proper authority of the state may use force in defense of its people.
3. War may only be waged by legitimate civil authority, and there must be a formal declaration of war.
4. The purpose for which the war is fought must be just.
5. The recourse to war must be a last resort.
6. The motive of war must be just.
7. There must be reasonable hope of success.

8. The good consequence to be expected from going to war must outweigh the evils incurred.
9. The war must be waged in such a way that only the minimum force needed to achieve the aims of the war may be used.[20]

It is important to note the continuing theme in thesis: the Christian has certain parameters within which to act ethically as one enlisted by a temporal power. The believer is viewed as both under temporal rule, and under the injunctions of the *civitas Dei*. Yet since the entire world—all its possible constructs—is within one schema of God, one must learn to live morally in all such dilemmas. Thus, Augustine attempts to codify even warfare under temporal regimes with a Christian ethic.

One remarkable distinction made by Augustine is the contrast between the justifications of going to war (*jus ad bellum*) and the just means of warfare (*jus in bellum*). This was further explained by such theologians as Isidore of Seville, who sought to advise the actual Christian soldiers in the midst of battle.[21] Augustine himself distinguishes between the perceived "blood lust" of the pagans and the love for enemies Jesus Christ demanded.

Augustine noted in *Contra Faustum* that the believer must live within the boundaries of nonretaliation, which demand a passive posture. Enlisted into warfare, the Christian must hasten to seek a nonviolent response first, and in last resort, enlist the sword. Still, Augustine's view of anthropology is clearly evident at this point. In his view, no war can ever be completely justified, since humanity is fallen. Conversely, Augustine believed, the death of a pagan can never be fully justified if all of humanity, however fallen, is still in the *imago Dei*.[22]

Therefore, Augustine arrives at a breach. Warfare is indiscriminate by design, and the innocent, no matter how careful the warrior, will die. Is there a possibility of immunity for noncombatants? It seems Augustine struggles at this point. Even if the motives for the war are just (point five of the criteria), the expected good consequences outweigh the evils (point six), and violence is directed only toward those in arms (point seven), the innocent and unarmed will suffer consequent horrors of war.

Therefore, Augustine leaves the soldier in a dynamic tension, between the vindication of justice and the nature of crusading militarism. The very people supposedly defended by *bellum justum* become victims of the conflict to secure the peace.

Notes

1. Thomas Aquinas, *Summa Theologia* (London: Blackfriars, 1951), 2.40, 1.
2. Louis Swift, *The Early Fathers on War and Military Service* (Wilmington, Del.: Glazier, 1983), 69.
3. Included among them is James Turner Johnson, *Just War Tradition and the Restraint of War* (Princeton, N.J.: Princeton University Press, 1981), 23.
4. Ambrose, *On the Duties of the Clergy* 16, in *NPNF*, 10:302.
5. Swift, *Early Fathers on War and Military Service*, 110.
6. Cicero, *De Officiis* 1.34–40, in *M. Tullius Cicero: The Fragmentary Speeches*, ed. J. W. Crawford (Atlanta: Merket, 1994).
7. Augustine, *Locutiones in Heptateuchum* (Paderborn, Germany: Schöningh, 1916), 6.10.
8. The Just-War advocates include James T. Johnson, *Ideology, Reason and the Limitation of War* (Princeton, N.J.: Princeton University Press, 1975); L. B. Walters, "Five Classic Just-War Theories" (Ph.D. dissertation, Yale University, 1971); Walter O'Brien, *The Conduct of Just and Limited War* (New York: Penguin, 1981). The influence of the theory continues, but the modifications in the church have radically changed the implementation of the policy so as to negate Augustine's premise, that is, "war is a result of sin, and the restrainer of injustice."
9. Augustine, *The City of God* 1.21, in *NPNF*, 2:15.
10. Ibid.
11. Ibid., 19.12–13, in *NPNF*, 2:407.
12. Walters, *Five Classic Just-War Theories*, 174.
13. Augustine, *The City of God* 22.6, in *NPNF*, 2:483.
14. Ibid. Also cited in Roland Bainton, *Christian Attitudes Toward War and Peace* (Nashville: Abingdon, 1960), 97. Therefore, the soldier's conduct

in war must be just as well. He cannot act as the heathen with vengeance and hatred, but rather he must fight with mercy.

15. Augustine, *Psalm 124*, 7, in *Patrologia Latina*, ed. Jacques Migne (Rome: Gregg International, 1982), 37:1654.

16. Thomas Aquinas, *Summa Theologia*, 2.40 (New York: Benziger, 1947), 10–12. In each citation, Aquinas quotes Augustine profusely, thus establishing him as the foundation for Aquinas's elaborations.

17. Ibid.

18. Ibid.

19. Ibid. Upon closer inspection, the crusading forces of the first expedition to Jerusalem seemed to violate the intention of each prohibition that Aquinas offered.

20. D. J. Atkinson, "Just War Criteria," in *Encyclopedia of Biblical and Christian Ethics*, by R. K. Harrison (Nashville: Nelson, 1992), 215–16.

21. Isidore of Seville, *Chronicon* 22, in *Patrologia Latina*, ed. Jacques Migne (Rome: Gregg International, 1982), 81:472.

22. Augustine, *Contra Faustum* 448, in *Patrologia Latina*, 38:635.

Comparison of the Speeches of Pope Urban II (1095) and Usamah bin Ladin (1998)

This is a theological comparison of the call to crusade by Pope Urban II on November 27, 1095, and the call to jihad by Usamah bin Ladin on February 23, 1998.

Pope Urban II Call to Crusade November 27, 1095	Theological Theme	Usamah bin Ladin Call to Crusade February 23, 1998
Most beloved brethren: Urged by necessity, I, Urban, by the permission of God chief bishop and prelate over the whole world, have come into these parts as an ambassador with a divine admonition to you, the servants of God.	Benediction	Praise be to Allah, who revealed the Book, controls the clouds, defeats factionalism,
I hoped to find you as faithful and as zealous in the service of God as I had supposed you to be. But if there is in you any deformity or crookedness contrary to God's law, with divine help I will do my best to remove it.	Statement of Desire	and says in His Book: "But when the forbidden months are past, then fight and slay the pagans wherever ye find them, seize them, beleaguer them, and lie in wait for them in every stratagem [of war]"; and peace be upon our Prophet, Muhammad Bin-ᵓAbdallah, who

said: I have been sent with the sword between my hands to ensure that no one but Allah is worshiped, Allah who put my livelihood under the shadow of my spear and who inflicts humiliation and scorn on those who disobey my orders.

For your brethren who live in the east are in urgent need of your help, and you must hasten to give them the aid which has often been promised them. For, as the most of you have heard, the Turks and Arabs have attacked them and have conquered the territory of Romania [the Greek empire] as far west as the shore of the Mediterranean and the Hellespont, which is called the Arm of St. George. They have occupied more and more of the lands of those Christians, and have overcome them in seven battles. They have killed and captured many, and have destroyed the churches and devastated the empire.

Threat of the Pagan Enemy to a Land They Consider Holy

The Arabian Peninsula has never—since Allah made it flat, created its desert, and encircled it with seas—been stormed by any forces like the crusader armies spreading in it like locusts, eating its riches and wiping out its plantations.

If you permit them to continue thus for awhile with impurity, the faithful of God will be much more widely attacked by them. On this account I, or rather the Lord, beseech you as Christ's heralds to publish this everywhere and to persuade all people of whatever rank, foot-soldiers and knights, poor and rich, to carry aid promptly to those Christians and to destroy that vile race from the lands of our friends. I say this to those who are present, it is meant

Slaughter of Our Fellow Believers by These Pagans

All this is happening at a time in which nations are attacking Muslims like people fighting over a plate of food. . . . First, for over seven years the United States has been occupying the lands of Islam in the holiest of places, the Arabian Peninsula, plundering its riches, dictating to its rulers, humiliating its people, terrorizing its neighbors, and turning its bases in the Peninsula into a spearhead through which to fight the neighboring Muslim peoples.

also for those who are absent. Moreover, Christ commands it.

	Obligation of Hearers to Help Defend Against the Infidels	

All who die by the way, whether by land or by sea, or in battle against the pagans, shall have immediate remission of sins. This I grant them through the power of God with which I am invested.

We—with Allah's help—call on every Muslim who believes in Allah and wishes to be rewarded to comply with Allah's order to kill the Americans and plunder their money wherever and whenever they find it. We also call on Muslim *ulema* [scholars with authority to pass judgment on Islamic life and behavior], leaders, youths, and soldiers to launch the raid on Satan's U.S. troops and the devil's supporters allying with them, and to displace those who are behind them so that they may learn a lesson.

	Forgiveness of Sin for the Warrior (Jihad)	

Let those who have been accustomed unjustly to wage private warfare against the faithful now go against the infidels and end with victory this war which should have been begun long ago. Let those who for a long time have been robbers, now become knights. Let those who have been fighting against their brothers and relatives now fight in a proper way against the barbarians. Let those who have been serving as mercenaries for small pay now obtain the eternal reward. Let those who have been wearing themselves out in both body and soul now work for a double honor. Behold! On this side will be the sorrowful and poor, on that, the rich; on this side, the enemies of the Lord, on that, his friends. Let those who go not put off the journey, but rent their lands and

Almighty Allah said: "O ye who believe, give your response to Allah and His Apostle, when He calleth you to that which will give you life. And know that Allah cometh between a man and his heart, and that it is He to whom ye shall all be gathered."

collect money for their expenses; and as soon as winter is over and spring comes, let them eagerly set out on the way with God as their guide.

O what a disgrace if such a despised and base race, which worships demons, should conquer a people which has the faith of omnipotent God and is made glorious with the name of Christ! With what reproaches will the Lord overwhelm us if you do not aid those who, with us, profess the Christian religion!

Fighting a Holy War Is a Sacred Task and Duty

Almighty Allah also says: "O ye who believe, what is the matter with you, that when ye are asked to go forth in the cause of Allah, ye cling so heavily to the earth! Do ye prefer the life of this world to the hereafter? But little is the comfort of this life, as compared with the hereafter. Unless ye go forth, He will punish you with a grievous penalty, and put others in your place; but Him ye would not harm in the least. For Allah hath power over all things."

You Are Obliged to Holy War Against These Demonic Infidels

All these crimes and sins committed by the Americans are a clear declaration of war on Allah, his messenger, and Muslims. And *ulema* have throughout Islamic history unanimously agreed that the jihad is an individual duty if the enemy destroys the Muslim countries. This was revealed by Imam Bin-Qadamah in "Al-Mughni," Imam al-Kisa'i in "Al-Bada'i," al-Qurtubi in his interpretation, and the shaykh of al-Islam in his books, where he said: "As for the fighting to repulse [an enemy], it is aimed at defending sanctity and religion, and it is a duty as agreed [by the *ulema*]. Nothing is more sacred than belief except repulsing an enemy who is attacking religion and life."

You Are Obliged to Holy War Against These Demonic Infidels (continued)	The ruling to kill the Americans and their allies—civilians and military—is an individual duty for every Muslim who can do it in any country in which it is possible to do it, in order to liberate the al-Aqsa Mosque and the holy mosque [Mecca] from their grip, and in order for their armies to move out of all the lands of Islam, defeated and unable to threaten any Muslim. This is in accordance with the words of Almighty Allah, "and fight the pagans all together as they fight you all together," and "fight them until there is no more tumult or oppression, and there prevail justice and faith in Allah."

BIBLIOGRAPHY

To the reader: Knowing that modern evangelicals understand very little about the Middle Ages, the Crusades, and Just War theory, we submit this rudimentary list of books for further study. Sadly, evangelicals are highly myopic; we are so near-sighted that we only understand as much Church history as we have experienced. This is not only tragic, it is dangerous. Muslims not only know these dark eras in our history—they constantly refer to them. When we ignore this period, we do so to our great peril. Read and study.

Primary Sources

Ambrose of Milan. *On the Duties of the Clergy.* In *A Select Library of the Nicene and Post-Nicene Fathers of the Christian Church,* edited by Philip Schaff. Buffalo, N.Y.: Christian Literature, 1886.

Ameoroz, Henry. *The Eclipse of the Abbasid Caliphate: Original Chronicles of the Fourth Islamic Century.* Oxford: Oxford University Press, 1920.

Arnobius. *Against the Heathen.* In *The Apostolic Fathers,* trans. by A. Cleveland Cox. Grand Rapids: Eerdmans, 1987.

Athanasius. *History of the Arians.* In *Patrologia Graeca,* edited by J. P. Migne. 31 vols. Paris: Garnier Fratres, 1884.

Augustine of Hippo. *Contra Faustum.* In *The Nicene and Post-Nicene Fathers.* 10 vols. New York: Christian Literature, 1887.

———. *The City of God.* In *The Nicene and Post-Nicene Fathers.* 10 vols. New York: Christian Literature, 1887.

————. *Locutiones in Heptateuchum.* Paderborn, Netherlands: Schoningh, 1916.

Bouquet, Martin, ed. *Recueil des historiens des Gaules et de la France.* 26 vols. Paris: University, 1806.

Brundage, James A. "The Army of the First Crusade and the Crusade Vow: Some Reflections on a Recent Book." *Medieval Studies* 33 (1971): 2.

Clement of Alexandria. *Paedagogus.* In *The Apostolic Fathers,* trans. by A. Cleveland Cox. Grand Rapids: Eerdmans, 1987.

————. *Stromata.* In *The Apostolic Fathers,* trans. by A. Cleveland Cox. Grand Rapids: Eerdmans, 1987.

Crawford, J. W., ed. *M. Tullius Cicero: The Fragmentary Speeches.* Atlanta: Merket, 1994.

Cyprian of Carthage. *De Bono Patientiae.* In *The Apostolic Fathers,* trans. by A. Cleveland Cox. Grand Rapids: Eerdmans, 1987.

————. *The Epistles of Cyprian.* In *The Apostolic Fathers,* trans. by A. Cleveland Cox, Grand Rapids: Eerdmans, 1987.

Devizes, Richard, and Geoffrey de Vinsauf. *Chronicles of the Crusades.* London: H. G. Bohn, 1848.

Dix, Gregory, trans. *Apostolic Tradition of Hippolytus.* London: SPCK, 1937.

Dubois, Pierre. *The Recovery of the Holy Land.* New York: Columbia University, 1956.

Duchesne, Lin, ed. *Liber Pontificalis.* 15 vols. Paris: Pontificalis, 1884–1892.

Eaton, Burton Scott, trans. *Apostolic Tradition of Hippolytus.* Cambridge: University, 1943.

Eusebius. *History of the Church.* In *A Select Library of the Nicene and Post-Nicene Fathers of the Christian Church,* edited by Philip Schaff. Buffalo, N.Y.: Christian Literature, 1886.

————. *The Life of Constantine.* In *A Select Library of the Nicene and Post-Nicene Fathers.* New York: Christian Literature, 1891.

————. *The Oration in Praise of the Emperor Constantine.* In *A Select Library of the Nicene and Post-Nicene Fathers.* New York: Christian Literature, 1891.

Guibert, Abbot of Nogent. *Historia quae dicitur Gesta Dei per Francos.* In *Recueil des historiens des croisades, Historiens occidentaux.* 5 vols. Paris: Bibliotheque, 1844–1895.

Hagenmeyer, Henrich. *Die Kreuzzugsbriefe aus den Jahren 1088–1100.* Innsbruck: Hilbar, 1901.

Hill, Rosalind M., ed. and trans. *Gesta francorum et aliorum Hierosolymitanorum: The Deeds of the Franks.* London: Penguin, 1962.

Irenaeus. *Contra Heresies.* In *The Apostolic Fathers,* trans. by A. Cleveland Cox. Grand Rapids: Eerdmans, 1987.

Isambert, Jean, ed. *Les Anciennes Lois de France.* 17 vols. Paris: Paris University, 1882.

James, Bruno Scott, ed. *The Letters of St. Bernard of Clairvaux.* Chicago: Henry Regnery, 1953.

Justin Martyr. *Dialogue with Trypho.* In *The Apostolic Fathers,* trans. by A. Cleveland Cox. Grand Rapids: Eerdmans, 1987.

———. *1 Apologia.* In *The Apostolic Fathers,* trans. by A. Cleveland Cox. Grand Rapids: Eerdmans, 1987.

Kelly, J. N. D. *The Oxford Dictionary of the Popes.* Oxford: Oxford University Press, 1986.

Krey, A. C., trans. *Baldric of Dol Version.* In *The First Crusade: The Accounts of Eye-Witnesses and Participants.* Princeton, N.J.: Princeton University Press, 1921.

———. *Getsa Version.* In *The First Crusade: The Accounts of Eye-Witnesses and Participants.* Princeton, N.J.: Princeton University Press, 1921.

———. *Guibert of Nogent Chronicles.* In *The First Crusade: The Accounts of Eye-Witnesses and Participants.* Princeton, N.J.: Princeton University Press, 1921.

Lactantius. *The Divine Institutes.* In *The Apostolic Fathers,* trans. by A. Cleveland Cox. Grand Rapids: Eerdmans, 1987.

Levi-Provencal, Etienne. "La 'Mora Zaida,' femme d'Alphonse VI," *Islam d'Occident: Études d'histoire Medievale.* Paris: Paris University, 1948.

Marcus, Jacob. *The Jew in the Medieval World: A Sourcebook, 315–1791.* New York: JPS, 1938.

Migne, Jacques, trans. *Athanasius' History of the Arians.* In *Patrologia Latina.* 220 vols. Rome: Gregg International, 1982.

———. *Isidore of Seville.* In *Patrologia Latina.* 220 vols. Rome: Gregg International, 1982.

———. *Prudentius' Contra Symmachum.* In *Patrologia Latina.* 220 vols. Rome: Gregg International, 1982.

———. *Theodosiani Libri.* In *Patrologia Latina.* 220 vols. Rome: Gregg International, 1982.

Monumenta Germaniae Historia, Legume. 8 vols. Hannover, Netherlands: University, 1837.

Munro, Dana C., trans. *Robert the Monk Chronicles.* In *Urban and the Cru-saders.* Philadelphia: University of Pennsylvania Press, 1896.

———. *Translations and Reprints from the Original Sources of European His-tory,* vol. 1. Philadelphia: University of Pennsylvania Press, 1896.

———. *Truce of God Proclaimed in the Diocese of Cologne in 1083.* In *Urban and the Crusaders.* Philadelphia: University of Pennsylvania Press, 1896.

———. *The Truce of God Proclaimed at the Council of Clermont—1095.* In *Ur-ban and the Crusaders.* Philadelphia: University of Pennsylvania Press, 1896.

Origen. *Contra Celsus.* In *The Apostolic Fathers,* trans. by A. Cleveland Cox. Grand Rapids: Eerdmans, 1987.

Peters, Edward, ed. *The First Crusade.* Philadelphia: University of Pennsylva-nia Press, 1971.

Recueil des historiens des croisades, Historiens Occidentaux. 5 vols. Paris: Bibliotheque, 1844–1895.

Ruinart, Stephen. *Acta Martyrum.* Ratisbon, Germany: UP, 1859.

Ryan, Frances Rita. *Fulcher of Chartres' A History of the Expedition to Jerusa-lem, 1095–1127.* Knoxville: University Press, 1927.

Stubbs, William, ed. *"The Chronicle of William of Malmesbury."* In *Willelmi Malmesbiriensis monachi De Gestis regum Anglorum.* 2 vols. London: SPCK, 1887–1889.

Tatian. *Oratio ad Graecos.* In *The Apostolic Fathers,* trans. by A. Cleveland Cox. Grand Rapids: Eerdmans, 1987.

Tertullian. *De Corona Militis.* In *The Apostolic Fathers,* trans. by A. Cleveland Cox. Grand Rapids: Eerdmans, 1987.

———. *1 Apologia.* In *The Apostolic Fathers,* trans. by A. Cleveland Cox. Grand Rapids: Eerdmans, 1987.

———. *On Idolatry.* In *The Apostolic Fathers,* trans. A. Cleveland Cox. Grand Rapids: Eerdmans, 1987.

Theodoret. *Historia Ecclesiastica.* In *A Select Library of the Nicene and Post-Nicene Fathers of the Christian Church,* edited by Philip Schaff. Buffalo, N.Y.: Christian Literature, 1886.

Secondary Sources

Armstrong, Karen. *Islam: A Short History.* New York: Modern Library, 2002.

Atkinson, D. J. *Just War Criteria.* In *Encyclopedia of Biblical and Christian Ethics,* edited by R. K. Harrison. Rev. ed. Nashville: Nelson, 1992.

Bainton, Roland. *Christian Attitudes Toward War and Peace.* Nashville: Abingdon, 1960.

Baker, Robert. *A Summary of Christian History.* Nashville: Broadman and Holman, 1994.

Battifol, Pierre. *Études d'histoire et de theologie Positive.* Paris: Bibliotheque, 1906.

Bornkamm, Gunther. *Christian Experience.* New York: Harper and Row, 1971.

Brehier, Letienne, *Histoire anonyme de la première croisade.* Paris: Champion, 1924.

Browne, L. E. *The Eclipse of Christianity.* Cambridge: Cambridge University Press, 1932.

Cadoux, Cecil John. *The Early Church and the World.* Edinburgh: T. & T. Clark, 1925.

Carroll, Vincent and David Shiflett. *Christianity on Trial.* San Francisco: Encounter, 2002.

The Challenge of Peace: A Pastoral Letter on War and Peace by the National Conference of Catholic Bishops. Washington, D.C.: United States Catholic Conference, 1983.

Churchill, Winston. *A History of English Speaking Peoples.* New York: Dodd, Mead, 1958.

Comnena, Anna. *The Alexiad.* Chicago: University of Chicago Press, 1926.

Deanesly, Margaret. *A History of the Medieval Church.* London: Routledge, 1991.

DeMolen, Richard L., ed. *One Thousand Years: Western Europe in the Middle Ages.* Boston: Houghton Mifflin, 1974.

Dowley, Tim, ed. *Eerdman's Handbook of the History of Christianity.* Grand Rapids: Eerdmans, 1977.

Duncan, Pope. *The Pilgrimage of Christianity.* Nashville: Broadman, 1965.

Egan, Edward. *The Beatitudes: Works of Mercy and Pacifism.* In *War or Peace: The Search for New Answers,* edited by Thomas Shannon. New York: Harper and Row, 1980.

Erdmann, Carl. *The Origin of the Idea of Crusade.* Trans. by Marshall Baldwin and Walter Goffart. Princeton, N.J.: Princeton University Press, 1977.

Finucane, Ronald C. *Soldiers of Faith: Crusaders and Moslems at War.* New York: St. Martin's, 1983.

Gilson, Etienne. *The Spirit of Thomism.* New York: P. J. Kenedy & Sons, 1964.

Gonzalez, Justo L. *The Crusades: Piety Misguided.* Nashville: Graded Press, 1988.

Goodsell, Daniel. *Peter the Hermit.* Cincinnati: Jennings, 1906.

Gray, George Z. *The Children's Crusade: An Episode.* Boston: Houghton, Mifflin, 1871.

Hornus, Jean-Michel. *It Is Not Lawful for Me to Fight.* Kitchener, Ont.: Herald, 1980.

Hunt, Noreen. *Cluny Under Saint Hugh, 1049–1109.* London: Blackwell, 1967.

Jenkins, Claude. *Medieval Contributions to Modern Civilization: A Series of Lectures Delivered at King's College University of London.* New York: Barnes and Noble, 1921.

Johnson, James T. *Ideology, Reason and the Limitation of War.* Princeton, N.J.: Princeton University Press, 1975.

———. *Just War Tradition and the Restraint of War.* Princeton, N.J.: Princeton University Press, 1981.

Kelly, J. N. D. *The Oxford Dictionary of the Popes.* Oxford: Oxford University Press, 1986.

Kemp, Waldram. *Canonization and Authority in the Western Church.* London: Oxford University Press, 1948.

Knowles, David. *The Evolution of Medieval Thought.* New York: Vintage, 1962.

Kramer, Martin. *The Jewish Discovery of Islam.* Tel Aviv: Moshe Dayan Center, 1999.

La Monte, John. *Feudal Monarchy in the Latin Kingdom of Jerusalem: 1100–1291.* Cambridge, Mass.: Medieval Academy of America, 1932.

Langland, William. *The Peasants Life.* In *The Vision of Piers Plowman,* trans. by H. W. Wells. New York: Sheed and Ward, 1935.

Lawrence, Charles. *The English Church and the Papacy in the Middle Ages.* London: Thames, 1965.

Lewis, Bernard. *Islam in History.* Chicago: Open Court, 1993.

Macdonald, A. J. *Berengar and the Reform of Sacramental Doctrine.* New York: Richwood, 1977.

Mahmud, S. F. *A Short History of Islam.* Oxford: Oxford University Press, 1988.

Mansthal, Pierre. *The Writings of Guibert.* New York: Pantheon, 1862.

————. *The Writings of Urban II.* New York: University, 1861.

Maurer, Armand. *Medieval Philosophy.* New York: Random House, 1962.

McGrath, Alister. *Christian Theology: An Introduction.* Oxford: Blackwell, 1994.

Menendez, Pidal. *La Espana del Cid.* Paris: University of Paris Press, 1944.

Merton, Thomas. *Faith and Violence: Christian Teaching and Christian Practice.* Notre Dame: University of Notre Dame Press, 1968.

Michaud, Joseph Francois. *The History of the Crusades.* New York: A. C. Armstrong, 1895.

O'Brien, Walter. *The Conduct of Just and Limited War.* New York: Penguin, 1981.

Oldenbourg, Zoe. *The Early Crusaders.* New York: Pantheon, 1964.

Pernoud, Regine. *Les Croises.* Paris: Hachette, 1959.

Placher, William C. *A History of Christian Theology.* Philadelphia: Westminster, 1983.

Prawer, Joshua. *The World of the Crusaders.* New York: Quadrangle, 1972.

Proctor, W. C. G. *Absolution.* In *Evangelical Dictionary of Theology,* edited by Walter Elwell. Grand Rapids: Baker, 1984.

Riley-Smith, Jonathan. *The Crusades: A Short History.* New Haven, Conn.: Yale University Press, 1987.

Runciman, Steven. *A History of the Crusades.* 3 vols. Cambridge: Cambridge University Press, 1951–1954.

Russell, Jeffrey Burton. *A History of Medieval Christianity: Prophecy and Order.* Arlington Heights, Ill.: Harlan Davidson, 1968.

Schaff, Philip. *The Creeds of Christendom.* 3 vols. New York: Harper and Row, 1931.

Setton, Kenneth M., ed. *A History of the Crusades.* 6 vols. Madison, Wis.: University of Wisconsin Press, 1989.

Shelley, Bruce. *Church History in Plain Language.* Nashville: Nelson, 1995.

Slaughter, Gertrude. *Saladin.* New York: Exhibition, 1955.

Stewart, Robert. *Charlemagne and On.* New York: Firebird, 1964.

Swift, Louis. *The Early Fathers on War and Military Service.* Wilmington, Del.: Glazier, 1983.

Thomas Aquinas. *Summa Theologia.* 3 vols. London: Blackfriars, 1951.

Tierney, Brian. *The Crisis of the Church and State 1050–1300.* New York: Prentice-Hall, 1964.

Tillich, Paul. *The Interpretation of History.* New York: Charles Scribner's Sons, 1936.

Ullmann, W. M. *The Growth of Papal Government in the Middle Ages.* London: Penguin, 1962.

Verduin, Leonard. *The Reformers and Their Stepchildren.* Sarasota, Fla.: Christian Hymnary, 1991.

Von Harnack, Adolf. *Militia Christi.* Tübingen: Tübingen University Press, 1905.

Walbank, Walter. *Civilization Past and Present.* New York: Scott, 1942.

Walters, L. B. "Five Classic Just-War Theories." Ph.D. dissertation, Yale University, 1971.

Widgery, Alban G. *Interpretations of History: Confucius to Toynbee.* London: George Allen & Unwin, 1961.

Yoder, James. *The Politics of Jesus.* Grand Rapids: Eerdmans, 1972.